FITZROY

FITZROY

Dyson Hore-Lacy

LION PUBLICATIONS

First published 2000

© Lion Publications
P.O. Box 336
Fitzroy
Victoria 3065

All rights reserved. No part of this publication may be reproduced, stored in a retrieval system or transmitted in any form or by any means, electronic, mechanical, photocopying, recording or otherwise without the prior permission of the publisher.

ISBN 1876 557 33 8

Printed in Australia by Doran Printing, Victoria.

Contents

Dramatis Personae
1

Foreword
7

Prologue
11

1 – Some Background
13

2 – Welcome to the Fitzroy Football Club
26

3 – 1992
47

4 – 1993
73

5 – 1994
103

6 – 1995
124

7 – Merger Movement
141

8 – The Pressure Mounts
192

9 – The Dust Settles
223

10 – Aftermath
232

Dramatis Personae

Ahern, Bernie — FFC 'White Knight'
Armstrong, Matthew — FFC player, later with North Melbourne FC
Atherton, Bill — Fitzroy director
Audi Dabwido, Dr David — Nauru Insurance Corporation chairman

Austin, Rod — FFC coach
Bahen, John — FFC player, real estate consultant
Baker, Robert — Westpac manager
Baldwin, Jason — FFC player
Bamblett, Alf — Aboriginal community leader
Basto, Greg — FFC director
Birt, John — FFC chief executive officer
Boyd, Brad — FFC player and captain, later with Brisbane FC

Brennan, Michael — Administrator of FFC
Broderick, Matthew — FFC player, later with Richmond FC

Browne, Jeff — AFL solicitor
Buchanan, Dr Peter — QC and legal adviser
Cahill, Ron — Head of 'AFL for Canberra'
Cain, Nancye — Number one FFC supporter
Capuano, Barry — AFL administrator, FFC chief executive officer

Carter, Colin — AFL commissioner
Casey, Ron — North Melbourne FC chairman and president

Clodumar, Kinza — President of Nauru, director FFC and Nauru Insurance Corporation

FITZROY

Coates, George	FFC president
Collins, Ian	Carlton FC chief executive officer, AFL general manager, Docklands manager
Conlon, Michael	FFC player
Conn, Malcolm	Journalist
Connolly, Rohan	Journalist
Costigan, Peter	Journalist and Lord Mayor
Crawford, David	Accountant, author of Crawford Report
Curl, Bruce	Solicitor, Williams Winter and Higgs
Daphne, Leon	Richmond FC president
Dawson, John	FFC finance director
Dawson, Mark	North Melbourne FC director
De Rauch, Peter	North Melbourne FC vice-chairman
Dundas, Matthew	FFC player, later with Richmond FC
Dunn, David	Brisbane Bears FC solicitor
Eales, Robert	FFC director
Elliott, Jamie	FFC player, later with Richmond FC
Elliott, John	Carlton FC president
Evans, Ron	Essendon president, AFL commissioner, managing director of Spotless Services
Findlay, Elaine	FFC director, vice-chairman
Gale, Michael	FFC player, later with Richmond FC
Gange, Alf	FFC supporter
Gordon, Noel	Brisbane Bears FC president
Gordon, Peter	Footscray FC president
Grollo, Bruno	Melbourne builder and developer
Guard, Jeremy	FFC player
Hammond, Bob	Adelaide FC chairman

DRAMATIS PERSONAE

Harding, Mark	*Journalist*
Hayes, Rod	*FFC finance manager*
Hobbs, Colin	*FFC player, FFC director*
Hogg, Jeff	*FFC player*
Hore-Lacy, Dyson	*FFC president and chairman*
Ireland, Andrew	*Brisbane Bears FC chief executive officer*
Jackson, Wayne	*Adelaide chairman, AFL chief executive officer*
Johnson, Chris	*FFC player, later with Brisbane FC*
Johnstone, Robert	*FFC director, McDonalds executive*
Kann, Brian	*Hawthorn FC director*
Kelleher, Max	*FFC general manager*
Kennedy, John	*AFL commissioner*
Khun, Ruben	*Republic of Nauru finance minister*
Lane, Tim	*ABC radio journalist and broadcaster*
Lauritz, John	*Hawthorn FC chief executive officer*
Lawrie, Grant	*FFC player, chairman of selectors and reserves coach*
Lehman, Kevin	*AFL finance manager*
Levy, Ken	*FFC director, Brisbane director*
Linnell, Stephen	*Journalist*
Lord, Geoff	*Hawthorn FC president*
Lynch, Alastair	*FFC player, later with Brisbane FC*
Mallick, S C	*Nauru Insurance Corporation general manager*
Malloy, Jarrod	*FFC player, later with Brisbane*
Mathieson, Bruce	*Hotel developer*
McAlister, Alan	*Collingwood FC president*
McArdle, John	*Solicitor, Williams Winter and Higgs*
McConnell, Allan	*FFC assistant coach and interim coach*

FITZROY

McMahon, David	*FFC player, Fitzroy director*
Miller, Greg	*North Melbourne FC chief executive officer*
Mitchell, Gus	*FFC chairman of selectors*
Mitchell, Peter	*FFC director*
Montgomery, Ken	*North Melbourne FC financial controller*
Murray, Kevin	*FFC player and coach*
Nunan, Michael	*FFC coach*
Oakley, Ross	*AFL chief executive officer*
O'Bryan, Michael	*Solicitor*
O'Connor, Terry	*West Coast Eagles FC president, AFL commissioner*
O'Neale, Warren	*Supporter, founding member of Fitzroy Foundation*
Osborne, Richard	*FFC player, later with Collingwood FC, Western Bulldogs FC, and Sydney FC*
Palmer, Scot	*Journalist*
Paton, Ray	*FFC director*
Pearce, Daryl	*Northern Land Council director, community leader*
Pert, Gary	*FFC player, later with Collingwood FC*
Petinella, John	*FFC director*
Pinskier, Henry	*FFC director*
Quinlan, Bernie	*FFC player and coach, media personality*
Reynolds, Tom	*Minister Kennett government, FFC number one ticket holder*
Ridley, Ian	*Melbourne FC president*
Roos, Paul	*FFC player and captain, later with Sydney FC*

DRAMATIS PERSONAE

Ryan, Kevin — *FFC director*
Samuel, Graeme — *AFL commissioner*
Sandground, David — *FFC director*
Scanlon, Peter — *AFL commissioner*
Serafini, Laurie — *FFC player, Brisbane director*
Shaw, David — *Essendon FC president, AFL commissioner*

Shaw, Robert — *FFC coach*
Sheahan, Mike — *Journalist*
Sherry, Graham — *Nauru Insurance Corporation solicitor*
Smith, Damien — *Player manager and agent*
Smith, Patrick — *Journalist*
Stephen, Billy — *FFC player and coach*
Stewart, John — *FFC finance manager*
Timms, Daryl — *Journalist*
Wallace, Don — *FFC finance manager and chief executive officer*

Warry, Glen — *FFC football manager*
Wiegard, Keith — *FFC president*
Wiegard, Leon — *FFC president and chairman*
Wilson, Arthur — *FFC football manager*
Winneke, John — *AFL commissioner*
Wynd, Jimmy — *FFC player*
Zanotti, Mark — *FFC player*

FITZROY

Foreword

I was fascinated by Dyson's account of the saga which surrounded the demise of the Fitzroy Football Club. To a lot of people it may not mean as much, but to genuine Fitzroy supporters it will recreate the heartache that surrounded us when the club went down.

At the time of writing this preface, four new seasons have started and yet somehow the fixture list still seems wrong when I look to see where the games are being played and there is no Fitzroy.

When I finished reading the draft of this book, I felt empty and again sickened by how it all ended. The pressure on the board of management and particularly Dyson must have been enormous. My opinion used to be that a certain amount of bad management by the board must come into play when a club loses its place in a league where it had won eight premierships and was the glamour side of the VFL in the early days. A club which has produced some of the greatest players ever in football. Yet, when I read of the events and efforts of the board to keep the club afloat I cannot be critical.

Certainly the club allowed itself to get into a position where it had no money. However many league clubs over the years have been in a position where they have virtually been broke, but they have all survived, except Fitzroy. By hook or by crook someone had to go! I am not against money in football as it has been in the game for as long as I can remember, however when money becomes the prime objective, look out – as someone or something has got to give.

My connection with the Fitzroy Football Club began at a very early age in the 30s. My parents used to take me to the football at the Brunswick Street Ground where I fell in love with Fitzroy and with football. Football in those depression days kept people alive. If your father couldn't answer a football question your mother could. If your brother couldn't teach you how to play your sister could. Every family barracked for a team and that was a lifetime commitment. Fitzroy was our team and I will always remember our footy days. I think in those days the footy started later at 2.30 pm or so and my memories of Fitzroy were the cold dark days, the dark maroon guernsey and the black shorts. In spite of my youth I can still see the players – Bunton, Dinny, Ryan, Doug Nicholls and many others (if anyone has a spare hour or two), as clear in my mind as they were then.

Haydn, of course was my first idol and he was the idol of all at Fitzroy. Like all kids I had his number seven on the Fitzroy guernsey knitted by my mother. In those days Victorian football was developing the culture that made our game into the best spectator event in the world. Every boy had an ambition to represent his chosen team. Many of us never saw a golf club or even picked up a tennis racquet. It was football in the winter and cricket in the summer. Most families were too poor to buy a football even if you could get one. So we used a paper footy – rolling one every night to take to school the next day. (It may seem unlikely to younger people, but football in those days was more a part of people than it is now. It was almost a religion.)

The Fitzroy Football Club was founded in 1883 with the idea that the community of Fitzroy needed a football team. The club was an immediate success both on the field and off it, attracting the support of the local people. Fitzroy was never a big area but the people ever since I have known them had an amazing loyalty to their team. I think that is one of the reasons why people were so hurt when their team went down, they felt lost, betrayed, wanting to blame someone but not really knowing who.

Over the years keeping the club going was getting tougher, yet our supporters never wavered, year in and year out, as requests for financial help and voluntary work to cut costs were made on the Fitzroy people. We were sandwiched between two powerful and financial clubs in Collingwood and Carlton, making it very hard to enlarge our supporter base and to attract recruits, as even in the early days a recruit wanted to go to the club who could offer the most – and generally it wasn't us.

The club had outstanding people as its leaders who fostered

FOREWORD

unity between committee, players and followers. Two of these were Lal McLellan and Percy Mitchell, who had such a love of Fitzroy that the club always had the respect and loyalty of all who associated with them. Percy was also a driving force behind the Australian National Football Council and the development of football generally for many years – there was no greater man for football.

The club had many bright moments, making the finals on many occasions, but a flag in 1944 was our last premiership. The club had six Brownlow Medallists, with Bunton winning three, for a total of eight. Many others were worthy of one but were not so fortunate.

1970 provided great memories for our supporters as Fitzroy defeated the reigning premiers Richmond in the first ever Sunday match. This game was played to commemorate a visit by the Royal Family. Two weeks later the club was involved with Geelong in the first ever game at Waverley.

In 1979, at the Waverley Ground, Fitzroy kicked the highest score ever recorded in the Victorian Football League – 36 goals, 22 behinds against Melbourne – a record winning margin of 190 points. A magnificent day for the club, yet ironically 16 years later we were out of the league after 113 years of service and entertainment. Certainly the history of events as recounted by Dyson Hore-Lacy in this book needs to be told.

I find it hard to get out of my mind the way the merging of the two clubs was engineered, however I must accept the fact that the merger is now history. I have to also accept the fact that if I want to have some living memory of Fitzroy in AFL football I have to follow and accept the Brisbane Lions. The Brisbane Lions face a hard battle to increase their support base in Victoria because they made mistakes and offended many people initially after the merger with their dogmatic and take-over attitude. Few games in Melbourne – and no training base – makes it very hard to give people that sense of belonging that is the heart of a football club. Nevertheless, we must try to keep all Fitzroy people together. They deserve better. I cannot see any other way.

W.J. (Billy) Stephen

Prologue

Writing this book has not been a labour of love. One of the reasons why it has taken so long is that it has been a painful exercise which has led me to turn away from the task for fairly long periods of time.

Fortunately I have been pushed and prodded by Colin Hobbs and Brian Norton and have finally completed it. Colin got so tired of me that he finally put out a flyer for the book and took orders so forcing me to finish it.

I have put pen to paper solely for the benefit of the tens of thousands of Fitzroy supporters, players and staff, and for the generations which went before them who are entitled to know the truth of what happened to their club.

This book is not about retribution against the AFL or anyone else. I have attempted to write it in an even-handed way although attitudes towards people and organisations will be obvious.

This book is not about me. It is about Fitzroy and the events leading up to the formation of the 'Brisbane Lions.' I have written something of myself because my loyal strappers believe that my involvement with football and events leading up to my joining the Fitzroy board would be relevant to the story and of some interest to readers.

There are dozens of people who were pivotal to the successful operation of the Fitzroy Football Club who have not been mentioned in this book. Members of our staff and of coterie groups such as the Lionesses, the Lion Hunters, The Pride, The Roys, The Cheer Squad the Cheer Leaders and the 'Ins and Outs' committee are just some of those people. People who gave their all for Fitzroy. I have not mentioned many of these wonderful people because I have attempted to concentrate on events which impacted on the course of the club whilst I was a director. I could write another three books about the contributions of other people to Fitzroy.

FITZROY

To the Fitzroy stalwarts – those who stood in the rain rattling cans during our appeal, the ones who consistently gave money to keep their beloved club alive, the ones who attended matches week after week even when the side was losing badly, and to the generations of players and supporters before them, this book is dedicated to you.

Brian Norton has been invaluable in helping me put together the contents of the book in some sequential order. Colin Hobbs, his wife Heather, and children Lori and Brett have been instrumental in keeping me 'focussed' through their friendship and encouragement. Colin has also helped with parts of the book dealing with our coaching and football department.

D. F. Hore-Lacy
August 2000

Chapter 1

People often ask how I got involved with Fitzroy. The answer is not simple.

I lived in Tasmania until the age of 13, and like most kids in Tassie, I had a favourite AFL team. The only names I recognised as a child were Melbourne and Geelong because they were well known places. Suburbs like Richmond and Fitzroy meant nothing to me, so I became a Melbourne supporter.

In 1954 I came to Victoria to live. I do not believe I missed a single Melbourne game during its golden era. At the end of the season I could repeat the scores of every game they played in, quarter by quarter. My favourite players were, of course, the Tasmanians. Athol Webb, Peter Marquis, Stuart Spencer (whom I met in his capacity as a Melbourne director more than 30 years later), and Tassie Johnson were just some of them.

In my final year at school I played for Ringwood Football Club which was in the Croydon-Ferntree Gully League (now Eastern District Football League). I was a reasonably good schoolboy footballer and in late 1959 as an 18 year old signed with Richmond.

Things were a bit different in those days. I do not recall much of a pre-season and the only weight training I can recall was being advised to eat plenty of Saunders malt extract over the summer to build up my then skinny frame.

I had been courted to some degree by eight clubs. Melbourne had been one of the teams interested in my signature. I remember being invited to a Melbourne dinner after one of its wins and being seated between legendary coach Norm Smith and Melbourne star Ron Barassi, which impressed me no end. All clubs except Melbourne and Collingwood offered some sort of inducement to sign. Those two clubs believed the honour and prestige of playing with their club was sufficient attraction in itself. Melbourne also offered the promise of MCC membership. Most clubs offered money even though it was contrary to the 'Coulter law'. Hawthorn promised me a place in the Melbourne University Medical Faculty assuming I passed my matriculation exams, which like today, was a very difficult course to get into.

The main reason I signed with Richmond was that Bobby Dummett, the Richmond full forward, had watched me play a number of school games. He recommended Richmond to me and me to Richmond. One lunch hour Dummett, Jack Dyer (Richmond legend) and president Bill Timms were discovered roaming around the school grounds amongst the kids looking for me. I was fairly impressed with this effort and eventually signed. My signing on 'fee' was 50 pounds ($100) and Richmond also got me a job at Russell Manufacturing in Burnley Street as a storeman/driver during the Christmas holidays.

In 1960, I played eleven games with Richmond seconds before retiring from VFL football.

I did not have the dedication which was required and was not fast enough, in any event. Half way through the season I returned to play for Ringwood in the finals and then played for Ivanhoe Amateurs for some years before finishing my distinguished career with Old Ivanhoe Grammarians reserves in 'F' grade.

In those days, the amateur competition was absolutely pure. Before being allowed to play, John Walker (who later kicked 150 goals for Preston) and I had to front the amateur officials to prove our amateur status. John had been with Hawthorn. We were asked such questions as, 'Have you ever bet when playing golf?' 'No', we replied, completely straight faced. In fact, I was very clean because I never accepted money from Richmond.

In succeeding years, I maintained an interest in football, but any club loyalty now took a back seat to a general interest in the game itself. Playing with Richmond had broken my previous attachment to Melbourne and I was not at Richmond long enough to develop any deep emotion for that club. Like most Tasmanians, I took an interest in the many great footballers who left the Apple

CHAPTER 1

Isle to play in the VFL. Over the years, I closely followed the careers of such players as Verdon Howell, Brent Crosswell, Peter Hudson, Ian Stewart, Darryl Baldock (my all-time favourite) and the like.

Occasionally I'd go to Glenferrie Oval just to observe the wizardry of Peter Hudson. I would watch him when the ball was up the other end just to see how it was that he managed to get free of his opponent all the time. He would start moving when the ball was two or three kicks away. Playing with long sleeves, he did not have the tough man image of a Ted Whitten, but his record is better than any full forward in any era.

In the early seventies I moved to North Fitzroy to live. At that time, Carlton and Hawthorn were sharing nearby Princes Park and I would occasionally go there to watch a game.

How did I come to barrack for Fitzroy? The fact that I lived in a suburb bearing the name Fitzroy had something to do with it. As well I was attracted by Fitzroy's underdog image. Looking back I cannot think of any definitive moment when I decided to follow the club. I suspect it was more of a gradual osmosis.

Initially when I began following Fitzroy, it was with interest but no real commitment. During the early eighties, I became a member and began to get more intensely involved. At two o'clock every Saturday afternoon a few other dedicated supporters such as Barry Dickens, Kevin Williams and I would assemble near the goalposts in the outer at Princes Park. At five o'clock when I left the ground my involvement ceased. During the eighties, the Lions were very competitive. Fitzroy made the finals five times, and I believe was very unlucky not to win at least one premiership during that period.

It was around this time that I first met Leon Wiegard, the president of the Fitzroy Football Club, through some close mutual friends. The club found itself needing legal representation and my support for Fitzroy presumably led to my name coming up.

In 1987, Keith Wiegard, Leon's brother and also a former club president, sued Fitzroy in the Supreme Court of Victoria for damages for wrongful dismissal. Keith had been sacked as a result of serious irregularities concerning, in particular, alleged false claims for expenses. One particular claim was for a trip to Tasmania for recruiting. Fitzroy asserted that Keith went to Tasmania for the weekend for purposes totally unconnected with the oval ball.

I was asked by barrister (and Fitzroy director) Dennis Connell if I would appear with him for the club in the Supreme Court action. Dennis Connell was 'Dennis Donohue' of *Lawyers, Guns and Money* fame, a popular show on community radio. I left a message for Dennis that I could not appear as I was otherwise engaged. The night before the case began, Dennis rang me and asked, 'When are we going to have a conference with our clients?' Dennis apparently had not received the message that I was unavailable. Rather than see Fitzroy left without a senior barrister, I reluctantly agreed to appear for the club after rearranging my schedule.

Dennis and I were instructed by Ross Campbell (Ross Stevenson, also of *Lawyers, Guns and Money*) who was then a solicitor with Slater and Gordon. At that time, *Lawyers, Guns and Money* had developed a cult following every Saturday morning, and I was an occasional guest, taking the pseudonym 'Mr. Francis.' At that time, lawyers, like doctors, were not allowed to use their real names when appearing on television or radio – even on a light hearted comedy show – for fear of being accused of advertising. Until recent times, I acted as a legal expert under two other pseudonyms – the first was 'Mr. Horse-Racy,' which was a little obvious, and was changed at very short notice on one occasion to 'Mr. GG.' *Lawyers, Guns and Money* went from 3RRR to 3AK and then, with a number of personnel changes, to the breakfast show on 3AW.

From the start the case went very well for the club. Keith's explanations for, on the face of it, incriminating evidence seemed implausible in the extreme. After hearing three days of evidence Keith's barrister offered to withdraw his claim if both parties paid

CHAPTER 1

their own costs. Even though we were extremely confident of winning, in which case we would have been awarded costs against Keith, in the final wash-up we believed Keith would have found it hard to pay our costs in any event. So we settled. After rejecting the club's original offer Keith ended up with nothing.

One of the more unfortunate aspects of the whole case was that Leon Weigard had to give evidence against his brother. They did not speak to each other for years. Fortunately they made peace before Keith's untimely death on December 17, 1992.

Leon, like many people, had not much respect for lawyers but was in court every day during the running of the case and seemed impressed with the job that we did. The fact that neither Dennis, Ross nor I charged a fee for our services probably impressed him even more.

We were, however, rewarded in other ways. Dennis, Ross and I were given a club pullover with leather shoulders. Even better, Max Kelleher (Fitzroy's general manager) gave me Fitzroy's number seven membership. Max had noted I worked in room seven on the seventh floor of my building. Fitzroy's Michael Gale wore number seven. This was a nice touch by Max because it was Keith Wiegard's recruiting trip to Tasmania to sign Michael that was central to the court case.

I suspect it was the result of the court skirmish that caused Leon's and others' minds to turn towards me as a possible director of the club. Every time I saw Leon over the next couple of years, he said things like, 'We must get you on the board.' Fortunately, the thought must have disappeared from his mind equally as quickly because no approach was made to me for a long time.

One day in mid to late 1990, however, Leon made a serious approach to me to join the Fitzroy Football Club board. He did not give me much of an option, come to think of it. He rang me and during our conversation said casually 'Incidentally, the directors have voted you onto the board.' I said, 'What's involved?' Leon replied 'A meeting once a month, that's all.' I accepted. I thought it would be impolite to decline. A bit of legal advice once per month would not constitute too much of a sacrifice, so I thought.

I was appointed to the board to fill a casual vacancy. Under Fitzroy's Articles of Association a casual appointee had to stand for election at the next annual general meeting. At the AGM Ray Paton, a very popular lifelong Fitzroy supporter, topped the poll and I finished second, securing one of the seats. At the first board meeting after the AGM, Leon Wiegard was elected chairman unopposed.

I was flattered to be asked to be a director of such a great and historic club. The position was absolutely honorary. I am surprised these days when I read of commercial directors of large companies receiving hundreds of thousands of dollars per year. At Fitzroy, we got nothing for free – we even paid our way at the chairman's lunches and other club functions.

In those days I do not believe that all football club directors were conscious of their legal liability, certainly not to the extent they are today. The most significant restriction was the Companies Law, which required companies not to trade if they were insolvent. That is, they could not trade if they believed they were not able to pay their debts when they became due. The old football club committees, run by presidents, secretaries and treasurers, etc, gave way to more modern business practices. When Fitzroy Football Club became Fitzroy Football Club Ltd, the company was subject to the strict provisions of civil law. Furthermore, under taxation law, if tax was not paid, the directors had certain personal liability.

Personal liability became an important issue for club directors in later years. I still believe there should be some way of separating 'normal companies' from sporting organisations like AFL clubs. With a community football club, the lives of tens of thousands of members and supporters revolve around the club, which makes it very difficult if not impossible to make decisions based solely on commercial reality and corporations law responsibility.

A person more street-wise than myself might have inquired about the club's finances before joining the board. Indeed a number

CHAPTER 1

of prominent people who we later asked to become directors of the club did make those inquiries and, as a result, most declined.

When I first joined, I had no idea that money was a real problem at Fitzroy. Before becoming a director I had attended a meeting at the Southern Cross Hotel where Leon Wiegard had mooted the possibility of playing games in Tasmania. At that meeting the 'Fitzroy Second Club Membership' proposal also emerged, which was based on the notion that Fitzroy was everybody's second favourite team, and that supporters of other clubs would take up our generous offer to become members of Fitzroy as well. It never really occurred to me that a VFL club that had been around for 100 years could have been threatened by serious financial problems, bearing in mind the huge popularity of VFL football. The Lions did not have a big membership but I assumed its traditional supporter base, backed up by the then VFL, would ensure the club's viability. I would quickly learn how naive that assumption was.

At the Southern Cross, Leon detailed financial projections on a whiteboard which showed hundreds of thousand of dollars coming in from the Tasmanians paying for Fitzroy membership and hundreds of thousand dollars coming in from all sorts of different areas. I must say that I was mightily impressed with the figures.

These financial windfalls did not eventuate, of course, although the club did play two premiership games and one pre-season game in Tasmania each year for two years. There were a number of reasons why the Tasmanian experiment did not wholly succeed. First, unlike the situation for most clubs in Melbourne, Fitzroy received no revenue from ground advertising or catering. In addition, unlike the position with all other clubs playing interstate, the AFL insisted we pay for all expenses (including air fares and accommodation) for both clubs. The North Hobart ground was too small for AFL football and the crowds averaged only about 10,000 people. At the end of the day we were paying for the privilege of playing in Tasmania.

I attended my first board meeting in early September of 1990.

FITZROY

At that meeting it became very quickly apparent that the club needed a major injection of funds to survive. There were also quite a few other problems that we had to deal with. Difficulties were being experienced in signing key players and in particular two of our champions, Gary Pert and Paul Roos. At the time the club's training headquarters were situated at Lakeside Oval, the old home of the South Melbourne Swans. In late 1990, the Albert Park Lake Trust, which leased the ground to Fitzroy, was so unimpressed at our lack of attention to paying the rent that it changed the locks to our training rooms.

The Fitzroy 'lock-out' was given wide publicity in the press, which was quite embarrassing, not only because our gymnasium equipment was locked inside but because it fanned the speculation which had been fuelled by the press for years concerning Fitzroy's financial viability. One proposed solution to the problem was to hire a truck and to turn up at six in the morning, hacksaw the lock and retrieve our equipment. I thought there had to be a better way of fixing the problem than that, and there was. We very quickly negotiated a settlement after drawing up a new schedule of payments.

But player contracts and training venues were not the only problems. During that first meeting our coach, Rod Austin, resigned in fairly controversial circumstances.

Rod had asked to speak to the board about his reappointment. The thrust of his address was that all other VFL clubs had appointed or reappointed their coaches for the following year whilst Fitzroy had not. The not so thinly veiled suggestion was that if we did not reappoint him then and there, he would resign. During the meeting we attempted, in vain, to ring Leon Weigard who was absent due to a speaking engagement somewhere on the Murray river. There was a feeling among certain directors that we should reappoint Rod to save embarrassment but we could not because the board had already appointed a sub-committee to make recommendations concerning all coaching positions for 1991. The board could not –

CHAPTER 1

and would not – be railroaded into making a decision before the recommendation was handed down.

Max Kelleher decided to talk to Rod outside the boardroom. When Max returned to the meeting he said that Rod wanted to know whether he had the full support of the board. If he did not, he wanted the opportunity to resign.

Even though it was a reasonable request the board was unable to give its unequivocal support at that time. However, I believe that it was almost certain that a new coach would have been appointed even if Rod had not pushed the issue. Rod had been senior coach of the club in 1989 and 1990. 1989 had been relatively successful for Fitzroy. Fitzroy had a win/loss record of 12-10, and only missed out on the final five in Round 20 when Collingwood, the club we were duelling with for fifth position, beat us by 33 points – a game which will be remembered by Fitzroy supporters more for Richard Osborne's sustaining of a serious knee injury.

The following year, 1990, was not a good one. In the first game Fitzroy were beaten by Essendon at Windy Hill by a mammoth 81 points and won only 7 games for the year. Many of the losses were by huge margins. There was a feeling amongst many of our supporters that Rod was not getting the best out of the team. Like all clubs, when the team is not performing the coach is the first person to come under scrutiny.

One of the great difficulties in football is determining who, if anyone, is responsible when a team is performing poorly. Unfortunately for coaches, one cannot change the playing personnel overnight. For the sake of the morale of members and supporters, not to mention sponsors, clubs must be seen to be doing something to bring about change. The ultimate responsibility falls on the coach and as such, he is usually the person who must go.

After discussing Rod's position with the board, Max left the room again and told Rod that he did not have its full support. Rod promptly announced his resignation and gave the club a serve in the press the next morning, as is the usual custom with disappointed coaches.

FITZROY

Within a few weeks Robert Shaw was appointed senior coach. He had played with and coached Essendon reserves. He had coached Fitzroy reserves for three years which included a premiership in 1989. He was desperate to coach at the premier level and was extremely confident in his ability to succeed. He lobbied the board individually and impressed us all with his energy and determination. Robert had served his apprenticeship successfully and with the supporting recommendation of Kelleher and the match committee, he was given a three year contract.

My second board meeting featured even more drama – an abortive coup against Leon Wiegard. A number of directors had decided that Leon should be replaced as chairman by vice chairman Paul Burke, who was a leading executive with Campbell's Soups, one of our major sponsors. (Burke was later to be a central figure, as Chief Executive Officer of Campbell's Soups, in the take-over battle with Arnott's Biscuits). Fortunately, being a newcomer and a friend of Leon's, I had not been approached in relation to the coup. The numbers had, apparently, been quietly organised before the meeting.

Unfortunately for the plan, one of the coup organisers, in a sudden and unexpected outpouring of guilt, revealed the plot and announced to the stunned directors, including Leon, that he had changed his mind. Then to the horror of other directors involved, he moved a motion of confidence in the chairman. I cannot remember if the motion actually was seconded or whether there was a vote but the attempted coup quickly collapsed. Wiegard and Burke almost came to blows after the meeting. Burke resigned at the next meeting and with this resignation Fitzroy lost its second largest sponsor.

I was rather bewildered by this, my first experience of boardroom politics and intrigue. Leon had been the public face of Fitzroy for years and had almost single-handedly stopped Fitzroy merging with Brisbane in the mid-80s. He had publicly carried the fight for Fitzroy's survival in a noble manner, and I had no

CHAPTER 1

inkling then that there was any dissatisfaction at board level. Later I would learn why this was so – Leon had a somewhat autocratic style and was not a great believer in lengthy debate.

I had been appointed to the board following a bitterly contested court case. My early board meetings featured a lock-out, a resignation and an attempted coup. But all of these issues were minor inconveniences compared to the financial projections presented to another early board meeting indicating that the Fitzroy debt was between $800,000 and $1.2 million which, in those days, was a lot of money. While star players today earn that much by themselves, a debt of such magnitude then meant that the Lions faced severe financial constraints. Fitzroy needed money desperately to remain competitive and ensure survival.

The Lions' on-field success had helped raise the club's profile during the eighties, but a crucial factor in the club's survival in those years had been one-off licence payments from new interstate clubs entering the AFL. We received $660,000 from the Adelaide Football Club licence fee when it was admitted into the competition in 1991, and earlier there had been a similar distribution from the West Coast Eagles entry in 1987.

In terms of yearly club income and expenditure, it was difficult to judge our real financial position. This was because money was always coming in and going out, and club accounts were not always up to date. There was a long list of creditors and debtors which was constantly changing.

In some ways Fitzroy was caught in the same bind as other sections of the community. In the early 90s interest rates were very high, as had been the case for some years. In order to fund football operations, we (like many other AFL clubs) had to borrow over a million dollars from the bank every year to fund our operations for the next year. This borrowing was secured against the following year's expected dividend which each club received from the AFL. This meant that the club was in effect operating one year behind its income. Fitzroy was paying out hundreds of thousands of dollars each year in interest and we believed if we could get rid of the debt the club could, with good business management, operate in the black every year. As every person closely involved in football knows, this is easier said than done!

In any event the board took the view that the only way the club could progress would be to eliminate the debt. Fitzroy had already conducted a major fundraising appeal in 1985 and it seemed inevitable that unless something extraordinary happened we would have to go to the public again, and quickly. We had seen what Footscray Football Club had managed to achieve two years earlier after the abortive attempt to merge that club with Fitzroy. Footscray succeeded in raising over two million dollars in three weeks. We set a target publicly of $800,000 to be raised by the end of June, 1991.

The appeal, born of necessity, was planned by Leon and the board and was launched at a grand ceremony at the Southern Cross Hotel in early 1991. By that time, I had been given a rapid promotion. After the annual general meeting Leon had been elected unopposed as chairman, but the previous vice-chairman, Paul Burke, had of course resigned and there was a vacancy for that position. I was nominated by Max Kelleher and elected unopposed. I am sure that the main reason for my elevation after only four months on the board was that no one was prepared to take on the position. I did not lobby for it nor did I want it. However by that stage I had become fairly heavily involved in a number of issues and had made a personal commitment to do the job as well as I could.

Leon's idea was that he would conduct the appeal and that I would be mainly responsible for the day-to-day running of the club. Such a structure never really operated, as we all became very involved in the appeal, the success of which was essential to the club's survival and future.

Our members and supporters and the Victorian football public in general both responded magnificently to our need. Our

CHAPTER 1

volunteers and Carlton and United Breweries distributed appeal tins to almost every hotel in Victoria. Our supporters took the tins to the streets and it was very difficult to move very far in any direction in Victoria without having a Fitzroy appeal tin thrust under your nose. We eventually raised over $200,000 from the tins alone. If all the tins had been returned, however, we would have made considerably more!

We also raised over $200,000 in our 'monster' raffle. The club had not conducted a major raffle in previous years. It relied on a number of smaller ones which accompanied the quarterly mail-out of our newsletter to members. In the major raffle the two main prizes were motorcars and, although GMH would not give us a vehicle, it did provide both cars at a reduced rate.

Nancye Cain, wife of then Premier John Cain, and our number one ticket holder, served as one of our trustees for the club's Grand Trust. Nancye, highly respected by the general community in her own right, was a great asset to the campaign. About $75,000 was raised by the trust. This consisted of $1000 donations which went into trust and was only to be distributed to Fitzroy if the appeal succeeded and Fitzroy continued in the AFL. Frank Gaffney, chairman of the AFL Tribunal for many years and a great Fitzroy supporter and former player, was another trustee as was Dennis Connell. The Fitzroy trust was the brainchild of a number of people, including Kevin Power, a dedicated Fitzroy supporter and father of Brisbane Lion's emerging star, Luke Power.

Every conceivable way of making money was investigated, and more often than not, implemented. There was a sense of urgency with all our functions. We held gambling nights, disco nights, theatre nights and even a Fitzroy concert. Due to this massive effort, we eventually managed to struggle past our $800,000 target in August 1991.

The appeal was to be Leon's last major contribution to the Fitzroy Football Club. By September of 1991 he had resigned and I had become acting chairman.

Chapter 2

The circumstances surrounding Leon Wiegard's resignation were more than a little acrimonious. In the end Leon incurred the wrath of all directors as a result of his involvement with Gary Pert's contractual dispute. This saga also taught me further lessons about how the AFL and its clubs operated.

Gary Pert had played for Fitzroy from a very young age. He came to the club at the same time as two of our other champions, Paul Roos and Richard Osborne. Gary had damaged his knee in the last game of 1990 which led to an immediate knee reconstruction. This meant he would not play a single game in 1991, the last year of his three year contract.

In those days, clubs used standard player contracts. Player payments were split into two categories: Base payments, which were a fixed amount to be paid regardless of whether or not the player played any games, and match payments. The amount of match payments received depended on the individual contract, the number of matches played and whether the player played in the senior team or the reserves. The contract also could include bonuses for such things as polling well in the club's best and fairest award.

Gary argued that under the terms of his contract he was entitled to the total of his base payment plus 22 senior match payments. The board argued that he was only entitled to his base payment because he would not be playing any matches. However we did offer an amount which included the base payment and made allowances for a substantial number of match payments. We also wanted Gary to enter into a new contract because we did not want to be in a position of paying him for a season he did not play and possibly losing him at the end of the year when his contract expired. It was no secret that other AFL clubs were interested in securing Gary's services.

CHAPTER 2

We attempted to negotiate with Gary. We received a solicitor's letter threatening legal action and a similar one from his manager. Gary also addressed the board and put his case. He spoke elegantly and forcefully. Gary was a very polished performer both on and off the field.

The Gary Pert dispute should be seen in the context of another decision taken by the board. We had to cut costs and we believed at that time that the team's performance did not justify the payments we were making to the players. We were very close to paying the players the maximum of the salary cap at that time. Consequently Max Kelleher was instructed to attempt to effect a 10% reduction in player payments across the board. Had the club been in a healthier financial position we would have been in a position to agree to Gary's request.

In the end, Gary was prepared to take less than his original demand and we were prepared to pay more. Unfortunately, the two figures did not meet.

The board recognised Gary's right to insist on what he believed was his contractual right. The board read his contract a different way. Gary's dispute became a public issue and there started to appear some very negative articles about the club with direct quotations attributed to Gary.

The board decided that it could not afford to pay Gary what he requested and it could not afford the continual negative publicity. Consequently, after discussions with the match committee, it took the dramatic step of de-listing him, the equivalent of sacking him. This was a huge shock to Fitzroy supporters and the football public in general.

When the dust settled, the club – and no doubt Gary – looked at all the options. The only way Gary could go to the club of his choice was if an arrangement could be made with an AFL club whereby Gary was exchanged for another player or players and/or draft choices. If this could not be arranged, then Gary would have to go into the November draft which meant that any club, and the least successful clubs had the early choices, could draft him. If this happened Fitzroy would get nothing and would lose a quality player into the bargain. It was obviously in both the club's and Gary's interests to agree to a satisfactory trade. To achieve this, however, the club would need to keep Gary on its player list for the 1991 season.

Consequently, we wrote to Gary's manager informing him that we would not immediately de-list him but would use our best endeavours to arrange a trade to the club of his choice sometime during 1991.

In the end, Gary was still a Fitzroy player and would remain one for the 1991 football season. As the year progressed, with the appeal going very well, the directors were increasingly hopeful that we could settle the dispute with Gary and that he would remain at Fitzroy. Morale-wise that would be a crowning moment to the success of the appeal, some of us thought.

In about mid-1991 a few of the directors became concerned that negotiations regarding Gary's future were taking place. Whilst the board did not often involve itself in player contracts and negotiations, we took the view that Gary's case was important enough to demand our involvement. Consequently the board directed that no deal could be done with Gary without the express approval of the board. This was recorded in the club minutes in early 1991. During the year, rumours abounded that Gary Pert to Collingwood was a 'done deal.' The rumours even appeared in the press but the directors kept denying them. They were hopeful that we could settle the dispute with Gary and that he would remain at Fitzroy.

Towards the end of the year I received a phone call stating that Gary Pert was most concerned because the AFL proposed to investigate a deal which had been done between Collingwood and Fitzroy during the year. I spoke to Don Wallace, our CEO, who told me that Leon Weigard and Max Kelleher had agreed with Collingwood chairman Alan McAlister and Graeme Allan, who

CHAPTER 2

was Collingwood's football manager, that Pert would be sold to Collingwood at the end of the season in exchange for $120,000 plus Collingwood's first two draft choices. This agreement was contrary to AFL draft rules, as players could not be sold. None of the other directors, I believe, had any knowledge that a deal had been done with Gary.

Don Wallace and I arranged to meet Gary Pert at his Prahran home where we had a very frank meeting. Don and I told Gary that the board always hoped that Gary and the club would resolve their differences and that Gary would re-sign with Fitzroy. Gary was concerned that he may be disqualified from playing football for some time although there was no suggestion that Gary was involved in anything contrary to AFL rules. I believe that part of the unauthorised agreement with Gary was that he would be paid for the year that he couldn't play football by one of Collingwood's sponsors although this was not mentioned by Gary. When we left Gary's home that evening, I believe that Gary, Don and I had an agreement in principle that Gary would come back to Fitzroy if the agreement with Collingwood could be undone.

At that time, with the appeal underway, we thought that the club could afford to pay Gary what he asked.

Don Wallace then informed the directors of what had happened. Collingwood had been given a supposed 'minute' indicating board approval for the agreement that was effected. The directors took the view that what had occurred was in direct defiance of the board decision, and were very, very, angry.

We wrote a detailed letter to Collingwood setting out what had occurred according to our information and informing them that if they did not relinquish their hold on Gary we would be making a formal complaint to the AFL setting out everything that had happened. The letter was ignored.

We then lodged a complaint with the AFL, setting out the history of the matter asking that the transfer of Pert to Collingwood be set aside for contravening the draft rules and also on the basis that it was in defiance of a board directive. Even though the action we took could have been severely embarrassing for Leon, he did not attempt to dissuade us from our course in any way. He knew, however, that the directors were extremely unhappy with the situation.

At the time we lodged our complaint, or shortly after, the AFL hierarchy were in London on one of their junkets officiating at an end of season promotional game between two AFL teams. Coincidently, Leon Wiegard was in attendance as the official announcer.

Barry Capuano, then a senior administrator with the AFL, was assigned to determine the complaint. I am told that Glen Warry, Fitzroy's football manager, and Don Wallace gave precise details of meetings with McAlister and Allan and of conversations between them detailing the agreement with Collingwood including the money. McAlister, Allan and Kelleher denied the allegations. Kelleher was no longer with us. I am told that Capuano asked McAlister and Allan to fill in a statutory declaration denying the events which had been so closely detailed by Warry and Wallace. This they did. Capuano officially found that the complaint was not substantiated.

Part of the fallout from this abortive attempt to have Pert's transfer set aside was that Don Wallace was threatened with a defamation suit by one of the Collingwood officials, a threat which caused a great lot of distress to Don who was approaching his retirement, and who was not well. In addition, Wallace was reminded by the AFL solicitor Jeff Browne that if the Fitzroy complaint was proved, Fitzroy could be fined $250,000 for its part in breaching AFL draft and salary cap rules. So much for truth in football.

Don had told me that there was documentation in existence which evidenced the agreement. This documentation could not be found, however, until the day after Capuano's hearing concluded. We now felt we could prove that payments were

CHAPTER 2

involved. It set out in detail how the payments would be made in instalments and disguised as membership income. Some of the handwriting was readily identifiable.

Word had obviously got back to the AFL very quickly that the documents had been found, because a short time later I received a telephone call from AFL solicitor Jeff Browne, stating that the AFL wished to see the documents if I had them, as the AFL did not want to be made fools of later. I did not admit or deny that I had the documents.

Early next year, Sandy Robertson, a Melbourne barrister, was appointed special AFL investigator to replace Max Croxford. He was assigned a number of matters for investigation. The main one was the circumstances surrounding the drafting of Nathan Buckley from Brisbane Bears to Collingwood. Another was the drafting of Gary Pert by Collingwood. It is extraordinary that no hint of the Pert allegations have reached the press to this day. It seems the AFL can keep a secret if it chooses to.

By the time the Gary Pert matter came up for its hearing before Sandy Robertson, the Fitzroy draft choices had arrived in Melbourne and were in training. Jeremy Guard was one of these. Our football people rated his potential highly. The Fitzroy directors discussed at length what our response to the investigation would be. In view of the threat of fining the club for 'our' part in the Pert deal and because so much water had flown under the bridge in the meantime, we decided to let sleeping dogs lie.

After informing the AFL solicitor, Jeff Browne of what I proposed to do, I went to Harrison House, the AFL headquarters at an appointed time for the commencement of the Pert hearing. I told Sandy Robertson that we did not wish to pursue the complaint, giving him the reasons why. And that was the end of the matter.

Gary Pert went on to become a very good player for Collingwood. Jeremy Guard became a good player for the Lions, but never achieved the heights we hoped he would.

Shortly after Leon Wiegard came back from London, he

tendered his resignation to the board and it was accepted. He was made a patron of the Club which was the highest honour we could bestow upon him. He was already a life member of both the AFL and of Fitzroy.

It was time for a change. Leon Wiegard has been and remains a great Fitzroy person. While some found his leadership style too undemocratic, his approach did have its benefits. I am told that in 1986, when the Fitzroy board voted for Fitzroy to re-locate to Brisbane, Leon refused to accept the decision and the club kept going for another ten years. Leon was a great public speaker and in the public arena was a very fine leader. While Leon was very cool towards the board at the time of his resignation, and I believe for some time thereafter, bad feeling from the events of 1991 eventually disappeared. He was always welcome at Fitzroy and indeed was asked to speak on a number of occasions, invitations which he readily accepted.

The irony of what had happened was that, at the end of the day, we lost Gary and the money. If we had turned a blind eye to what had happened and gone along with the 'secret plan', the club would have benefited by $120,000, money we very much needed. The directors took the view, however, that if Fitzroy Football Club could not function with integrity, it would not function at all.

I declined the invitation to assume the chairmanship until after the next annual general meeting, but filled the position in an acting capacity.

What I thought would be a quiet introduction to life as an AFL football club director turned out to be the exact opposite. From the outset I was kept busy putting out spot fires which were continually fanned by the media. Extremely harmful reports were appearing in the press concerning different aspects of Fitzroy's operations. At the end of 1991 I drafted a long letter to the major newspapers – signed by the directors – asking the press to get off our backs. The administration seemed to spend half its time hosing down negative press stories about Fitzroy.

CHAPTER 2

Fitzroy lashes 'critical' reports

Angry Lions roar
Club pleads for unity, blasts critics

Bruce Matthews
Herald Sun
Tuesday 19/3/91

Ron Carter
The Age
Tuesday 19/3/91

Many of the problems we were experiencing, such as difficulty in signing key players, were problems that all clubs experienced. Any problem that Fitzroy had, however, was always highlighted by journalists, some of whom seemed to have free access to sensitive AFL information concerning Fitzroy. This was to be another constant source of annoyance over the years.

One such incident occurred in 1995 when the Holiday Inn in Sydney sent a letter of complaint about the behaviour of a couple of our players. It was headlines in the Melbourne press within hours. I rang the manager of the Holiday Inn to discuss his complaint. He told me that within half an hour of faxing his complaint to the AFL, and to the AFL's travel agent, he was bombarded by press from all over Australia asking him questions about the incident. The publication *Inside Football* must have received a copy of the Holiday Inn fax because, in the fax, Doug Hawkins was incorrectly listed as one of the occupiers of a damaged room instead of another one of our players Simon Hawking. The magazine rang asking me to confirm that Doug Hawkins was the occupier of the damaged room. I warned the magazine that the details were incorrect without being specific. They published the story anyway and Doug later successfully sued them for defamation.

Dougie was then an emerging star on 'The Footy Show' and he told me that within hours of the complaint being made by Holiday

Inn, one of the Channel 9 executives confronted him, saying that he had information from 'very high up' that Doug had been involved in damaging a room at the Holiday Inn. As it turned out, neither he nor Simon Hawking had been involved in any damage whatsoever or in any untoward behaviour.

On another occasion, Fitzroy had made an application to the AFL Commission to extend the time for repayment of an AFL loan of $250,000 that the AFL had advanced to us. The only people at Fitzroy who knew of our approach to the AFL were three directors, such was our concern for confidentiality. At the time we made the application we specifically told the commissioners that we did not want to read about our application in *The Herald Sun* the next day.

About a week after our meeting with the AFL Commission, Ross Oakley rang me in my chambers and informed me that the AFL had rejected our application. I deliberately decided not to inform anyone else, including the other directors.

I was out of Melbourne that night, and the press did not know where to find me. Usually with leaked information, the press would ring me or our CEO and say, 'I have heard this or that, do you have a comment?' Depending on the answer the story would read 'Fitzroy Chairman denies etc' or 'Fitzroy Chairman admits etc.' If the press could not get any meaningful response it would just print the story with the information coming from 'reliable sources'.

Later on that evening, knowing the press did not know where I was, I was curious to see whether anyone had rung Barry Capuano, now our CEO, but a former senior administrator with the AFL. I rang Barry at home and he told me that he had been rung by Daryl Timms of the *Herald Sun* about the rejection of our loan submission. Of course Barry knew nothing about it. He did not even know about our approach to the AFL. When Barry asked me if I knew what Timms was talking about, I said that I would tell him later. I was determined that no Fitzroy person apart from myself would know about it.

CHAPTER 2

Sure enough, next morning's blazing headlines on the back page of the *Herald Sun* trumpeted Mike Sheahan's article giving precise details of our application and the AFL's rejection!

I was furious. I spoke on radio stations 3LO, 3AW, and 927 Sport, stating exactly what happened. Of course the AFL denied it and Sheahan wrote a lame article saying the leak did not come from the AFL and suggesting I had told somebody at Fitzroy and had forgotten about it. Everyone at Fitzroy and many of the football public in general had a good laugh about the AFL being so blatantly caught out.

Involvement with the public appeal and dealing with an often negative media began to take more and more of my time. My hope was to help guide the club out of stormy waters, at which time I would quietly resign and fade back into the relative anonymity of my previous life. Unfortunately the security and stability that the members and supporters craved was never achieved except in fleeting moments. Oh, for a Joe Gutnick![1]

During 1991, there were a number of changes in Fitzroy's administration. Our chief executive officer, Max Kelleher, was replaced by Don Wallace, our finance manager. Max, I think, got worn down by the job. The board had directed Max to reduce player payments and there is no tougher job in football. As a result of this Max became very unpopular with some of our key players.

With a new coach, a good football staff and a fresh outlook we looked forward to the start of the 1991 season with a heart full of hope. Glen Warry had replaced Arthur Wilson as our football manager after years of devoted service from Arthur. Gus Mitchell, a former very successful coach of St. Bernard's Old Boys in the Victorian Amateur Football Association was chairman of selectors. Our match committee included former star player, captain and coach Bill Stephen.

---

1. Mining magnate Joe Gutnick came to Melbourne Football Club's rescue in 1996 when he injected millions of dollars into the club.

For years Fitzroy had played a free running, handballing, attacking style of football. Robert Shaw was determined to inject a hard competitive edge to the team. This meant a completely new style of football and like most changes, the first few steps were backwards rather than forward. We did not expect the steps to be quite so far backward however! Our first game for 1991 was in the pre-season competition at North Hobart on February 3. Everyone at Fitzroy was hopeful for a good start to the season to help launch our appeal on a positive note. It was not to be. We got belted by Carlton by 85 points.

In Round 1 of the premiership season the club had a bye. We met Melbourne in Round 2 at Princes Park. Melbourne, not one of the stronger teams, won by 131 points. Then followed losses to Collingwood (69 points), Footscray (16 points) and Richmond (24 points). These last two results gave us some heart and we were confident of a good showing against Hawthorn in Tasmania on April 10, 1991. Hawthorn was one of the elite teams, however, and proceeded to demolish Fitzroy to the tune of 157 points. I remember watching the match on television in Melbourne and thinking, at sometime during the game, that if Hawthorn continued in the vein that it had started it was going to break Fitzroy's record for the highest winning score in the AFL. But Robert was apparently conscious of this as the game progressed and towards the end stacked the back line which made scoring more difficult for the Hawks.

During the appeal we had promised people that they would have their money refunded if the appeal was unsuccessful and Fitzroy could not continue. During one of our worst losses at Princes Park (now Optus Oval), during a quiet period in the game, a lone voice yelled out 'Give back the money now.' One thing constant about Fitzroy supporters was their sense of humour!

It was not until Round 10 at Princes Park against Geelong that Fitzroy had its first win for the season. This 21 point victory provided a great lift to the club. The second half of the season,

CHAPTER 2

however, was even more encouraging. Although Fitzroy lost the next eight games the losses were not as bad as earlier ones and the Club finished on a high by winning three out of the last five games, including the defeat of competition leaders West Coast Eagles at Princes Park in the last game of the year by 10 points.

How many Fitzroy supporters can forget the nightmare of the loss to the Crows in Adelaide during Round 12? It had been teeming with rain all night and with two minutes to play, in a very low scoring game, the umpires awarded four very questionable (we would say wrong) free kicks in a row to the Crows. These penalties constituted the last four kicks of the night which resulted in Adelaide kicking two very quick goals to win by three points after the final siren. Our gallant team, which had played its heart out all night, was shattered.

It seemed the whole of Victoria watched the last quarter on television, all willing a Fitzroy victory; and there was general outrage over what had happened.

Our match committee actually wrote to the umpires' advisor complaining about each of the free kicks and we were most surprised to get a letter back agreeing that none of the free kicks was warranted. Who said umpiring decisions cannot affect the result of a game?

Throughout the year while the appeal was running, the board kept what it believed was a close eye on the club's financial position. John Dawson, a very senior executive with the National Bank of Australia, served as our finance director and tried to monitor our accounts. Towards the end of the year, however, it became increasingly apparent that the club had not traded as well as we had believed. We became progressively aware that a projected profit was turning into an increasing loss. We were shocked to learn from the information we were regularly receiving that the loss could be as high as $300,000, excluding money from the appeal, and that the figure was continuing to blow out alarmingly.

The board was meeting weekly at this time, trying to cope with the deteriorating financial position. I recall ringing John Dawson who was in Perth on business and hearing him ask, 'Not another hundred thousand?'

Every week the board would be informed of an additional loss. These losses were attributed to such basic things as accounting errors or treating short term loans as income. When the books were closed off for the full football financial year, our real trading loss added up to around $860,000.

This shattering result meant that we had lost more in trading for the year than we had raised in the appeal! This was going to be very difficult news to break to our members – many of whom had stood in the rain for hours rattling tins to keep their beloved club afloat.

Roys still in the red

James Weston
Herald Sun
19/12/91

In the meantime, it was left to me, as acting chairman, to explain to the Fitzroy faithful how we had managed to lose more in trading than we had raised in the appeal. This was perhaps the most unpleasant and difficult task I ever undertook as chairman.

There were good reasons to account for about half of the loss. Traditionally, many expenditure items had been deferred to the next year's accounting period. As a result of some highly publicized company failings including the Tri-Continental crash, and the Victorian Economic Development Corporation (VEDC) debacle, auditing procedures had tightened up considerably in Victoria. The board had made a decision some time before to clean up the books so that the club's financial reporting more accurately reflected trading for that year. We also had a large list of debtors, many of

CHAPTER 2

which should have been written off. Relating expenditure items to their correct year increased the loss for that year.

To soften the blow, one week before the annual general meeting held on December 18, I gave an interview to a journalist renowned for his integrity, Mark Harding, who was writing for the *Sunday Herald Sun*. Mark wrote a story which faithfully recorded my given reasons for the loss and put the position in perspective.

At the annual general meeting I was treated well by our faithful supporters who were largely very supportive. Even those who disagreed with the directors' performance managed to do so without being condemnatory.

This was, perhaps, partly because the bad news about our trading position was somewhat tempered by other, more positive announcements at the AGM. The first concerned our planned return to Brunswick Street oval, the traditional ground of the Lions and the place where it all started for Fitzroy.

We had been liaising with the Fitzroy Council during that year, seeking approval to return to the Brunswick Street Oval as a home base. A very supportive Fitzroy Council had approved our application. All that was needed was renovation of the old heritage grandstand, and the building of a modern gymnasium over the existing community room, for a total amount of $250,000, and we were back to our roots! Some local residents had objected to our proposal, but with the help of architect and town planner Lou Sayer, we won the objectors' appeal in the Administrative Appeals Tribunal. Unfortunately we never had the money to complete our plans.[2]

Even better news was to follow. I was able to announce the acquisition of the Fitzroy Club Hotel as a social centre for the club, complete with a gaming room facility. Our members knew what a big step this was, and greeted the news enthusiastically.

---

2. The Brunswick Street oval is once more being used for football. Fitzroy Redz in the Victorian Amateur Football Association and Fitzroy Juniors in the Yarra Junior Football League play home games at the venue in the traditional Fitzroy colours.

Roys set up home in Northcote pub

Michelle Griffin
Melbourne Times
22/1/92

In 1991, legislation was introduced by the Victorian parliament enabling the establishment of gaming machines in hotels and clubs. The legislation provided for clubs to receive four percent and hotels to receive three per cent of total turnover as commission. Fitzroy, with Melbourne Football Club, was one of only two AFL clubs in Victoria which did not have a social club. We were very keen to establish a base for our supporters in any case, but it now became a financial necessity as well. The pokies were going to be the saviour of all Victorian clubs, so everyone thought, and Fitzroy did not want to be left wallowing in the wake of other AFL clubs. If we were going to participate in gaming machine revenue, we had to acquire a hotel.

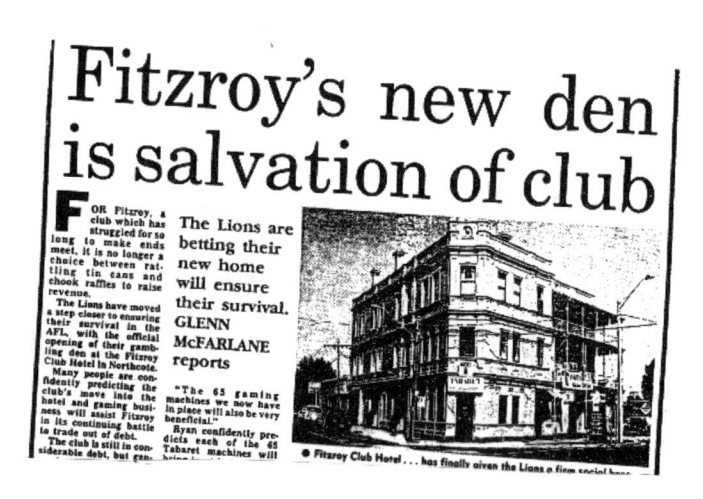

Fitzroy's new den is salvation of club

FOR Fitzroy, a club which has struggled for so long to make ends meet, it is no longer a choice between rattling tin cans and chook raffles to raise revenue.

The Lions have moved a step closer to ensuring their survival in the AFL, with the official opening of their gambling den at the Fitzroy Club Hotel in Northcote.

Many people are confidently predicting the club's move into the hotel and gaming business will assist Fitzroy in its continuing battle to trade out of debt.

The club is still in considerable debt, but gen-

The Lions are betting their new home will ensure their survival. GLENN McFARLANE reports

"The 65 gaming machines we now have in place will also be very beneficial."

Ryan confidently predicts each of the 65 Tabaret machines will

● Fitzroy Club Hotel... has finally given the Lions a firm social base

Glenn McFarlane
Herald Sun
15/3/92

CHAPTER 2

One of Fitzroy's former players, John Bahen, worked for leading real estate agents, McGees. He was on the lookout for us for a suitable hotel and had been for some time. For obvious reasons, we wanted a hotel in the Fitzroy area. We looked at quite a few, but most were unsatisfactory. A hotel called The Loaded Dog, on the corner of St. Georges Road and Holden Street, North Fitzroy was the initial target. A leading Melbourne accounting firm, Bongiornos, put a proposal to us whereby it would purchase the hotel, pay for the renovations, and lease it back to Fitzroy Football Club. On the face of it, this appeared quite an attractive proposition.

While we were negotiating with Bongiornos, another hotel was brought to our attention – The Albion Charles, on the corner of Charles Street and St. Georges Road, Northcote. This grand Georgian structure overlooked Merri Creek and had off-street parking for around seventy vehicles, whereas The Loaded Dog suffered the serious disadvantage of having no off-street parking. The Albion Charles had a turn-over of around $30,000 per week, its bar trade inflated by the presence of topless barmaids.

The Loaded Dog was publicly auctioned and, on the day of the auction, was passed in unsold. Bongiornos were not prepared to pay the asking price, and it was with some relief that our proposed joint venture came to nothing because by now most of the directors believed that the Albion Charles would be a more suitable acquisition. One of the part owners of 'The Albion', Max Novelli, was a long-time Fitzroy supporter and he had two partners keen to sell and we were just as keen to buy[3].

The problem with the Albion Charles was that unlike the Loaded Dog at the time, it had an established trade and therefore, we would have to pay more for a lease of the business. The going figure at that time to acquire a long term lease was about $500,000, but because of the constant adverse publicity surrounding the club, it was impossible for us to borrow from any financial institution.

---

3. The hotel's previous tenant had walked out of the hotel forcing Max and his partners to run the hotel themselves.

We had to raise money to acquire and set up the hotel ourselves. In the end, the club acquired a twenty-year lease for a purchase price of $150,000. Because of the lower purchase price, our monthly rent was much higher, $22,500 to be exact, indexed to the Consumer Price Index.

The club's advice, from John McArdle of law firm Williams, Winter & Higgs, who specialised in liquor licensing, and Charman and Tierney, well known hotel accountants, was that it was a good deal. John Bahen's own opinion made it unanimous.

I signed the contract for the lease on the day of the annual general meeting, in the offices of Williams, Winter and Higgs. Shortly before I signed, I raced out to a chemist shop and bought a disposable Kodak camera to mark the momentous event. The snaps did not come out too well in the gloomy office but somewhere one day I will find photos of a smiling, optimistic acting chairman (myself), John McArdle, and the solicitor acting for the owners, John Leadston, holding the lease agreement.

Before the lessors would sign a lease, the vendors insisted that I guarantee the purchase price ($150,000) of the hotel. I did this in the confident expectation that we would be successful in raising the money. The other directors said later that they would stand by me if the worst happened and we had to forfeit the purchase price. To finance the hotel, I wrote to about 400 people enclosing a solicitor's letter from John McArdle setting out what the company structure would be. For the protection of the football club and of the hotel, it was imperative that the Fitzroy Football Club Limited and the hotel be kept completely separate. I would not have asked our members and supporters to invest if I had thought either entity could adversely impact on the other. The people I wrote to were the major shareholders of Fitzroy Football Club Limited (we had about 700 shareholders in total) and those of our supporters whom we believed may have had a capacity to lend the club money.

The only way we could fund the hotel was from our club folllowers. In order to protect their investment, we decided to set

CHAPTER 2

up a company, Fitzroy Finances Limited, which would be the investment company. A trust company, the Fitzroy Hotel Trust, was set up and a shelf company, Bondborough Pty Ltd was set up as the trustee company. Bondborough was to hold the licence. Under the terms of the trust, income from the hotel could be allocated to Fitzroy Football Club, its players and coaches or any other like entity, in what is known as a discretionary trust. The practical effect of this arrangement was that the club would almost certainly receive hotel profits, as long as it stayed in the AFL competition. No person, including directors, could receive a cent of any profits. In setting up the structures, we acted on the advice of our solicitors and in particular the accounting firm KPMG.

None of us knew at the time that the setting up of the hotel was to become a huge issue five years later when the Fitzroy Football Club administrator claimed the hotel as an asset of the football club. (This hopelessly doomed claim was to be funded by the Brisbane Football Club through the Supreme Court of Victoria and up to the Court of Appeal.)

We set the hotel up in the way we did for two main reasons. First, we hoped to make substantial profits from the hotel and our advice from KPMG was that the profits from the hotel would not be subject to taxation if it was done that way. Second, in the event of either the hotel or football club folding, the creditors of the failed entity could not touch the assets of the other.

Investors were to be paid an interest rate of ten per cent – which was more than competitive at the time it was struck. Their investment was protected by a debenture over Bondborough's assets (including the twenty year lease). Eventually the directors put in $70,000 and others contributed around $65,000, which was enough to get the hotel up and running.

There were five directors of Bondborough: myself, Elaine Findlay, Vince Flynn, Ray Paton and Ken Levy. David Sandground was also a director for a very short time. Ray Paton was a former hotelier and builder who completed much of the renovations at bargain basement rates. All the directors of Bondborough Pty Ltd were required to be directors of Fitzroy Football Club Ltd.

I remember very clearly the first board meeting of Bondborough. Fitzroy was playing a practice match at Bulleen Park, our summer training ground, against Melbourne Football Club. I used to enjoy these matches – there wasn't the same pressure as there was with the genuine article. Everybody was in a post-Christmas, pre-season mood. At that time of the year, the team was as good as one's imagination. The weather was perfect, sunny and warm with cloudless skies. We sold barbequed sausages on bread for a dollar each.

It was just such a day on February 8, 1992. Again a number of grinning Bondborough directors were photographed. At that time we passed key resolutions which formally secured for Bondborough Pty Ltd a twenty year lease of the hotel. After the game, a number of us went back to the hotel. For the first time in years Fitzroy had a social club to call its own. Just sitting there having a quiet drink, knowing that the place was ours, was contentment itself.

We took possession of the hotel on March 12, 1992, and shortly thereafter it was officially opened, with great pomp and ceremony, by Paul Roos who cut ribbons with Fitzroy colours to mark the occasion. John and Judy Patterson were our first managers. Unfortunately – and I say that for financial reasons only – we had to dispense with the services of the topless barmaids. It is a fairly sad indictment on the male population, which comprised around ninety per cent of our public bar trade, that patronage of the public bar fell away significantly when the girls left. Before they departed, however, they did have an impact. I recall getting a letter of complaint from one of our elderly supporters who related how he was proudly showing his wife around the hotel when he took her into the public bar to be confronted by a pair of 'bare bosoms from close range'. I experienced the same shocked reaction from a number of other people. It is very hard to please everybody!

CHAPTER 2

The first formal occasion at the hotel was a black tie dinner, held on March 23, 1992 to mark the commencement of the premiership football season, where a proud group of players, coaching and other football staff attended along with close supporters of the club. It was a great success. Thereafter all the coteries held most of their functions there, and during the football season, the 'Ins and Outs' night was created. For the price of $10, members could get a two course meal on a Thursday night and be entertained by one of the match committee announcing the team selected for the weekend. Usually an injured player or two attended.

After the games, supporters and the team would go back to the hotel. The players would have a drink and something to eat upstairs and at about 6.30 pm would go downstairs to be greeted by their adoring fans. When we won, the place was packed. I recall one year when we beat Collingwood by three points at Princes Park the hotel took $25,000 (for liquor sales alone) on the Saturday, a massive amount of money for that venue.

At that time the club's administration offices were at the corner of Lygon Street and Brunswick Street, Brunswick. We were paying $35,000 per year rent and it was only a matter of time before we moved our administration to the first and second floors of the Fitzroy Club Hotel.

In all, we had to find approximately $200,000 to renovate the hotel and set it up for gaming. Ray Paton had done a wonderful job in planning and overseeing the renovations to the hotel and he would be sorely missed when he left the board in August of 1992.

1991 had been a year of ups and downs for the Fitzroy Football Club. Almost all management positions were filled with new personnel, the club had struggled publicly to free itself from debt, and there was growing difficulty in keeping our key players. None of us thought that the Lions were out of the financial woods yet, but the encouraging on-field results from the season's second half was a reason to look forward to 1992. The hotel was the kind of money-spinner we hoped might offer a long-term alternative to appeals and loans.

At the first board meeting after the annual general meeting I was voted chairman and John Dawson vice chairman. Both positions were unopposed. A special position of senior director was created and filled by Elaine Findlay in recognition of her contribution to the board.

But new financial crises would arise to test the new people, and problems with the AFL and its corporate vision would soon cause us to forget this brief moment of contentment.

Chapter 3

The newly named Fitzroy Club Hotel helped fuel the directors' optimism somewhat, but we knew that the club would live or die by its on-field success, and the situation there showed great promise. The first few months of 1992 were to become the most enjoyable for Fitzroy supporters since the successes of the eighties.

We had a large core of very good players in 1992 – Paul Roos, Richard Osborne, Paul Broderick, Matthew Armstrong, Ross Lyon, Alastair Lynch, John Blakey, Michael Gale, Jimmy Wynd and others.

We got off to a flying start in the pre-season competition with a gutsy win over North Melbourne at North Hobart Oval by two points in late February, and two weeks later we whipped Sydney by 58 points at Waverley. The improvement in the side was dramatic and it was with some confidence that we faced up to Adelaide in the semi-final on March 6. Fitzroy played terrific football in that game to win by 31 points. On March 14, 1992, in front of over 50,000 people, we met AFL powerhouse Hawthorn in the Fosters' Cup grand final at AFL Park. This was a fantastic experience for our supporters and players, but unfortunately we were no match for the very powerful Hawthorn side who, after an even first 45 minutes or so, went on to win by 65 points.

Over the years Fitzroy's colours had changed to the extent that the traditional maroon had gradually become closer to a red. I remember looking out over the crowd when we scored a goal and noting different coloured flags from different eras being waved. There is nothing like success to bring out supporters! A crowd of 50,000 was considered to be very good for a pre-season match, showing that a successful Fitzroy team could draw crowds. At the pre-game dinner, AFL protocol was to invite competing club presidents plus other dignitaries to sit at their table. The Hawthorn president at that time was Trevor Coote and Premier Jeffrey

FITZROY

Kennett, a keen Hawthorn supporter, was at the table as well. For want of something better to talk about I brought up the subject of mobile phones which received a fairly cool reception. Most readers will recall the colourful tape-recorded conversation between Jeff Kennett and Andrew Peacock, which if my memory serves me correctly, was none too flattering of our current Prime Minister, John Howard.

Despite the fact that we were beaten fairly convincingly, our good form gave us all hope for the remainder of the season. After an annoying first-round bye, Fitzroy met Essendon at the MCG for our first premiership contest. I was working in Darwin at the time and had to ring Melbourne for the scores. I recall ringing my wife and hearing her reply, 'Haven't you heard what's happened?' My heart sank. I answered 'No, I haven't, what's happened?' She told me that Fitzroy was over 90 points ahead at three-quarter time! I couldn't believe it. Essendon rattled on goals in the last quarter but Fitzroy still won by 52 points.

After the first nine games we had won six and lost three. The last of those wins was against Collingwood at Princes Park by only three points. It was one of the best games I have ever seen. Fitzroy led all day only to relinquish the lead as a result of a freak Collingwood goal from the boundary and another, kicked by former Lion Gary Pert, in the dying minutes of the game. Then, with seconds to spare, Paul Roos snapped a left foot goal to give us victory by three points.

Thereafter our form commenced to slip. We were beaten by Footscray at Princes Park by 62 points the next week, and then by Hawthorn by 56 points. We recovered somewhat to beat Carlton by 19 points at Princes Park before losing to Melbourne by 22 points and then regaining form against Sydney at the Sydney Cricket Ground to win by 53 points. On July 12 we met Essendon at North Hobart Oval. That match was very hard fought, with Fitzroy well ahead deep into the last quarter. Some very good late goals by Essendon gave them a win by three points. I believe that

CHAPTER 3

this match was a turning point for us for the rest of the year. We were all extremely disappointed, but no one more than Robert Shaw who, having played and coached at Essendon, was very keen to have another win over his mentor, Kevin Sheedy. We then lost five games in a row before beating Richmond in the second-last game and losing to North Melbourne in the last, a very disappointing finish to the season considering our good start. However, nine wins was an improvement on our previous two years.

But on-field success must be backed by sound finances, and our performance in the account books failed to match the players' success on the scoreboard.

Early in 1992 the board began to be increasingly concerned about some aspects of the club's administration. Don Wallace started as finance manager in 1990, the same year that I was appointed to the board. He had a distinguished work history in banking. During our 'Appeal Year' (1991) we appointed Don as general manager, partly on the recommendation of our resigning general manager, Max Kelleher. Don did not have the ideal qualifications for the job but the state of the club was so fragile that we were probably over-sensitive about negative publicity from more changes to key personnel, and he had worked very well in the finance area.

Don Wallace, along with his replacement as finance manager, Rod Hayes, controlled club finances. One of Don's biggest responsibilities was the negotiation of player contracts. This resulted in a large increase in player payments of nearly $350,000. The positive aspect of this policy was that the players went into the 1992 season much happier than the group which succumbed so easily in the first half of 1991.

In mid-year Rod Hayes rang up and asked to come in and see me. He revealed additional debts totalling approximately $250,000 that had not been disclosed to the board. One was an overpayment to the players of $45,000 at the end of 1990. These payments had not been recovered in 1992. There was also $54,000 in salary paid to a staff member included in expenses for the previous year. Other amounts not disclosed included taxation penalties for non-payment of tax owed. In addition, repayments were made to a past club official who had apparently loaned the club money out of his own pocket to help pay Paul Roos.

Don had been working under a lot of pressure and it was starting to take its toll on his health. His condition became serious enough to require him to be hospitalised for a short period. The directors took the view that to allow him to continue in the position may very well exacerbate his already precarious state. Although Don was reluctant we felt we had no choice but to insist he resign.

We approached Kevin Ryan, a board member with vast commercial accounting experience with a leading trustee company, who had recently retired, and he agreed to assume the role of chief executive officer.

The board then co-opted a finance committee consisting of myself, John Dawson vice chairman, Kevin Ryan, David Sandground a financial advisor and Gus Mitchell – our chairman of selectors and also a qualified accountant. After examining the financial position, it became fairly quickly apparent that the club was going to suffer another substantial loss in 1992 and that we would need further financial assistance.

We felt we had no alternative but to go, cap in hand, to the AFL. After preliminary discussions between Kevin Ryan and AFL commissioner Graeme Samuel in late July, we arranged to meet the full AFL Commission in early August, 1992.

At that meeting we laid all our cards on the table and said we would need assistance in the order of $1.5 million in order to continue. For many years Fitzroy (like most other clubs) borrowed against the next year's annual AFL dividend payment. The dividend, which was paid at the conclusion of every AFL season, was expected to be $1.1 million or thereabouts for 1993. What we sought was the early borrowing against our dividend as had been the case in the earlier years plus a loan of $400,000 to make up the

CHAPTER 3

difference. We were accorded what we thought was a reasonably sympathetic hearing by the AFL commissioners.

Prior to the implementation of the Crawford Report in 1993, the clubs controlled the AFL. Each club appointed a director and every three months there was an AFL director's meeting attended by the director nominated from each club. The AFL Commission managed the day to day running of the competition, but the directors had control.

After the recommendations of the Crawford Report were implemented, a new company structure was adopted whereby AFL club directors were replaced by club appointees, who retained very little power. Each club was represented by one appointee, and every three months, instead of the old director's meeting, the AFL Commission would hold an " information" night, at which time the clubs were supposed to be kept up to date with what the AFL was doing. In addition the Commission sought and received the views of the clubs on various issues. After the Crawford Report, apart from powers in relation to mergers or cancellation of a club's licence to compete, the only power the clubs retained was the power to sack the Commission. This power was more illusory than real however. The interstate clubs generally supported the AFL Commission as a block and there were enough Victorian clubs beholden to the AFL Commission to render the possibility of sacking the AFL commission a remote one indeed.

Lions' $1.5m debt puts future in doubt

Mike Sheahan
Sunday Age
16/10/92

Adrian Dunn
Herald Sun
19/10/92

Lion boss hits out
Club to trade out of debt

51

FITZROY

I was not able to participate in initial discussions due to a lengthy work period in the Northern Territory, but all the reports indicated that negotiations were going well. I was told that the AFL Commission would probably agree to redirect our 1992-93 dividend to Westpac Bank and that the AFL would recommend to the AFL club directors that the AFL Commission guarantee us a loan of $400,000. This would give us the $1.5 million required.

I finished my work in Darwin and flew back to Melbourne on Tuesday, December 1, one day before the scheduled AFL meeting which was to discuss our application. We fully expected the AFL Commission to recommend that both the re-direction and loan be approved. The proposal was that the AFL would take a debenture security over the Fitzroy Club Hotel behind other investors. This meant that the AFL's $400,000 guarantee would be fairly well secured. At that time the hotel lease was valued at $750,000, which meant there was ample equity in the hotel to pay out the AFL if required.

At about 7 o'clock in the morning of the AFL meeting on Wednesday I had a call from Noel Gordon, president of the Brisbane Bears. He wanted to know why Fitzroy Football Club was on the agenda for the AFL meeting later that day. I told him. He said that a number of other clubs were curious. After talking to Kevin Ryan we decided that all the clubs should be notified of the reason we were appearing on the agenda. I asked Kevin to do a ring around for the purpose of informing them.

I was in my chambers at about 10.00 a.m. when I received a phone call from a very heated Ross Oakley the chief executive officer of the AFL. Ross accused us of undermining him and making him look like a 'bloody idiot.' He said the AFL had had a meeting the night before and it was 'very difficult' to convince all the commissioners to support our request. He said he had planned to present the proposal himself. I apologised and told him I would ask Kevin to stop ringing. He had by this time contacted six presidents.

CHAPTER 3

At the meeting later that day, Oakley presented a recommendation to the directors supporting our proposal. He said that in his view the AFL had good security over the hotel for $400,000 which constituted their only risk. The most important reason for supporting us, he said, was that it would be very difficult to 'redraw' the schedule for the 1993 season. After his presentation, John Dawson very capably answered a number of financial questions. Kevin Ryan was also in attendance and answered questions when requested. I wasn't required to say much. The proposal was supported unanimously by the other AFL clubs.

We hoped to have all the necessary documentation completed by that Friday, December 4, as the club was virtually supporting itself from hotel proceeds. Most (if not all), players were supposed to have been paid by that day according to their contracts.

On Friday the AFL's solicitor, Jeff Browne, prepared a proposal agreement and sent it to me. I had two small queries and suggested amendments which I conveyed to Jeff who said he did not believe there would be any problems concerning them.

As time went by, it became increasingly apparent that the agreement would not be ready to be signed until Monday December 7, at the earliest. Monday came and went.

On Tuesday I got a phone call from Kevin Ryan saying there had been a hitch. Westpac now said it was not prepared to accept a re-direction of our 92-93 dividend as it had received legal advice that it may not be 100% secure!

The bank was apparently concerned that if Fitzroy Football Club was forced into liquidation, Westpac might have to compete for the dividend against preferred creditors such as the Taxation Department. At that stage I did not worry, mainly because I believed it would be quite simple for the AFL to guarantee the payment of the dividend. If the AFL guaranteed that the money was to be paid to Westpac, there would be no problem.

However, we quickly became concerned when we were advised by the AFL that it was up to us to convince the bank 'to change its mind.'

FITZROY

I had an uneasy feeling that the AFL was having second thoughts about backing us, despite our apparently straight forward proposal.

I spoke to Kevin Ryan, John Dawson and Kevin Lehman (finance manager of the AFL) at length concerning their previous discussions with Westpac. From what they told me I formed a view that Westpac had agreed to the proposal that the AFL club directors had sanctioned on December 2. Furthermore, I did not believe that the AFL would have presented its case to the AFL presidents on the basis of a mere indication from the bank.

A further concern was the fact that Westpac were the AFL's bankers as well as ours. I suggested to Kevin Lehman that what the bank wanted was not significantly different to what the directors had originally approved on December 2.

We continued to hear nothing from the AFL. By Tuesday, December 8, we were starting to be most concerned with the delay. I was to address the players at 5.00 p.m. that night. I rang Ross Oakley at 3.00 p.m. that afternoon. Oakley said that the AFL was going to meet over the weekend and that they wanted to meet with us on the following Tuesday afternoon. During that conversation we discussed many things. At one stage I asked Oakley about our equity in the assets of the AFL including Waverley Park. He said the club had no equity or financial interest in the league. Oakley stated that the life members and other members owned the assets. He said the Fitzroy Football Club licence was 'worth nothing.' It only conferred a 'right to participate in the AFL.'

Disturbed by what I perceived to be a sudden change in attitude, I asked Oakley what he proposed to do with Fitzroy? His reply was chillingly matter-of-fact: 'Well, anything can happen. You can liquidate. Perhaps the directors may approve a guarantee. Or you might merge.' I said merger may be a long term possibility but what could the AFL offer us in the short term? Oakley said, 'Oh no, you could do something fairly quickly. You could invite all AFL clubs to tender in writing an offer to merge within 14 days.'

I was dumbstruck. After taking a moment to recover, I said that

CHAPTER 3

mergers took time. If it was not carefully approached – and on an equal basis – the merged entity would lose all the Fitzroy supporters. I reminded him that many people had reacted negatively to the catastrophic Footscray-Fitzroy merger proposal in 1989 because it was seen more as a takeover than a merger. Oakley disagreed. He thought the Fitzroy-Footscray merger proposal was 'very good' and completely equal.

Ross Oakley's words convinced me that the AFL had now decided it was quite prepared to let Fitzroy go to the wall.

The next day, December 9, I ran into the AFL's solicitor, Jeff Browne, and had a fairly lengthy conversation with him. I asked him why the AFL could simply not guarantee Westpac the payment of the dividend. If the AFL was concerned about our financial viability, Fitzroy would assign to the AFL any rights we had to a dividend. He said that that might be construed as entering into an arrangement to defraud creditors or some such thing. I said all right, that in exchange for an AFL guarantee, we would not seek a dividend. He said he would get legal advice. I did not hear back from him. The silence from the AFL told us all we needed to know.

On Monday, December 14, I informed Oakley that we did not propose to attend the next afternoon's AFL full commission meeting. The Fitzroy board of directors unanimously agreed there was no point in attending. It was quite obvious the AFL had cut us adrift.

During this conversation with Oakley, I also said we were very keen to have a full meeting of the AFL board of club directors as soon as possible. I added that if it did not convene a meeting very soon the Fitzroy Football Club would have to consider a Supreme Court injunction forcing it to. Later it was confirmed that an AFL club directors meeting had been scheduled for Thursday morning at 8.00 a.m. on December 17.

What was most frustrating was that we did not believe that what Westpac wanted was any different from what the directors had authorised back on December 2. On Tuesday morning I spoke to two AFL club directors, Peter Gordon, Footscray's president and Errol Hutchesson, Collingwood's delegate. Both advised me to attend the AFL meeting scheduled for Tuesday December 15.

Their advice prevailed and John Dawson, Kevin Ryan and I attended the AFL offices at 4.30 p.m. Present were Peter Scanlon (a former Elders-IXL director), Graham Samuel, Alan Schwab, Ross Oakley and two other commissioners.

Oakley commenced the meeting by saying words to the effect of 'Well, your application to the bank has been rejected, what do you propose to do now?' Hours of debate over the finances then began.

We pointed out to them that nothing had changed since the time that the AFL decided to support us. Graham Samuel was putting what we believed were exaggerated figures on the whiteboard suggesting that the AFL would be at risk to the extent of $2.8 million if it proceeded with its guarantee. John Dawson and Kevin Ryan, in my view, destroyed Samuel's numbers with ease.

Samuel then said their legal advice, not yet in writing, was that a guarantee of our dividend may not be secure from creditors and that it might have to pay the creditors as well as Westpac if Fitzroy defaulted. I said that was contrary to our legal advice. I had previously spoken to Dr Peter Buchanan QC (now a Justice of the Victorian Court of Appeal. Peter gave us a lot of advice over the years. He never charged us a cent.) Peter informed me that he took the view that as Fitzroy had no legal right to a dividend, their creditors could not call upon it to declare one. Peter's advice was, in effect, that the AFL's investment was totally secure.

Next day I asked Dr Buchanan to put his advice to writing, which he did willingly and very quickly. At about 2.00 p.m. the advice was completed and we forwarded it, as promised, to AFL solicitor Jeff Browne.

On December 16 we woke to some very negative press coverage

CHAPTER 3

– coverage that could only have emanated from a leak within the AFL. But our immediate task was to contact all the AFL directors we could. We did not ask directly for support although many unequivocally offered it. We were more intent on informing the directors of what had occurred. Those who said they would back us included Errol Hutchesson (Collingwood), Peter Gordon (Footscray), Ron Hovey (Geelong), Stuart Trott (St. Kilda), Peter Weinert (Sydney) and Noel Gordon (Brisbane). Mike Humphries (Richmond), Peter de Rauch (North Melbourne) Bob Hammond (Adelaide), Brian Kann (Hawthorn) and the Melbourne representative were non-committal.

Essendon's David Shaw said if we could substantiate Buchanan's legal advice, we would have Essendon's support. Carlton's Ian Collins and John Elliott were not available.

The last president I contacted was Terry O'Connor (West Coast Eagles). He said with disarming frankness, 'Well Dyson, we believe there are too many clubs in Melbourne anyway. We will be supporting the AFL recommendation.' This was further confirmation that the AFL had decided not to support us.

Our worst fears were confirmed at 10.00 p.m. that night, less than 10 hours before the meeting was to take place. Oakley rang me at home and said that they had received legal advice from Ron Merkel QC and junior counsel that was contrary to Peter Buchanan's advice. He said we could come in early to AFL headquarters to look at that advice. Oakley added: 'Unfortunately, the AFL will not support you.' This came as no surprise.

John Dawson picked me up at my place at 6.45 a.m. on the Thursday morning. We arrived at AFL headquarters at about 7.15 a.m. There we waited approximately 20 minutes for Oakley to arrive. We asked to see Merkel's advice and were informed that Samuel had it. Samuel was not there so I spoke to him on the phone. It turned out that no formal advice existed, all Samuel had were notes taken from a conference he said he had had with Merkel.

I rang Peter Buchanan at home and told him what had been

told to me concerning Ron Merkel's advice. Peter said he would further look into the matters that had been raised by Merkel when he got into chambers. I asked him to ring me back as soon as he could.

The AFL meeting commenced a little after 8.00 am. I addressed the delegates first, inviting them to direct financial questions to our finance director, John Dawson. John was soon to be appointed manager for the National Australia Bank in the UK and Europe. At that stage, NAB was funding the development of the Great Southern Stand at the MCG and John was one Fitzroy person the AFL respected. I related the history of our application and submitted that what we were asking was not essentially different to what the delegates had approved on December 2. The only difference was that the AFL would need to guarantee the dividend of $1.1 million in addition to the guarantee of $400,000.

Ross Oakley replied, stating that the AFL Commission was very much against guaranteeing the dividend. Oakley implied that if the AFL guaranteed Fitzroy, banks accepting re-directions from other clubs might ask for guarantees and if this occurred the financial viability of the AFL itself was in jeopardy. Graham Samuel said that Westpac had decided Fitzroy was a 'cot case,' at which stage I interrupted saying that that was quite misleading and untrue. In fact, Westpac's real worry was that it did not believe that the AFL's promise to redirect Fitzroy's AFL dividend was 100% secure, in other words it was more distrustful of the AFL than us.

Samuel kept raising the same figures concerning the AFL's potential loss that Dawson and Ryan had demolished two days earlier. Samuel's major point was that the AFL's financial position was not secure.

During the debate Peter Buchanan rang. I took the phone call. He made it absolutely clear that Fitzroy could assign its right to a dividend in circumstances which would not make the AFL vulnerable. I asked him if he could come straight to the meeting. He agreed. When I went back to the meeting I informed the

CHAPTER 3

directors he was on his way and that he would be available to explain the legalities to them.

Suddenly, Samuel took a different tack, saying that the legal opinion was not really relevant — the real question was one of principle, whether or not the AFL would give guarantees. When Dr Buchanan arrived I informed the meeting that he was available. The AFL Commission were not interested in hearing from him. If the AFL club directors were, they did not have the courage or initiative to say so. What had previously been the whole basis of the AFL refusal to guarantee the loan had suddenly changed. The AFL then quickly called for a vote. Greg Durham, Geelong's CEO, said he did not like what was happening. No one else spoke up for us. Before the meeting Alan McAlister had been on television saying Collingwood was going to support us. When the vote came, however, Errol Hutchesson, the Collingwood AFL official delegate, was the first hand to go up against us. Only two clubs supported us, Geelong (Ron Hovey was true to his word) and Footscray.

Some clubs abstained from voting which, for many of them, was probably the most courageous thing they could do.

A number of the directors did not seem to understand the figures being mentioned. Samuel kept talking about $2.8 million which was, according to Dawson and Ryan, a demonstration of Samuel's non-understanding of accounting. But as in so many other situations, the club directors were like babes in the wood when it came to dealing with the AFL Commission.

After the vote I then made a short statement to the assembled throng. I told the meeting that, as it may be my last directors' meeting, there was something I wished to say. I raised the leaking of confidential information to the media and carefully told of the events of the past thirty-six hours.

I related how, on the Tuesday evening, Kevin Ryan, John Dawson and I had met with Oakley, Samuel, Scanlon and Schwab, finishing at around 7 o'clock. After the meeting the three of us watched Australia and the West Indies in a day-night match at the

MCG for a while, then John gave me a lift home. When I got home there were urgent messages from the *Herald Sun* waiting for me. Channel 7 was attempting to contact me through another director. The *Herald Sun* had been trying to contact me at the Fitzroy Club Hotel. Press interest was feverish, which was always a bad sign. I contacted the *Herald Sun* and answered what seemed to be regulation questions.

I knew exactly what the intense press interest meant. It already knew about our meeting with the AFL! We had only decided to attend the meeting with the AFL commissioners some six hours before it took place and only a handful of people from Fitzroy knew anything about it.

The next morning (Wednesday) after the meeting with Oakley and the others, I caught the train to work at about 8.00 a.m. I noted the headline 'Death Knell' on the back of the *Herald Sun* that someone was reading. There was nothing in *The Age*. I thought the 'Death Knell' headline must have related to the cricket until I had an opportunity to read the whole article.

DEATH KNELL
Tony De Bolfo
Herald Sun
16/12/92

LAST-GASP LIONS
DEATH IN FITZROY
Herald Sun
16/12/92

CHAPTER 3

Fitzroy 'faces liquidation tomorrow' the article read. It reported rumours that the Gaming Commission had blocked the use of the hotel as security – which was quite untrue. Trevor Grant's rhetoric described us as an 'itinerant drunk... subsisting on handouts... unashamedly hung out the begging bowl.' He finished by condemning 'those administrators who governed so recklessly.'

Past hits the Roys hard
Trevor Grant
Herald Sun
16/12/92

A number of Fitzroy stalwarts were rounded up for comment on Fitzroy's demise.

There were interviews with Kevin Murray, past Fitzroy champion and Brownlow Medal winner, and a host of other 'Fitzroy people.' Words like 'death,' 'demise' and 'crisis' were liberally used. In so quickly putting together this multi-page section, the *Herald Sun* obviously knew something that we did not.

I eventually spent the rest of that Wednesday morning attempting some form of damage control. I did a hurried interview with Neil Mitchell on 3AW and did interviews with Channels 7, 9 and 10, refuting the story. At this stage we had spoken to most other AFL directors and we were very confident of their support.

Whilst telling the AFL club directors on that Thursday morning of the events of the previous couple of days, I held up the copy of Wednesday's *Herald Sun* so that each director could see the headline, 'Death Knell.' I reminded them that only three Fitzroy people knew we were meeting with the AFL, and that 'We did not tell the press.' Confidentiality, I stated, is constantly asked of us by the AFL but is not given in return. I said how sad it was that the people clubs pay to look after our interests are the people we fear most. I then asked my colleagues, 'How long are we, the directors, going to sit here like cowering sheep taking this sort of treatment?' I was extremely angry.

61

Clubs wait on Roys

Tony De Bolfo and Michael Stevens
Herald Sun
17/12/92

Having expressed my anger at the leak, I then recounted other disturbing aspects of the media's AFL reporting. I told the directors that for some years certain reporters had been writing anti-Fitzroy articles. Fitzroy had been concerned for a long time about the accuracy of information related by these journalists – and how they obtained it in the first place.

I gave details, for example, during a meeting back in August of that year when we disclosed to the AFL Commission our precise financial details we impressed upon the AFL Commission the necessity for confidentiality, something we had had trouble with in the past. About a month later an article by Mike Sheahan appeared which set out our financial circumstances to the dollar!

After I finished my speech about the AFL leaks to the media, Ross Oakley replied that the AFL Commission was also concerned with the source of the leaks. He asked me if I knew who it was. I almost fell off my chair. I replied that I had my suspicions and looked at another person in the room. His face went bright red.

As the AFL club directors left the meeting we were approached by Hawthorn's Brian Kann and David Shaw of Essendon, who said they believed the club directors would have approved a straight loan from the AFL to us. Both clubs indicated their support, for which we were extremely grateful.

Kevin Ryan, John Dawson and I met with the AFL Commission for about a quarter of an hour after the vote. There was some discussion concerning what had occurred at the meeting. Finally Peter Scanlon put the proposal which we believe their strategy may have been heading towards all along.

Peter told us that they may back us financially – if we entered into a secret agreement with the AFL to merge in the following year!

CHAPTER 3

MERGER MOVE
Lions look to Bears, Dees

Tony De Bolfo
Herald Sun
18/12/92

Kevin, John and I all declined the AFL offer. I told them I would rather go to gaol than come to an agreement like that without going to the members first. We were then left to talk amongst ourselves. Whilst we were discussing what we would do next, John Dawson quietly rang up Robert Baker from Westpac and told him of the vote. Robert Baker was the senior Westpac officer from the branch handling the Fitzroy account. Robert said words to the effect that it may be possible that Westpac would reconsider their position. This gave us new hope.

While we were at AFL House after the vote, Ross Oakley was extremely jovial, whistling to himself as he attended to his chores. At a press conference with Ross Oakley later that morning I stressed that the AFL club directors had merely voted to the effect the AFL Commission was not authorised to guarantee the loan, and that it went no further than that. This in fact was the situation and it was the constant theme of the many media interviews I conducted afterwards. The press conference was reported almost verbatim in the *Herald Sun* the next day. Both John and Kevin stayed with me for the press conference, which was a comfort.

The Fitzroy directors decided that we would use the press to put increasing pressure on Westpac and the AFL to compromise. Consequently all interviews contained the fact that we believed Westpac had earlier agreed to accept a re-direction but had backed out of their agreement.

I also said that Fitzroy was also very disappointed with the way in which the AFL opposed our application and the vigour with which they opposed it. We did not want to rock the boat too much while negotiations were continuing, however, so we were forced

63

to temper our comments against the AFL and Westpac somewhat. As far as the press was concerned, Fitzroy was now finished. Not quite!

On Thursday afternoon, on the same day as the club directors meeting at about 3.00 p.m. I received a call from Alan McAlister, president of Collingwood, asking if he could come and see me, and an appointment was made for 4.00 p.m. During that meeting Alan said how much Collingwood wanted to help us. He pointed out the similarities in our historical origins and a number of other things and said that Collingwood wanted to merge with us.

I said that we were duty bound to listen to all propositions and asked him what he had in mind. He mentioned that Collingwood would pay off our debt and would house all our honour boards and other records and memorabilia. I said that I believed the main things worth preserving in a merger were the name, logo and colours and I couldn't imagine Collingwood giving up or diluting any of these things. At one stage in the conversation I said that if any merger was to take place, Fitzroy would have to keep its name in some form. Alan looked a bit crestfallen as he said, 'Yes, you'd have to keep your name.' Little did I know what he had in mind.

During our conversation, Alan (who had a mobile phone with him) mentioned that he was soon to be interviewed by Peter Costigan on 3LO (now Melbourne's controversial Lord Mayor). Alan then did the interview, unbeknown to everyone but myself, from my chambers.

During the interview Alan was asked on air if Collingwood had ever had any thoughts of merging with Fitzroy. 'Oh no,' said Alan, apparently aghast at the thought, 'No, nothing like that had ever crossed our minds. The Fitzroy directors are doing a wonderful job'.

I also had received a message to ring Costigan, which I had declined to do. I could hear the telephone conversation and whilst Alan was answering questions I felt like loudly shouting, 'Hello Peter, this is Dyson Hore-Lacy here. We are both together in my

CHAPTER 3

chambers, and guess what we are discussing'.

After Alan concluded his interview, and towards the end of our discussion, I said something to the effect that the AFL Commission would not approve of the merger between a strong club and a weak club in any event, as it was their stated policy. Alan then told me that it was an AFL commissioner who proposed the idea!

On Friday, December 18, we got a message that Robert Baker, and their legal adviser wanted to meet with Kevin Ryan and John Dawson (who had both been involved in negotiations from the outset) and the AFL and their legal adviser. I asked Kevin whether he thought I should be there. He said yes.

At 4.00 p.m. that evening we all met at the Westpac offices on the corner of Toorak Road and St Kilda Road.

At the meeting the AFL was represented by Kevin Lehman, their finance manager, and Jeff Browne, their solicitor. From very early on it became obvious that the dispute was essentially a dispute in principle between the AFL and Westpac.

The AFL was prepared to re-direct Fitzroy's dividend to Westpac at the end of the '93 season and to guarantee that the dividend would be at least $1.1 million. Westpac very quickly saw the flaw in this offer, that is the AFL were not guaranteeing that Fitzroy would **receive** a dividend. The AFL argued that it could not legally guarantee a dividend to Fitzroy because the payment of a dividend was discretionary under the Memorandum & Articles of Association. But the AFL also told Westpac that it was certain Fitzroy would get one, because no club had never not got one. The AFL argued that Fitzroy was only entitled (legally) to a dividend after it played its first premiership game in the following year.

When the AFL commissioners left the room and we were discussing matters with Westpac on our own, we argued that we must be entitled to a dividend from an early stage as receipts were not only earned from the playing of football, but came from royalties on merchandise, etc. At one stage I said I would go out and buy a Fitzroy guernsey to make sure we would qualify!

The meeting closed at about 6.00 p.m. and Jeff Browne and Robert Baker were to discuss the matter over the weekend. We believed the dispute was very close to resolution.

On Saturday afternoon I rang Robert Baker at home. He had not heard from anyone, and was a little surprised. In fact, the main reason why I rang him was to warn him about the Sunday papers, which I knew, would have something prejudicial and sensational in them.

Bingo!

Next day, there it was. Headlines in the *Sunday Herald Sun*, 'Collingwood to take over Fitzroy.' A major story, in great detail. When the reporters rang me, I refused to confirm or deny that there had been any discussion between Collingwood and Fitzroy. Someone from Collingwood had apparently leaked the story for their own purposes, possibly to sink our delicate negotiations with Westpac.

SECRET AFL OPTION FOR LIONS

COLLINGWOOD TO TAKE OVER FITZROY

Scot Palmer
Herald Sun
20/12/92

If we go, so will others – Fitzroy

Herald Sun
20/12/92

PIES TAKEOVER

Herald Sun
20/12/92

CHAPTER 3

Robert Baker and I spoke again later that Sunday after I had made a number of unsuccessful attempts to phone him. He said that the AFL and Westpac were further apart than they ever were. He said the AFL were only prepared to guarantee the dividend if the club played the first premiership game in 1993, This only crystallised Westpac's fears about the security of their loan if the club folded sometime between December 1992 and April 1993 (when the first premiership game would be played). For the first time I went into a cold sweat as I was talking to Robert and realising that the parties were drifting apart. I immediately rang Jeff Browne and at my request he agreed to frame the undertaking in such a way that the dividend to Fitzroy would be guaranteed from the first of April but that any rights Fitzroy had before then would be preserved.

He also said he would get instructions to defer $250,000 owing to the AFL from Fitzroy until after April 1993, to ease our cash flow situation. At this stage we were desperately trying to satisfy Westpac that we had the ability to continue trading until April.

In Monday's *Herald Sun*, in an article by Scot Palmer, it was clear that Collingwood thought Fitzroy was gone beyond recall. If they survived beyond 1993, they would go no further according to Collingwood. The offer to merge with Fitzroy was publicly proclaimed. The proposal to merge was such a blatant 'takeover' that even the most naive person could see through it. As far as the retention of our name was concerned it was said that perhaps the seconds could be called Fitzroy!

I was so annoyed I immediately rang the *Herald Sun* and gave them a further interview. I then said what subsequently appeared in the later edition of the *Herald Sun*: a blast aimed at McAlister who I claimed was holding out one hand of friendship while stabbing Fitzroy in the back with the other.

Meanwhile, life was going on. 3UZ (now 927 Sports) was playing *'Good Old Collingwood Forever'* and having a good laugh about it, talking about 'good-hearted Collingwood coming to our rescue' and other such things.

For us, however, all the conjecture about the club was no laughing matter, for at that stage we believed that Westpac was almost ready to respond positively to the AFL's offer and we were most concerned about the effect of these stories on the minds of the Westpac people.

That afternoon, Monday, December 21, our worst fears were realised. Robert Baker rang me on a conference line in the presence of Westpac's lawyer and politely but firmly told me that our application for credit had been refused.

Individual guarantees from our supporters had been organised by our senior director, Elaine Findlay, to the extent of $130,000 and we thought, if necessary, we could use that as collateral. I asked Robert if that would make any difference. Robert said if we had another application to make we would have to submit it. I said we couldn't possibly do that in the time available. It was then only three days before Christmas. Furthermore, I pointed out that unless we knew what was required, it was almost impossible to be able to submit another application in the time available because that, in turn, may be declined.

He said, 'I'm sorry, all I can say is that your application is refused. We do not believe the draft letter the AFL has sent us secures the loan.' I asked him if he would be kind enough to fax me the letter and I said I'd get back to him. Robert faxed me the letter almost straight away.

I rang Kevin Ryan and John Dawson and told them they had better get up to my chambers. After they arrived the three of us stared at each other contemplating what in the hell we would do. I wondered what I was going to tell the press. What could I say? I remember looking out over the docks (the view of which was years later to be blotted out by Colonial Stadium) wondering, 'Is this really the end?'

I looked at the AFL letter again. I was convinced that what Westpac was demanding was no more than what the resolution of the club directors had authorised back on December 2. I rang

CHAPTER 3

Robert Baker back and asked him what Westpac would do if the AFL guaranteed three things:
1. That Fitzroy would be paid a dividend.
2. That the AFL would pay Fitzroy's dividend to Westpac on or before September 30, 1993.
3. That the dividend would be at least $1.1 million.

Robert said subject to legal advice, that would satisfy them. I repeated the three matters so there would be no mistake.

After I hung up I asked Kevin Ryan and John Dawson whether I was going mad or had not the AFL club directors meeting of December 2, authorised the AFL to give Westpac what it now sought? They both agreed that it had. John rang the AFL's Kevin Lehman again. John asked him to fax me a copy of the resolution of December 2, which he did very promptly. I then told Lehman what Robert Baker had said that Westpac would accept and that we believed that the AFL directors had authorised what Robert wanted. Kevin said he would speak to Ross.

In the meantime I had rung two club directors, both lawyers, Peter Gordon (Footscray) and David Shaw (Essendon). I read out the three conditions that Westpac wanted, and asked them if they believed that was what the AFL directors had authorised weeks earlier. Both agreed that it was in accordance with their understanding. David Shaw volunteered to ring Ross Oakley and tell him.

After reading a copy of the directors' resolution of December 2, our spirits rose because we believed it was quite clear – the AFL had authorised what Robert Baker requested. We now had a legal avenue open to us. We could take legal action to compel the AFL Commission to comply with what the club directors had authorised on December 2. In addition, we now had another avenue of applying leverage to the Commission.

At approximately 5.30 p.m. that evening, Ross Oakley rang back. He asked me to repeat what Westpac had indicated it would accept. I did. He then said that he was going to recommend to the other commissioners that they accept the Westpac stipulation, and if the AFL agreed then they would do a ring around of directors on Tuesday to have it approved.

But, he added, we would have to give some assurances. We would have to undertake not to throw up our hands in a couple of weeks' time and say 'Oh, it's all too difficult' and then let the club go into liquidation. We couldn't believe it! We had fought so hard I did not believe anyone could doubt our resolve. Other assurances he mentioned included not signing cheques without AFL approval. After putting down the phone the three of us just stared at each other. In the space of three hours we had come from despair to almost victory. I do not believe, to this day, any of us have ever felt more relieved.

Then came the waiting. Next day I was informed that Jeff Browne was preparing a list of undertakings for us to sign. I kept ringing and he kept saying they would be ready in 'ten minutes'. Kevin Lehman then mentioned an 'agreement' being drawn for the directors to sign. Before then we had no hint of what was in store.

When 4.00 p.m. arrived and no documentation had come, I was starting to get most anxious about the delay. I was constantly stalling the press by saying to them that negotiations were continuing and that we were hopeful. We hadn't informed them that the matter had almost been resolved.

At about 5.00 p.m. on Tuesday December 22, Jeff Browne faxed me a seven page document – a binding agreement consisting of forms giving personal guarantees.

As I read them, I again began to despair. I could not allow directors, who were acting in the community's interest and in a totally honorary capacity, to sign any personal guarantees. That night I rang Peter Buchanan and he agreed to have a conference with all of the Fitzroy directors at his chambers at 9.00 a.m. on the following morning (Wednesday).

At the conference, Peter carefully went through every paragraph,

CHAPTER 3

explaining what liability the directors were exposed to. While I was in his chambers Jeff Browne rang, and at Peter's request I asked Jeff to come up to Buchanan's chambers. Fitzroy's solicitor John McArdle, a partner at Williams Winter & Higgs, solicitors, also attended the conference. He had been doing terrific work for us all year in connection with the hotel and other matters.

I won't go into detail. Suffice to say negotiations dragged on concerning the exact wording of the agreements. In the end we were satisfied by Peter that by signing the document we were not exposing ourselves legally to anything more than the law exposed us to anyway. At about 1:30 pm, the 'agreement' was finally signed.

Later Jeff Browne rang up to tell us there were two charges on the hotel. None of us knew anything about them. They were in fact charges securing old debts that had been paid off years ago by the previous owners. John McArdle acted very promptly in getting them removed. The AFL had also insisted on a new charge of its own over the hotel as security for the $400,000 it was guaranteeing in addition to our dividend.

As soon as we reached final agreement with Jeff Browne, Kevin Ryan rang his staff to tell them we had been saved, and he organised a press conference at the Fitzroy Club Hotel for 3.00 p.m. that day.

I specifically asked John and Kevin to join me at the press conference because of their fantastic work during the negotiations and the very solid support they provided during the crisis. We invited our senior director, Elaine Findlay, to be there because of her great service to the club over a long period of time.

ROY RESCUE
Loan deal lifts Lions

Geoff Poulter
Herald Sun
16/12/92

LIONS CASH RELIEF
Michael Stevens
Herald Sun
3/12/92

Lion fans sweat on bank decision
Geoff Poulter
Herald Sun
16/12/92

Roys keep head above water
Stephen Linnell
The Age
12/92

Because I have related events from my perspective, it may appear to the reader that I was making all the decisions. That was not the case. It should be recognised that all finance committee members – John Dawson, Kevin Ryan, Gus Mitchell and David Sandground – contributed substantially to the overall thrust of what we were trying to do. Whilst I was regularly consulted about what was happening, I played no part in negotiations leading up to the decision by the AFL to initially support us. John Dawson and Kevin Ryan did most of the preparation and footwork relating to cash flow that was absolutely critical to our application.

The uncertainty cast over Fitzroy's future by the 'Westpac saga' caused great hurt and anxiety to thousands of Fitzroy supporters. It was totally unnecessary and was brought about by the AFL trying to be cute with legal niceties. They took advantage of an opportunity, on the kindest of interpretations, to place us under extreme pressure. This method of operation – a corporate – driven philosophy which is blind to the wishes and sensitivities of the average football supporters who make this game — was to become, many would argue, the AFL's trademark.

Chapter 4

After putting the Westpac debacle behind us, the club moved confidently into 1993. We had an excellent team list, a good coach and match committee and we could have been excused for believing we would play in the finals that year.

Melbourne Review
RELIGION
Royboys: a '93 revival?
They're buggered but they'll go on forever

Barry Dickins
Melbourne Review
21/4/93

We started the 1993 season in fine style by defeating Geelong at Waverley Park by 12 points in the pre-season competition. This was followed by a fighting five point win against Footscray before succumbing to Richmond by six points in the semi-final: the Lions had narrowly missed playing in two pre-season grand finals in successive years.

The start of the premiership season could not have been better. We played Carlton at Princes Park before a crowd of almost 25,000. With about a minute to play in a match Carlton had seemingly won, we clawed our way back to be only six points down. Fitzroy then goaled, and I remember thinking they should ring the bell immediately and we'd be happy to settle for a draw. At the following centre bounce, the ball was hurriedly kicked out of a pack and found our new recruit, Michael Dunstan, unguarded. With seconds to go, Michael (playing his first premiership game) kicked truly giving the Lions a win by six points – much to the shock, dismay and disbelief of the large contingent of Carlton supporters.

Unfortunately, some heartbreaking losses followed – to Footscray by three points and to Adelaide at Football Park by a single point in a controversial game before we returned to the winning list by caning Sydney by 93 points at Princes Park. A loss to Brisbane at the Gabba preceded three wins against Melbourne, West Coast Eagles (at the WACA) and Collingwood. After nine rounds we had five wins and four losses, and it might have been better with a bit of good fortune.

Once again, though, the game against Essendon became a turning point for the season. At the MCG on Friday night, May 28, before a crowd of more than 50,000, Essendon won a great game by four points. Fitzroy squandered their early dominance with a number of missed chances from very close range by Alastair Lynch and the mercurial Darren Wheildon, who was one of the best – if not the best – on ground that night.

We then lost the plot, losing six of the next seven games, including a massive loss to a still-stung Carlton, by 86 points at Princes Park. We dropped out of contention for the finals but finished the season on a high note by winning the last four games against Adelaide, Sydney, Brisbane and Melbourne.

Alastair Lynch had a marvellous year and as we demolished Melbourne in the last game we were all hoping he would put in a big one. Alastair was one of the leaders in various media awards and was one of the favourites for the Brownlow Medal. He played a good game that day – and eventually won a number of awards – but unfortunately missed out on the Brownlow. Alastair had shown promise since arriving at Fitzroy five years earlier but had often struggled partly due to unreliable kicking. About half-way through the year, however, Matthew Armstrong, our skilful centreman gave him a valuable tip – and from then he became one of the competition's longest and straightest kicks for goal.

With players like Alastair and others starting to show form, Fitzroy was a competitive and exciting team to watch. The club's hotel was up and away and the gaming room had commenced operation in early October 1992, which was a pretty good achievement. In only ten months we had completed the

CHAPTER 4

renovations, managed to set up the different companies to run the operation and gained Liquor and Gaming Commission approval (which was no simple matter). In 1992 Fitzroy suffered a further loss in trading but not of the magnitude of the previous year. It was to be our last loss.

With no Westpac-type crisis immediately facing us, we could devote our energies to other issues – and there would be many issues to face in 1993. One nagging problem was our playing venue. We had been trying to obtain a secure, long-term home ground for years.

Our six year occupancy lease with the Carlton Social Club at Princes Park was due to expire at the end of 1992 and we were keen to renegotiate a new one. At that time three clubs, Carlton, Hawthorn and Fitzroy were using the ground.

Ian Collins, (AFL operations manager until recently and now head of Colonial Stadium) was CEO at Carlton at the time, and Fitzroy believed it was being continually disadvantaged by Carlton over its occupancy agreement. Some years earlier, before I became a director of Fitzroy, Carlton refused to allow us to use the modestly-named 'John Elliott Room' in the equally modestly-named 'John Elliott Stand' for our chairman's luncheons which, we believed, was contrary to our agreement. The case went to arbitration. A friend and colleague of mine, David Byrne QC (now Justice Byrne of the Supreme Court), appeared with me for Fitzroy and 'Coodabeen Champion' Simon Whelan (now a QC) appeared for Carlton. We won this part of the claim.

Successive Fitzroy administrations found it very difficult to deal with Carlton. We kept changing negotiators in an attempt to achieve a breakthrough but to no avail. There are certain areas of income for ground managers which are lucrative, the biggest three being ground advertising, catering and income from reserved seating. Under the terms of our old six-year lease, Fitzroy received a certain amount for perimeter fence advertising, nothing from all other ground advertising, nothing for catering rights and a small amount for reserved seating. This was far from satisfactory, as far as we were concerned, but it was better than what was offered with our new lease, which was next to nothing. Collins argued that the use of the ground for home matches rent free more than offset any other benefits.

We became so frustrated with our lack of progress with Collins that we asked the AFL to help us in our negotiations. Carlton and Fitzroy met at the AFL headquarters where senior AFL commissioner Graeme Samuel attempted to mediate. All to no avail. Collins was resolute. He knew he had us over a barrel. Where else could we go? To compound matters further, in an inducement to prise Hawthorn from its long term agreement with Carlton (enabling the Hawks to be co-tenants at Waverley Park with St Kilda), the AFL had guaranteed 22 matches per year at Princes Park until 2006, regardless of whether Fitzroy played there or not. Any bargaining power we may have had was completely eroded by the AFL's guarantee. This deal was subsequently amended in 2000 by the AFL because of the necessity of moving games to Colonial Stadium – no doubt Carlton received substantial compensation.

We even sought assistance from the head lessor, Melbourne City Council, but it was powerless to intervene as Carlton had a lease until 2006.

Collins complained to us that we were continually changing the negotiator. The reason we did this was to give a new person an opportunity to succeed where others had failed. Nothing was ever achieved and we continued to play our home games at Princes Park in 1993 without a formal lease. Not only did Fitzroy receive no income at all from Princes Park, when accounts were finalised at the end of the year, but we received an invoice for $6,000!

John Dawson, Vince Flynn, David Sandground, Kevin Ryan and myself were all at different stages involved in negotiations over the venue. A minute of the board meeting on February 24, 1993, summed up the situation perfectly:

CHAPTER 4

'The General Manager reported on the meeting held with Ian Collins and Graham Samuel. The latter represented the AFL in a conciliatory role. The meeting was inconclusive and a further meeting was to be arranged by Graham Samuel.' Another minute, of May 26, recorded that:

'David Sandground advised that Ian Collins remained intransigent and that Graham Samuel suggested Ross Oakley may be prepared to assist. David was to meet with Graham Samuel soon.'

These problems with our 'home ground' put extra pressure on our finances. Any hoped-for income from the ground would have to be found elsewhere. While we had successfully avoided liquidation or merger in the previous year, we now faced the task of attempting to both service debt and run the club with a shrinking revenue base.

Our 1993 budget was predicated on receiving profits in excess of $400,000 from the hotel plus a continuation of existing levels of sponsorship. However, whilst the hotel was returning a healthy profit, it was not quite the cash cow we had hoped for.

Sponsorship was down, with the Quit program decreasing its amount yearly. Cash flow once again became a matter of concern as 1993 progressed. One problem was that the AFL had lent us $250,000 in the previous year, which was repayable in April 1993, and it held a second charge over our hotel to secure this amount.

This made it very difficult, if not impossible, to borrow further on the hotel. To make matters worse, I had also received a letter signed by several senior players, spurred on no doubt by constant negative media stories, requesting an assurance that the club would meet the players' contractual payments when they became due.

The club had no general overdraft facility and by early April 1993 we were also faced with a problem in paying staff.

We were not unique in this respect. I recall a story told at a St. Kilda luncheon by one of its directors. He said the CEO rang him up one day and said he did not have any money to pay the staff.

The director said to the CEO, 'Look out the window. Do you see a two tone blue Holden sitting there?' 'Yes,' said the CEO, 'Well go and sell it,' said the director. 'But that's my car,' protested the CEO.

At Fitzroy such a story was not so amusing. If we were one day late with payments it would be in the press the next day. The financial situation was starting to become desperate as we exhausted all avenues.

Carlton and United Breweries – which had been a minor sponsor of Fitzroy for many years – came to the rescue, however. It entered into a five-year sponsorship agreement with Fitzroy for $250,000, all of which was paid in advance. Of the $50,000 per year, $25,000 was to exclusively sell its products in the hotel and $25,000 was for general sponsorship. CUB had already painted the hotel for us without charge and we were extremely grateful to them for bailing us out on this occasion.

Lions hit rumor
Paul Gough
Herald Sun
9/5/93

CUB was the AFL's major sponsor at this time and, of course, the AFL were very quick to find out about the $250,000. They wrote us a letter demanding that we hand over the money straight to them. Too late! It was gone. They were furious and they continually hounded us for the money for the rest of the year – even threatening to sue the Fitzroy directors. Towards the end of the year, Ross Oakley was reported in the press as saying that the annual dividends to the other clubs may have to be reduced because of our failure to pay back the $250,000. I replied publicly that the threat was straight out 'bloody-minded.'

However, pressure from the AFL over that $250,000 could not

CHAPTER 4

be ignored. By now we no longer expected support from the league, and their constant hounding of us for the $250,000 became the precipitating reason for the Lions playing their home games at the Western Oval in 1994.

Footscray, in those years, was determined to stay at the Western Oval (later the Whitten Oval). It was sole tenant and it was extremely keen to have another AFL club play there to maximise the use of the oval.

Footscray's Peter Gordon initially approached us in mid-1993 about the possibility of Fitzroy playing its home games at Footscray. The problems we were having with Carlton were well known. A formal offer was tabled at the Fitzroy board meeting in June of 1993. The offer from Footscray included:

1. All revenue from nearly all the advertising space at the ground;
2. All reserved seat revenue;
3. All car-parking revenue;
4. Free access to all corporate facilities;
5. Outer ground catering rights.

Most of these income sources were denied us by Carlton.

Footscray would receive revenue from catering rights from functions, including the chairman's luncheon and other coterie gatherings on match days, plus other advertising revenue. We were later to learn that this amounted to a profit of about $100,000 a year to Footscray.

In addition, Footscray offered an interest free loan to enable the club to repay its AFL debt of $250,000. Although we initially mooted transferring our home games to Western Oval as a tactical ploy in our negotiations with Carlton, as time went by, it became apparent that we would cease to exist if we had no additional income stream. We were also concerned that the AFL would use the $250,000 debt as an excuse to force us out of existence. The

Footscray offer became more of a reality as time progressed. On our financial projections the move would mean a yearly increase in revenue of approximately $400,000, which in those days was a large amount of money.

Tenant Lions look to Dogs

Mark Harding
Sunday Herald Sun
21/5/93

On September 22,1993, Peter Gordon addressed the Fitzroy board, club staff and supporter group representatives in respect of the 'positive aspects of the move to the Western Oval.' All who attended were enthusiastic about the proposal, especially as by this time the cash flow situation was again becoming critical. On the same night that Peter addressed the Fitzroy people the board held a meeting. The Minutes reported the following:

> 'The chairman reported on the current position of the club. It was noted that the cash flow predictions of the club would reach critical stages during October and it was felt necessary, in light of the requirements of Westpac regarding their future financing requirements, to approach the AFL seeking a $200,000 guarantee. A meeting was scheduled for Monday morning, 27 September.'

Although it was indicated that the club shortfall was in the vicinity of $400,000 it was anticipated that $200,000 could be generated internally. Board members were asked to consider their own situations in this regard and speak to the chairman individually. The chairman suggested that in the event of a negative response from the AFL there would be a need to call a meeting of members.

We felt we had no alternative but to inform them of the situation.

The application to the AFL to guarantee an extra $200,000 was, as mentioned previously, rejected in a blaze of publicity.

CHAPTER 4

Lion chief blasts the AFL over story leak

Patrick Smith
The Age
1/10/93

Our cash flow problem was eased, to some extent, by a very successful Schweppes promotion done in conjunction with Fitzroy. Schweppes wished to launch a high profile advertising campaign for its Solo lemon squash in order to head off a major competitor which was introducing a similar product to the market. For every can of Solo sold, Fitzroy would receive 10 cents. Paul Roos' picture was on billboards all over Victoria promoting the product. This proved very successful and we benefited to the tune of approximately $110,000 from this venture. Not before running foul again of the AFL, of course. Coca Cola was a major sponsor of the AFL and the league took the view that Schweppes, as a company, was a competitor of Coca Cola. Consequently it objected, to the AFL logo appearing on Paul's jumper which he was wearing on the billboards. Paul assisted in this promotion for no extra pay, by the way, a service which was greatly appreciated.

1993 was the year of the Crawford Report. A number of club presidents, including Peter Gordon, Alan McAlister and myself had been extremely critical of certain aspects of the AFL's operation for some time. In an inspired move, the AFL Commission asked high profile accountant David Crawford to prepare a wide-ranging report on the AFL's operations and its relationships with AFL clubs. The report was, as should have been anticipated, very pro-AFL Commission, and suggested increased power to the AFL Commission in a number of key areas.

FITZROY

A Fitzroy board minute of March 8, 1993 summed up our feelings:

'The board considered the contents of the Crawford Report which had previously been circulated to directors. General concern was expressed at the proposed concentration of power with the Commission. In particular the board was concerned at the power covering expulsion, relocation and merger.'

This report was subsequently implemented with some minor changes. The two worst things that came out of it were the new solvency rules and the changes to the draft rules.

The new Solvency Rule provided that if the AFL Commission formed the view that a club *may* not be able to pay its debts when they become due it may serve a notice on the club requiring the club to prove (to the AFL's satisfaction!) that it will be able to meet its financial commitments for the next twelve months. There was no right of appeal.

If the club could not so prove, the AFL could in effect take the club's licence.

We believed that this rule was aimed only at Fitzroy and it wasn't long before we received our first notice.

Of more significance to Fitzroy, however, was the changing of the draft rules. The existing draft rules provided for clubs to be able to draft new players, or 'out of contract players.' Each year the clubs held a draft meeting in November (now televised) and a second one in March. The order of choices was determined by the club's position on the AFL ladder. Consequently the club that finished last would have first choice, the club that finished second last, second choice and so on. The premiers would have last choice and the order would be commenced again until the process was exhausted. What protected clubs was that if a player was out of contract, he could not go to the club of his choice. This meant that a badly performing club could draft him and the player could only hope to be offered a reasonable contract for his services.

CHAPTER 4

This, coupled with the salary cap rules, which limited all clubs to a designated maximum amount for player payments, was designed to even up the competition.

Rather than strive for a level playing field, the AFL Commission decided to put its might behind AFL clubs Brisbane and Sydney. It changed the rules by allowing the Bears and Swans to sign a number of uncontracted players – without those players going into the draft, and without any compensation to the donor club. The AFL also somehow devised a performance formula which protected Richmond but not Fitzroy from the Bears and Swans. We had finished above the Tigers in 1992 but below them in 1990 and 1991. The formula devised provided a performance test just sufficient to give protection to Richmond but not Fitzroy. With seemingly unlimited AFL financial support, money was no object so far as Brisbane and Sydney were concerned. The passing of this rule was the blow from which Fitzroy never recovered. Our player list was plundered.

This support for Brisbane and Sydney was in marked contrast to the AFL's attitude to those clubs the year before.

Back on October 14, 1992, the AFL convened a meeting to discuss the future of the Sydney Swans, which owed the league two million dollars. The Swans was privately owned with big backers such as Mike Willesee and Peter Weinert. Sydney was running at a substantial loss and it had got to the stage where the owners refused to put one more cent into the club. At the meeting, Weinert made an impassioned plea to the AFL club directors and the AFL Commission for assistance. That assistance really meant postponing the $2 million AFL debt indefinitely (it has since been wiped by the AFL). In addition Sydney needed other short-term assistance.

During that meeting Adelaide's chairman, Bob Hammond, asked Ross Oakley if the AFL Commission had given consideration to merging the Swans and the Brisbane Bears. The Bears at that time were performing poorly and had been for some time. Ross replied that it had, but the financial figures did not stack up and he gave a number of other reasons why the AFL would not support such a move. The matter was not concluded and the meeting was adjourned for one week, when a final decision was to be made about Sydney's future.

Whilst Fitzroy was very strong in its belief that the AFL Commission should support the Melbourne clubs, it was never opposed to the existence of the interstate clubs then competing in the competition. Indeed, a minute of the Fitzroy board meeting held one day before the second Swans meeting records:

> *'The chairman reported on a recent meeting of the AFL board of directors which considered the future of the Sydney Swans in the competition. The board expressed general support for the Sydney Swans, and although final details of the financial support required were not known, instructed the chairman to note the mood of the board when voting on the Sydney Swans future.'*

At first it was our view that most of the Melbourne-based AFL clubs were disinclined to support the Swans. Indeed, Alan McAlister, Collingwood president, had been very vocal in Collingwood's opposition.

Just before our board meeting commenced at Lygon Street, I received a call from Peter Weinert. He said to me, 'You won't guess what they are trying to do to us. They are trying to make us merge with Brisbane.' I could not believe my ears after what had been said the week before.

The next evening, October 21, all the AFL club directors reassembled in the AFL Commission boardroom at the MCG. When I walked into the room I thought I must have been seeing things. Written on a large whiteboard was the heading 'East Coast Bears' along with all sorts of figures and financial projections! Ross Oakley spoke to the proposal, setting out the financial advantages of merging Brisbane and Sydney. The club directors were stunned.

CHAPTER 4

Brian Kann, Hawthorn director, tentatively reminded Ross of what he had said the previous week concerning the viability of such a union and asked what had caused the change of heart. I do not recall the response.

At some stage during the meeting, while Collingwood's official AFL director, Errol Hutchesson, was sitting there, I suspect with contrary instructions from his board, judging from the look on his face, Alan McAlister rose to his feet and said that after hearing Peter Weinert speak he had been impressed at what he said and he had changed his mind – Collingwood was now supporting Sydney.

In the end a vote was taken and Sydney received the support it desired from the AFL clubs. I believe the main reason the support was given was that the AFL club directors took the view that the AFL had no idea what it was doing in relation to the issue and in the short term at least it would be better to maintain the status quo with Sydney and Brisbane than be party to a hastily-arranged marriage between the clubs.

At Fitzroy, the discontent and concern demonstrated by some of the players in early 1993 had not evaporated. Late in the season in 1993 I was asked to attend a meeting of senior players at Paul Roos' home in North Carlton. Present were Paul, Alastair Lynch, Matthew Armstrong, Ross Lyon, Paul Broderick and Jimmy Wynd. The players expressed dissatisfaction about playing home games at the Western Oval. I outlined the reasons for the decision. At one stage during our discussions Paul said that he was concerned about losing players if we moved. Paul said, 'I can't of course leave but I am most concerned about Lynchy and others going.' I am sure Paul meant this at the time. Alastair Lynch said he was leaving Fitzroy in any event. Most if not all of the others said that if Alastair left they would leave as well. Within a little over 12 months all were gone.

At that time Alastair was our biggest asset. He came to Fitzroy as a skinny youngster who could take a very good mark but could not kick straight. In the few years he was at Fitzroy he had bulked up and become one of the competition's elite footballers and one of its strongest kicks for goal. Our coach, Robert Shaw, publicly described him at that time as, 'About the best going around.'

The last year of Alastair's contract was 1993 and we had been fearful for some time that he would be poached by Sydney or Brisbane by virtue of their new 'concessions.' In fact, a number of other AFL clubs were chasing him.

We made Alastair what we thought was a very generous offer but it couldn't match the seemingly bottomless purse of the Brisbane Bears. Another less-wealthy club at the time, St. Kilda, was about to lose its best player and arguably the greatest full forward of all time, Tony Lockett, under the same rule. The richer clubs, with their vast financial resources, were not troubled by the new rule. It was only the weaker clubs who could not match the financial inducements offered by Brisbane and Sydney. Also, for a number of AFL clubs, as was later proved, 'salary cap restrictions' meant no more than three words in the dictionary.

In any event the inevitable happened. I picked up the paper one day to see a large picture of Alastair reclining in the Queensland sun next to a swimming pool with a drink in his hand and a smile on his face. No wonder. Brisbane was reported to have offered him a minimum of $200,000 a year for 10 years, bank-guaranteed, regardless of whether he played a game or not.

Since then player payments have skyrocketted, but at that time, $200,000 a year for 10 years was a huge inducement.

Lynch Bears pledge

Mike Sheahan
Herald Sun
20/10/93

I do not blame Alastair for leaving the club (or Paul Roos, for that matter). We lost Paul the following year when Sydney made him a similar fabulous offer he couldn't refuse. He had his family

CHAPTER 4

and his future to think of. Fitzroy people do blame, however, the AFL for bringing in the rule which allowed most of our quality senior players to be poached without any compensation. By the end of 1994 we had lost Alastair Lynch, Paul Roos, Ross Lyon, Matthew Armstrong, Paul Broderick and Michael Gale. These were our elite players. No team can be decimated to that extent and expect to recover quickly.

If the AFL was serious about evening up the competition, it would have protected the weaker clubs such as ours when it implemented its new draft rules. It wasn't as if the AFL were unmindful of what could happen as it granted Richmond protection under the same mysterious formula which left Fitzroy exposed. Yet Fitzroy had a much smaller revenue base than Richmond and unlike Richmond, had finished at or near the bottom of the ladder for years.

We were very disappointed with the role the AFL played in the 'Alastair Lynch affair.' Unknown to us, the AFL Commission had been advising Damien Smith, Lynch's manager, as to whether or not various salary structures proposed by Smith would be in breach of salary cap guidelines.

We knew that moving to the Western Oval would not prove popular with all our players and supporters. We felt we had no choice, however. In late 1993 we had held a meeting in the Fitzroy Town Hall to explain to our members why we were going to play our home games at Western Oval. From the response of the people who spoke at that meeting we received almost unanimous endorsement.

Lynch's departure shattered our football people. Fitzroy had finished the season on a high note and felt, if we could have kept that team intact, we had the nucleus of a very, very good team for 1994.

After Alastair announced his departure, a meeting was called by coach Robert Shaw and the match committee with the football directors, Elaine Findlay and myself. Paul Roos was also in attendance (Elaine Findlay had been voted vice-chairman when John Dawson moved overseas).

The mood of the people at the meeting was extremely gloomy and the general feeling was that we should try to find a merger partner, or look at some other option such as relocation. Robert later publicly declared that at that stage he was in a state of depression. We gave them a bit of a pep talk and suggested that they get out and try to find a replacement for Alastair – and told them we were not merging.

It was two weeks of agony, says Shaw

Mike Sheahan
Herald Sun
20/10/93

CLUB WAS GONE

Shaw boycotts draft

Mike Sheahan
Herald Sun
29/10/93

Matthew Dundas and Paul Broderick had told the match committee earlier in the season that they also wished to leave the club. A swap was, we thought, arranged between Richmond and Fitzroy – Jeff Hogg for Dundas and Broderick. This seemed a good deal for us. Hogg had been a very good key forward for Richmond and had dominated whenever Fitzroy played Richmond. However, when the November national draft was conducted, Richmond would not trade unless Michael Gale was

CHAPTER 4

included. The coach and recruiters had seconds to make a decision, otherwise no Hogg. They made it. Michael Gale was included in the swap.

History records how Michael Gale and Paul Broderick went on to become very good players for Richmond. Dundas played a handful of games. Jeff Hogg was a terrific club man and a very fine person but injury unfortunately stopped him producing his best for Fitzroy. At the end of the day we had lost two very good players for little return.

As if losing key players wasn't bad enough, our financial squeeze continued to tighten towards the end of 1993. After continuing discussions with Westpac during the year, the bank notified us early in November, 1993, that it would not renew our financial arrangements unless the AFL gave an unconditional guarantee for the funds, payable on demand by the AFL to Westpac. We knew this meant serious trouble.

We asked the AFL to provide the guarantee on the promise that, in the event the club was substantially unable to meet its profitability and cash flow projections for 1994, we would use our best endeavours to facilitate a merger or relocation suitable to Fitzroy and the AFL. This action we suggested would take place based on the financial accounts as at July 31, 1994.

In other words a promise to merge if we did not perform. We could not make an unconditional promise because it was our view that we first had to get the consent of our members and shareholders. This offer was not made lightly. The board's position on a merger or relocation was that it was an option to one thing only – extinction. Without continuing to borrow against the following year's dividend, Fitzroy could not survive.

I would be surprised if the AFL took more than a few seconds to reject our proposal. It had us over a barrel: serious cash flow problems and no banker. It must have thought that it was just a matter of time before we folded.

We then went on a hunt for a bank or some other lending

institution. Just about every known bank was approached. They would give us a polite hearing but look at us with the 'dead fish' eyes that only bankers can give when being asked for money. They all refused. As well as the major banks, we approached all the less well-known banks such as Challenge, but were rejected out of hand except by Metway Bank. We went a long way down the road with that organisation with a major financial sponsorship proposal which we believe they were seriously interested in. At the last moment however, they knocked us back and shortly afterwards became a sponsor for Melbourne Football Club.

This minute was recorded at our board meeting on Tuesday, November 16, 1993:

'To determine attitude of board in respect to Westpac bank and the AFL's refusal to support banking facilities.

The general manager tabled the following documents:

i) Actual club financial position;
ii) Copy of AFL letter of 15 November;
iii) Copy of Westpac correspondence of 16 November;
iv) Cashflow projections for 1994;
v) Potential options available.

General discussion took place in respect to the various options available to the club, following which it was determined that the club would continue to pursue other financial institutions seeking their support as a banking facility. It was noted that a number of financial institutions had been approached but at this stage no positive confirmation had been received. In view of the club's current cash flow position the board felt it appropriate to set a time frame of Friday November 26, at which stage if no bank facility had come forth then the club would need to pursue its other options.

In regard to other options, the preferred option of the club was to seek a merger with another Melbourne-based club and in this regard the chairman indicated that he would seek preliminary discussions with potential clubs.'

CHAPTER 4

This minute is an indication of how serious our position had become.

The problem with our finances was not that the club was currently running at a loss. The problem was cash flow. Our funds were being continually squeezed. In fact Fitzroy declared a profit for the 1993 season of $29,939 which was a remarkable turnaround from the years before. Furthermore, with a team performing well at that time on the field, we were extremely optimistic about the future – if we managed to hold our star players and meet our short-term debts.

Our financial predicament was well known and was almost daily news in the press. Everyone seemed to know we were getting no support from the AFL or Westpac. However, we never gave up hope. We were still pursuing options when I had a late night call from Melbourne businessman Bernie Ahern on Thursday November 18.

Bernie was and is a seriously wealthy person. As a young man he was hospitalised for an extended period of time with a long-term injury. To fill in time, and, I suspect, to make a little money, Bernie commenced an SP bookmaking business whilst lying on his back. When he was discharged from hospital, Bernie had enough money to buy a truck. The one truck became two and before long he had a fleet, B J Ahern Transport. Bernie was a keen follower of harness racing and had been a member of the Trotting Control Board for years. He was a breeder and racer of pacers including Hunter Cup winner 'Royal Gaze.' Folklore has it that he plays the international futures market every night. He is the most astute of astute businesspeople. His philosophy is that if he can borrow money at X dollars and lend it at X plus dollars he will do business.

One of Bernie's great passions in life is the law. Although not formally-qualified, he has worked for years with Galbally and O'Bryan, a leading Melbourne firm of solicitors, as a 'law clerk.' He used to spend most of his time assisting Frank Galbally when Frank was still practising.

FITZROY

In my legal practice I had done a lot of work for Galbally's office and on a number of occasions, Bernie had instructed me. He always knew the material backwards. Galbally's office acted for Peter McEvoy, one of the accused in the Walsh Street murder trial. I am told Bernie was one of the few people who had read every word that was said at the committal hearing and at the trial, which amounted to thousands of pages of transcript.

Bernie seemed to be particularly pleased with me because I got a fair result in a criminal trial for the chef of his favourite restaurant; and this restaurant was the only restaurant in Melbourne that let him smoke cigars!

I had not spoken to Bernie for a long time, so I was fairly surprised to hear from him late that night. Bernie had read of our plight in the papers and he wanted to know why the AFL would not guarantee the AFL dividend. I told him that there was no reason, it was perfectly secure. I added that the advice of Peter Buchanan QC was that the security was 'watertight.' Bernie said that if his independent legal advice was the same, he would act as our banker. All we had to do was to get the AFL to agree. No small order.

Bernie rang the AFL and a meeting was organised between Bernie, Kevin Lehman, the AFL finance manager, and myself at Bernie's place in East Ivanhoe for Saturday morning, November 20, 1993. Bernie put a very simple proposition to Kevin: B J Ahern Pty Ltd would lend the AFL the money (the equivalent of the dividend) for twelve months, the AFL would pay our dividend in advance, and at the end of that 12 months the AFL would repay B J Ahern Pty Ltd. Deducted from the amount paid to Fitzroy was interest which was paid up front to B J Ahern Pty Ltd. We did not think the AFL could possibly squirm out of the offer. None of its money would be used to finance us and it could not argue that it was at risk. The only entity at risk would be Ahern Pty Ltd if the AFL happened to go to the wall. But Kevin could not commit himself to the proposal. He said he would take it back to Ross Oakley.

CHAPTER 4

There had been a fundraising rally organised for Sunday, November 21, at the Brunswick Street Oval. Like most of our functions at the Brunswick Street Oval the official dais was the back of a truck. I addressed the crowd and publicly announced that the club had found somebody prepared to finance us. Somehow Alf Gange (a prominent Fitzroy supporter) must have got wind of the fact that we had a saviour. Suddenly in the midst of festivities, a knight dressed in medieval armour on a white charger went galloping across Brunswick Street Oval much to the amusement of the Fitzroy supporters. Alf had managed to hire the act for the occasion. The 'White Knight' was born!

Lions find a savior
Ashley Browne
The Age
22/11/93

At that rally empty chairs were lined up on the tray of the truck with a sign to indicate that the chairs were placed there for AFL commissioners who, of course, were not present. Barry Capuano, our general manager who had been with us for a short time, told the crowd that the chairs represented the AFL commissioners who had been invited to the rally but who had failed to attend. He then flung a chair over and proclaimed that we could do without the AFL – which was greeted with loud cheers. This episode was given wide prominence in the press and a number of AFL directors took exception to what had happened. On this occasion they had good reason, because, as it turned out, some had not received their invitations. Not that any would have attended if they had.

Commissioners upstaged as Lions breathe again
The Age
22/11/93

93

We wanted to put as much public pressure on the AFL as we could to accept Bernie's proposal. I told the assembled Fitzroy supporters at the rally that the AFL would have no option but to accept our benefactor's offer – although Bernie was not named at his request. In my press interviews I spoke of the funding as a foregone conclusion, but we knew that the AFL could not always be relied upon to do what we wanted.

The following week there was almost frantic speculation in the press as to who the 'White Knight' was. Although the directors knew, no one said a word. We were quite enjoying the moment. As it turned out, Bernie attended the rally as one of the crowd. Leon Wiegard, who was compare of the *Good Sports* morning show on 3UZ (now Sport 927), recognised Bernie and put two and two together, although he did not publicly name him.

During the week Scot Palmer (legendary columnist), who had always supported Fitzroy in his column, rang me and asked me if he could speak to the 'White Knight'. I got in touch with Bernie and prevailed upon him to do an interview with Scot.

In the *Sunday Herald* edition of the November 28, Bernie's head almost filled the whole of the front page! The photo was accompanied by a very good article by Scotty.

Early next week the AFL reluctantly agreed to Bernie's proposal. Late on the evening of Wednesday, December 1, Bernie was with me in my chambers in Lonsdale Street with AFL solicitor Jeff Browne. Bernie had been carrying a cheque around in his pocket for days. Bernie was a great person for getting things done 'now.' He was known to ring up lawyers and accountants at two or three in the morning when he wanted information or wanted something done. Jeff told us on the Wednesday night that Ross had the agreement at home and that he would sign it and we would exchange the cheque for the agreement the next day. Bernie said, 'Don't worry about that, I'll send the cheque around to Ross' home with my chauffeur and he'll collect the agreement and bring it back to chambers.' Jeff obliged, rang Ross Oakley and within five

CHAPTER 4

minutes Bernie's chauffeur was motoring out to Richmond in Bernie's beautiful grey Rolls-Royce. Within an hour the deal was done and we had the signed agreement in our hands.

While that was occurring, Elaine Findlay was conducting a Fitzroy board meeting in my absence. At that particular time, we were meeting weekly because of the crisis. On the way home, I invited Bernie to meet the other Fitzroy directors. The last note of the minutes of that board meeting record: 'Due to the arrival of the Chairman, Dyson Hore-Lacy, together with Bernie Ahern, it was felt appropriate that the meeting be adjourned to a later date.'

We adjourned to the bar downstairs for a celebratory drink.

Why I saved the Lions

Scot Palmer
Sunday Herald Sun
28/11/93

Bernie is a very private person and he initially wanted his identity to remain a secret. However, I think he secretly enjoyed this episode in his life. Even though he denied it, I know he cherished some of the lovely letters he got from Fitzroy supporters.

Whilst Bernie was instrumental in securing our funding for the following year, we were by no means out of the woods. We still had about half a million dollars extra to find (the $250,000 loan from the AFL was eventually paid back principally out of monies advanced to us from our Footscray agreement, that is, from catering rights and advanced seat bookings).

The Gange brothers had advanced us a substantial amount of money in late 1993 by way of 'sponsorship for life' for the family. Alf was one of the avenues we turned to in desperation in late 1993. His family had supported Fitzroy for generations. Alf and his two brothers, John and Kevin, were partners in Astoria Taxis and owned a lot of property in the city and surrounding areas. All three brothers and their families were great supporters of the club and always took tables at the chairman's luncheon. John and Maureen's daughters, Rebecca and Fiona, used to babysit for my children. The Gange family had also lent a further amount which was secured on the hotel and later repaid. In recognition of their assistance to us in our hour of need, Alf was offered and accepted a position on the board but unfortunately later declined.

Player payments were due in late December of every year but with Bernie's money and other amounts we managed to scrape together, we had enough to pay them.

The advance from the Ahern arrangement, however, was for only $676,412, about $500,000 less than our AFL dividend. This was because the AFL had to pay back $1,500,000 to Westpac which we had borrowed in 1992. The AFL therefore subtracted the balance it had to pay over the dividend ($400,000) from our expected 1994 dividend ($1,100,000). Coupled with other debts which had accrued to the AFL, we were left with only $676,425 to run the Fitzroy Football Club from the AFL monies. We needed another $400,000 to bring us up to the dividend level of $1,100,000.

The only way to raise the necessary operating funds was to borrow more money against the hotel. The problem was that the AFL still held a debenture charge over the hotel for the $250,000 we owed it – even though we had paid the money back – and it was most reluctant to release that charge so that we could borrow more money using the hotel as security. The AFL had no legal right to hold the charge and would only remove it after we were forced once again to contemplate legal action.

Once the AFL loan was paid back the only money secured by the hotel was the initial charge. This secured borrowing of about $200,000 had been raised to pay for its purchase price and start up costs.

We then began the lengthy process of trying to raise more money. We organised meetings with major shareholders and supporters where we would explain the club's predicament and invite further

CHAPTER 4

investment. We went to great pains to ensure potential investors obtained independent legal and accounting advice. As it turned out, no one who lent money to the club in this way lost a cent, including interest.

We did not always accept money that was offered to us. Once we received a phone call from a supporter who was left over $100,000 in a will, wanting to lend us the money. She said that all she wanted was a small amount of interest because she was a pensioner. After a couple of questions it was apparent that the money was her only asset. Next morning I went around to her place with a bunch of flowers and a card thanking her for her very kind gesture but suggesting she put the money in the bank because we could not absolutely guarantee the repayment.

It was obvious that we needed one large contribution and a number of smaller ones to make up what was needed.

Once again we turned to Bernie Ahern in late January, 1994. He agreed to lend us a further $150,000 provided it was secured by way of a first debenture on the hotel and that all the other lenders moved out into a second debenture with the first one, of course, having priority. We held a meeting with all the initial debenture holders and all agreed to move into a second debenture except for two small investors who were paid out. In addition, we managed to raise about another $150,000 half of which came from directors, which then was included in the second debenture.

All in all, about $600,000 was borrowed against the hotel

Lions ease crisis with repayment offer
Michael Davis
The Australian
16/2/94

Lions: We can pay AFL
Daryl Timms
Herald Sun
16/2/94

company which held the lease. The legal arrangement was that Bondborough borrowed the money which on-lent it to Fitzroy Football Club Limited. With the gaming machines performing well we had our twenty year lease valued at $750,000, so we believed the investment by our lenders was fairly secure. In addition, the investment returned 10% per annum in interest to lenders – which at that time was a very competitive rate.

Despite the mixed feelings caused by future events, I still have wonderful memories of the many people who worked so hard to keep the club afloat during the various crises. The crowds of ordinary people who reached into their pockets to assist us reaffirms my faith in traditional football supporters. Even today, many of those who fought for Fitzroy still meet to exchange memories and repeat a myriad of stories and incidents.

Not all my time at Fitzroy was attended by drama and gloom and the struggle to stay competitive. There were many moments of satisfaction and amusement. Even my dealings with the AFL hierarchy had their moments.

Some of the best arose out of the AFL Club directors' meetings. These meetings took place every three months and were akin to 'feeding the chooks,' with the AFL being the feeders.

At one of my first directors' meetings, one of the agenda matters was the requirement that the clubs nominate the winner of the Jack Titus award. Jack (Skinny) Titus played 294 games (including 204 played consecutively) for Richmond between 1926 and 1943. This award was presented every year to an individual for outstanding service to AFL football, usually over a long period of time.

One of the eventual recipients of that award was Billy Stephen, who Fitzroy nominated yearly and who deserved to win the award many years before he did. Ironically Billy finally won it in the year that Fitzroy left the competition!

At this particular meeting, Ross Oakley advised us that the AFL recommendation was that Alan Cooke[4], from Richmond, be the

CHAPTER 4

recipient and we were asked to vote accordingly. After the motion was put one of the interstate directors asked who the other nominees were. 'I am afraid we are not allowed to tell you that,' said Ross 'It's confidential.' The West Coast Eagles director said, 'That's fine, but could I ask a question, Ross?' 'Allright,' replied Ross, 'Go ahead.'

'Who is Alan Cooke?' asked the Eagles man.

On another occasion, Ross Oakley was reviewing a series of disastrous games played outside Australia for promotional purposes. These games were perceived by some as overseas junkets for the favoured AFL clubs, their administrators and AFL personnel – which the remaining clubs had to help fund. Ross' review went something like this:

'The game in New Zealand was a bit disappointing. Only five hundred people turned up. Unfortunately, on the day, we had to compete with a sail past of the New Zealand Navy.' A despondent Ross continued by expressing his disappointment at games in Canada and England: 'Unfortunately we had to compete with the annual passing out parade of the Royal Canadian Mounties. The London game was a bit better. About two thousand people turned up. Unfortunately we had to compete with the World Cup in Rugby.'

Undeterred by this series of misfortunes, towards the end of the meeting a somewhat cheery Ross told us, 'I have some very good news. The South African Ambassador has approached us with the proposal to play a promotional AFL game in South Africa.' At this point, Carlton president, John Elliott, never lost for words, spoke up. 'Ross, there is only one place to play the game and that's Jo'burg.' 'Well, I would oppose that,' said Peter Gordon from Footscray. 'And why is that?' said an impatient Ross. 'Most of our supporters live in Soweto,' said Peter.

It took about two minutes for the laughter to subside.

---

4. Alan Cooke played 116 games for Richmond between 1949-58. He was chairman of selectors for many years.

FITZROY

From time to time, Fitzroy became tired of the continual public statements of the larger supported clubs, particularly Collingwood, complaining that there were too many clubs in Melbourne. The chairman's speeches at home lunches were our best opportunity to defend ourselves as they were often given wide publicity. Sometimes humour was used to make what were actually serious points. Sick and tired of AFL policy and Collingwood's bleating, I read a fictitious newspaper report from the year 2005 to our luncheon audience before our game with North Melbourne in 1995:

Newspaper Report – Year 2005
Long serving Collingwood president, Mr Alan McAllister, slammed the AFL today. Collingwood, which now owns every property in the area bordered by Johnson Street, Nicholson Street, Brunswick Road and the Yarra, is on the verge of going broke said Mr McAllister. 'We're sick of subsiding the other teams in the AFL,' he added.

Presidents of the two remaining clubs in the competition, the Sydney Swans and the Brisbane Bears, refuted Mr McAllister's claims.

Mr McAllister also criticised the 25 draft priorities given to both the Swans and Bears before Collingwood had its first choice.

The sole AFL commissioner and chairman, Mr Graeme Samuel, defended the AFL draft policy. 'It is working,' said Mr Samuel. 'As a result of our policies the Bears and the Swans are currently second and third on the AFL ladder,' he added with pride.

As far as the long term future of the game was concerned Mr Samuel welcomed the key recommendation in the second Crawford Report – that the AFL prune its football operations.

'These are very exciting times. Our policy of economic rationalism is really working,' said Mr Samuel. 'Unfortunately the playing of games is proving to be an unwarranted drain on the finances of the AFL.

Consequently, in our new five year plan, we propose to merge Collingwood, the Swans and the Bears into one club to be called 'Corporate Raiders.' We will sell AFL Park, AFL House and

CHAPTER 4

sublet the MCG for rock concerts and concentrate all our activities in property development.'

When asked what the new team would do. Mr Samuel said that it would be principally engaged in shopping centre promotions.

We will also have a Top Ten players list which we will utilise as guest speakers at corporate breakfasts, Mr Samuel added. Within five years the AFL could be one of the biggest and most profitable companies in Victoria.

Graeme Samuel rang me up and asked for a copy of what I said. I soon received a fax back saying that he thought what I said was very amusing, but I had one thing wrong – it would happen much earlier than the year 2005! I had to laugh.

On another occasion, I took the opportunity to have a swipe at the AFL's policy on racial vilification. I took the view that racial abuse should be treated the same way as any other offence on the football field. Half-an-hour's mediation (in secret) is not going to change anyone's view. A more effective deterrent I thought would be the disgrace of public exposure. At one luncheon I had this to say:

A special welcome to AFL commissioner Colin Carter. The AFL commissioners allocate themselves around the grounds each week. Colin was saying how pleased he was that this week he had first choice.

I have been told that the AFL are so buoyed by the success of its policy on racial slurs, that it is going to introduce 'mediation' for a whole range of offences. The penalty for abusing an umpire will no longer be a fine or suspension, but mediation. The umpire and offending player will be sent into the same room. The mediation will go something like this:

Umpire: Player, I don't like being called a blind, dirty, cheating, mongrel, weasel dog of a white leghorn.

Player: Sorry ump. I think you must have taken it the wrong way!

Umpire: Okay, then. Sorry for wasting your time. See you next week.

The answer to abuse of umpires is not in penalties. It is in educating the community that it is no longer acceptable to call umpires 'white leghorns.' An educational program will be implemented by the AFL to educate footballers that umpires are no different to the rest of us.

A similar policy will be implemented for striking charges. In future, anyone charged with striking will be sent into a room with the victim to settle their differences. Next week the AFL will announce that the new Dispute Mediation Resolution Centre will be Festival Hall!'

I received a lot of correspondence over the years from interested Fitzroy supporters. One of the most amusing was a letter from Perth which read:

'Please, I beg of you, don't merge. My in-laws live in Melbourne and are fanatical Fitzroy supporters. If Fitzroy disappears there will be nothing to stop them moving over to Western Australia to live.'

I wrote back and assured him that we were doing all we could to help him!

Chapter 5

Bernie Ahern's assistance plus loans from our dedicated supporters had placed us in a much better financial position. Bernie had also informed us that he would be willing to enter into another such arrangement for the following year. The AFL had other ideas though. Not long after we secured the Ahern loan the AFL announced that it would not enter into any more arrangements similar to the one it had entered into with B J Ahern. While we were disappointed that the AFL would not repeat an arrangement that assisted us at no risk to itself, we were not surprised.

Despite this, things were looking up. With the increased borrowings on the hotel, the generosity of the Gange brothers and the hotel itself running profitably, we had reason to believe our immediate cash flow problems were over. In addition the club had undergone some major administrative changes.

This overhauling had started more than a year earlier. In 1992 Kevin Ryan had come out of retirement to replace Don Wallace as general manager. Kevin had jumped into the breach to help us out when illness forced Don's resignation. Kevin was an extremely valuable board member and a loyal Fitzroy person.

In 1993 we commenced to look around for a top professional CEO, someone experienced in the world of commerce. The major professional employment agencies were approached. There was one suitable person who was available, but he prevaricated over the job for so long that we lost interest. Also he seemed to be more interested in finer details of his financial package than the challenge of running an AFL club.

Barry Capuano had lost his job with the AFL in early 1993 for his perceived responsibility (according to the AFL) for the substandard playing surface at Waverly Park. We decided to approach him for the Fitzroy position. Barry had impeccable qualifications. He played football for both Essendon and Victoria and served as both a general manager at Essendon and as a senior AFL administrator. We approached Barry for the position of CEO at Fitzroy and, after some initial uncertainty, Barry finally agreed to take the job as CEO for a period of three months effective from September 6, 1993. We were hopeful we could convince him to stay on. From the first day of his appointment Barry gave added public creditability to the club administration and his professionalism was welcomed by everybody at Fitzroy – including the players.

My right hand man, John Dawson, unfortunately left Fitzroy in 1993. John, an old school friend of mine and a friend of Leon Wiegard as well, was appointed CEO of the National Australia Bank in the UK and Europe. John was extremely well respected in the commercial world and his departure in April 1993 was a sad loss to the club. Elaine Findlay, who had been a director for longer than any of us, became vice-chairperson when John left. When the contribution of women in AFL football is assessed historically, Elaine should be at the forefront of discussions. She worked tirelessly for the club and loved it to death. To this day, she remains as loyal as ever.

John Stewart, a partner in Frank Jones and Associates, high flying accountants and the forerunner to Horwath & Horwath, was appointed in John Dawson's place, and we were fortunate in finding such a competent and professional replacement. He and his family were lifetime supporters. John and David Sandground controlled finance, with David also responsible for the running of the hotel. David was helped enormously by Peter Mitchell, the club's largest shareholder and someone with extensive experience in the running of hotels and restaurants. Other directors at the beginning of 1993 were Ken Levy, Kevin Ryan and Dr Henry Pinskier, who looked after marketing and public relations. David McMahon, a former Fitzroy champion, was our football director and was also involved in marketing. David was the second longest serving director and had played 219 premiership games with Fitzroy. (240 including

CHAPTER 5

pre season and night series games.)

John Petinella was appointed to the board by members and shareholders at our AGM in February 1993. John, a longtime supporter of the club who for years had employed players part time, is a very successful fruit and vegetable grower. He was the board member closest to the players, an extremely good director possessed of excellent judgment and common sense. John Petinella and Elaine Findlay worked with our social club and coterie groups, and later John was involved in marketing. By 1994 we had a system much like a cabinet, with each director responsible for specific areas.

In December, 1993, Colin Hobbs, another former Fitzroy player (captain of Coburg and playing-coach of Northcote in the VFA), was invited to join the board. Colin was an inspired choice. A former teacher turned business man, Colin quickly demonstrated an acute perception of what was important. His contribution from the start was significant and he very quickly became one of the most respected board members. He, like David McMahon, who also possessed very good judgment, were two football directors whom the players were able to relate to.

The club also benefited from the work of some talented administrators. Maria Galiano (our marketing manager), Glen Warry (football manager) and Allan McConnell, our assistant coach, served with distinction throughout my time with Fitzroy.

People often complain about the quality of directors on AFL boards, but by and large Fitzroy was served extremely well by the directors I was privileged to work with. Most were intelligent, successful and loyal. They fought their hearts out for the club and put their own personal finances and credibility on the line for the sake of the club. There were no tangible benefits in being a director of Fitzroy but they shared an intangible desire to keep the Fitzroy club going and to make it successful.

We were used to dealing with financial crises, but one thing we counted on was having a competitive football team. This was made more difficult by the loss of key players, of course, but we hoped the younger brigade would rise to the challenge. With the new administration in place, all we wanted was a reasonable year on the field. Our coach Robert Shaw had recently signed a new contract, providing the stable leadership we needed.

We were still being harmed by a lot of negative speculation in the press. On February 1, 1994 a well known *Herald Sun* reporter rang me and said, 'There is a very strong word around that you won't make it to the first game.' I said 'Who told you that?' He replied, 'Someone from the AFL.' I told him to print the story but also print the name of the source.

On February 10, the same reporter from the *Herald Sun* rang again and told me that two different sources from the AFL had said that we wouldn't make it to the first game. This time I denied it. The 'story' was not going to go away The AFL was familiar with our financial situation. Indeed in the last two years of our existence they knew to the dollar what our finances were. In both these years it had served one of their notorious solvency notices upon us which required us to satisfy the AFL as to our solvency by providing financial details.

The constant negative media speculation continued to have adverse effects on the club. We began to experience problems with the players even before the season started. On February 11, we were confronted with a major article on the back page of *The Herald Sun* under the heading '7 Days or We Walk.' Paul Roos' picture accompanied the article. A number of Fitzroy senior players had met at the home of the manager of many of them, Damien Smith, accompanied apparently by a photographer and a reporter from *The Herald Sun*. The gist of the article was that if the club was not able to give certain assurances, the players would refuse to play.

CHAPTER 5

Fitzroy players give club ultimatum

7 DAYS OR WE WALK

Players in secret meeting over future

Mike Sheahan
Herald Sun
12/2/94

LIONS CRISIS TALKS

Daryl Timms, Mike Sheahan and Scott Gullan
Herald sun
11/2/94

The directors were disappointed in this action to say the least. I and other directors, we believed, had regularly kept the players informed of relevant circumstances. We appreciated that at times it must have been hard for them with all the negative publicity surrounding the club. We would have been more than happy to answer any query that they had – as we had done in the past. In conjunction with the *Herald Sun* article, we received a solicitor's letter from Smith and Emerton, solicitors acting on behalf of most of our senior players. The letter demanded the following information:

a) A statement as to the current financial position of the club certified by its auditors;
b) A business plan of the club in respect of the 1994 football season;
c) The budget to which the club is operating in respect to the 1994 football season;
d) Copies of the 1993 accounts of the club.

A response to the letter was required by 5.00 pm on Friday, February 18. A minute of the board at a hurriedly convened directors meeting which took place February 13, reads:

'The directors took the view that it was inappropriate to supply all the details requested.' We agreed however to a meeting to be held between the players' solicitors, Damien Smith, myself, our chief executive officer, Barry Capuano and our finance directors, John Stewart and Kevin Ryan.

Barry Capuano and I also addressed the players on February 14 at our training headquarters, the Lakeside Oval, and told them precisely what the club's financial position was.

A few days later a meeting with the players association was held in my chambers. We told the assembled throng, including the grim-faced lawyers from Smith and Emerton, everything they wanted to know. The following day, Barry Capuano met with Damien Smith and discussed the budget and cash flow projections for 1994, following which Damien Smith indicated that he would instruct the players that in his opinion, the club was in a position to meet its commitments to players during 1994. The 'strike' was averted. Regardless of what the financial position of Fitzroy Football Club was, the AFL was a party to all player contracts and in our view would be obliged to pay out the players in any event.

Damien Smith was one of the first player managers in Melbourne. He represented most of our senior players, including Paul Roos and Richard Osborne. We never had cause for concern over Damien's credibility. He was always fair and upfront in his dealings with us while I was at Fitzroy.

We started 1994 with Lynch, Broderick, Michael Gale and Dundas all gone to other clubs. As well as snaring Broderick, Dundas and Gale, Richmond managed to snatch Jamie Elliott with the priority draft choice it had secured under the AFL's magic formula. At the time, Fitzroy believed it had a verbal contract with Elliott and consequently we took Richmond to the Appeals Tribunal which determined that as the contract was not in writing

CHAPTER 5

it was not valid. Tribunal members Peter O'Callaghan QC, Brian Bourke and Colin Stubbs gave us a fair hearing but decided, in effect, that unless a contract was signed it was not worth a cent.

Elliott had shown terrific promise at Fitzroy and Robert Shaw was extremely upset at losing him. Ironically he was never to recapture his form at Richmond. He was traded to St.Kilda and then slowly drifted out of AFL Football.

With a weakened player list, we still began the pre-season campaign with a win, this time by 14 points against Geelong before being beaten by Adelaide in Round 2. We started the premiership season optimistically, but were disappointed by the AFL's attitude to scheduling. The AFL draw, as it was commonly called, was not a draw at all. The scheduling of games was manipulated to maximise crowds. Consequently the big drawing clubs such as Essendon, Collingwood and Carlton always played each other twice and usually on select days, such as Queen's Birthday Monday or ANZAC Day – and usually at the MCG. Smaller crowd drawing clubs such as ours were used to fill in the gaps.

It was very important for membership and general interest purposes to have early home games, and preferably the first game.

It was crucial in 1994, as this was our first year playing our home games at the Western Oval, that we be given a favourable draw and that the venue be promoted. This did not happen. Our first 'home' game was in Round 2 – at Princes Park! Our first home game at Western Oval was not until Round 3. The first two games at the Western Oval were against Brisbane and Sydney, clubs which have little following in Melbourne.

In our first game we were beaten by Collingwood at Victoria Park by 11 points, before rebounding with a 13 point win against Essendon at Optus Oval. A win against Brisbane by 33 points followed, our first game at Western Oval as a home ground, before losing to West Coast at the WACA by 76 points. We then beat Sydney at the Western Oval by eight points. Three wins out of five wasn't a bad start for the season.

Unfortunately, after the bye in Round 6 we then lost five games in a row before beating Hawthorn in Round 13 by 13 points. In our last eleven games, our lack of depth and experience began to really tell and we won only one of them, a 28 point win against Sydney at the SCG in August. We lost our last ten games by an average of ten goals a game. As our form slipped during the season so did the gate receipts.

Bernie Ahern had secured our funding for the year – but finances were still very tight and we needed to secure our financing for the next year. Our returns from the sale of reserved seating from the Western Oval were good but did not reach the figures anticipated. Crowds there had not lived up to expectations but we did not think it was the fault of the location. Most of our supporters were ready to follow us anywhere. We believed more significant factors affecting our attendances were our poor performances on the field and the unattractive matches which were scheduled there. 'Back of the jumper' advertising was now permitted by the AFL but we had difficulty in obtaining a suitable sponsor.

In mid-March 1994, the club received another jolt and this one was major. Barry Capuano rang me at work and told me that he wanted to come in to see me. I asked him what about, but he said it was best he told me personally. My heart sank because I feared the worst. When Barry arrived he told me that he was going to take the position of CEO with the Melbourne Tigers basketball club. Barry had been a thoroughly professional administrator and a major reason for our renewed confidence. He had only ever guaranteed us three months but he seemed to be enjoying the challenge and was working very well with the board, the administration, football staff and particularly the players. Barry did, however, agree to stay on for a further month to assist us in finding a suitable CEO.

Once again we were without a chief executive officer and the press saw Barry's departure in a very negative light, even though we had originally announced his appointment as a temporary

CHAPTER 5

position only. As soon as Barry's resignation became public, Paul Roos was on the phone wanting to know what was going on, such was his concern. Even though when we first engaged Barry we stressed publicly it was only a temporary appointment, his leaving was very difficult to publicly explain.

As football club operations were expanding, so too was the required expertise of the CEO. Not only was the person responsible for football operations but also for merchandising and marketing, fund raising, overseeing the hotel operations, player contracts and a whole host of things unique to an AFL football club. The directors decided that Fitzroy would look for an expert commercial businessman in preference to an administrator who had come through traditional football ranks. Preferably, the two could be combined. We engaged professional employment agencies for assistance, but very few, if any, suitably qualified people were prepared to give it a go.

Through the grapevine, we had heard that John Birt, membership manager at Collingwood, was interested in taking over the chief executive spot at Fitzroy. John had as much general experience in football as anyone. Like Barry Capuano, he was a former Essendon champion footballer, had coached at a number of AFL clubs and had extensive experience in football administration. In an earlier life he had been a junior school headmaster. John took over the reins as CEO on June 1, 1994.

Other problems surfaced from unlikely sources. For many years Fitzroy had used the Lakeside Oval as its training headquarters. One of the side effects of Melbourne's successful grab for the Australian Grand Prix from Adelaide was that Fitzroy got turfed off the Lakeside Oval – no conversation, no negotiations, no discussions, no compensation. The Lakeside Oval, the former home ground for nearly a century of the South Melbourne Football Club, was converted to a soccer ground.

Our match committee looked at a number of alternative venues including Toorak Park in Prahran, Preston City Oval in Preston,

Northcote Football Ground, the AG Gillon Oval in Brunswick and City Oval in Coburg. For a number of reasons Coburg was selected, and for the price of about $30,000 which included provision of lighting (plus a couple of working bees) the venue near Bell Street and Sydney Road became our training headquarters. This association between two famous clubs continues today in the revamped VFL.

At about the time the match committee recommended Coburg, we were hunting in earnest for funding to replace the Bernie Ahern loan. Despite what we felt were very positive vibes from a couple of financial institutions, our overtures came to nothing. To compound our financial problems a number of our sponsors such as SouthCorp Wines were expressing a reluctance to continue. VicHealth – via the Quit campaign – had been reducing its sponsorship for years and its attitude was becoming very negative[5].

A board minute of the 30 August 1994 summed up the general feeling concerning potential sponsors:

'Sponsorship – J Birt reported that various companies had been approached about major sponsorships. Companies are interested but are anxious (sic) if we will be going on next year.'

A number of schemes were introduced to boost revenue. For example, the Fitzroy Foundation was formed. This was a trust (still continuing to this day) which comprised businesspeople investing money in projects, the profits of which would go to Fitzroy. Our former football manager, Arthur Wilson, and supporter Greg Basto devised a 'dollar a day' fundraising scheme, whereby members would contribute $1 per day to the club for 2 years.

In 1994 the AFL placed a $3 million inducement on the table for two AFL clubs to merge. For years the AFL had been pursuing a 'rationalisation' of Melbourne clubs so that they could introduce

---

5. Quit had been our sponsor for at least ten years and was, according to some surveys, the most identifiable sponsor in AFL football.

CHAPTER 5

more interstate sides into the competition. The AFL decided to push the issue by calling a meeting of all AFL club presidents, general managers and directors later in the year. A straw vote at the meeting saw the inducement rise from $3m to $6m. Footscray's Peter Gordon pushed for $8m. Finally a figure of $6 million was settled on. The irony of the voting process was that it was the wealthier clubs (Essendon, Collingwood and Carlton being three of them) which fought the increased inducement.

These three clubs, of course, were among those continually claiming that there were too many clubs in Melbourne. They also constantly complained about the equal sharing of marketing revenue. One of the great misconceptions about revenue distribution was that there was gate equalisation in the AFL. The fact was that competing clubs shared the gate – except for $3.20 which was taken out of each adult ticket for 'equalisation.' This $3.20 amount had not changed since it was introduced in the mid-eighties. As club memberships increased (with the clubs keeping all this revenue) the amount available for equalisation was reduced. Other amounts were paid to various clubs out of this fund including compensation to Essendon for leaving Windy Hill and an amount to Carlton for something which was never disclosed. By the mid-nineties, the amounts available for distribution from the 'equalisation fund' were negligible in comparison to attendances.

Since the big games were always scheduled at the MCG, often on public holidays, Essendon, Carlton and Collingwood would invariably play each other in these matches. In one of these games Essendon would receive more in gate receipts than Fitzroy would in a season. By 1994 Essendon, Carlton and Collingwood were receiving over a million dollars in gate receipts compared to Fitzroy's $100,000. Considering we were receiving approximately a million dollars less from membership than the larger Melbourne clubs – and considerably less in sponsorship – the difficulty in competing successfully can be readily understood. In 1994 we were running the club on a turnover of approximately $5 million per year compared to $11m or $12m being spent by the larger clubs. Once again our financial position was becoming critical.

We had been blocked by the AFL with our proposed loan arrangement with Bernie Ahern. The banks seemed lukewarm to any of our proposals and income was harder than ever to come by. This was the situation that compelled the Fitzroy directors to look at options for merging with another AFL club in 1994.

Brisbane had been making public overtures for years concerning a merger between Brisbane and Fitzroy. This idea was also being promoted by a number of Fitzroy people including former president George Coates.

On June 16, 1994, Damien Smith, manager of Fitzroy stars Roos, Lynch and Osborne, rang me with a detailed proposal for a merger between the Lions and Bears. He said that he was not acting on behalf of Brisbane but on his own initiative.

The Fitzroy directors took the view that if Fitzroy had to merge we would prefer it to be with a Melbourne – based AFL club. The board discussed all the possible alternatives. It is fair to say that most AFL clubs in Melbourne had, in the past, expressed interest at some level in a merger with Fitzroy.

None of the Fitzroy directors wanted to merge. Our real and stated policy was that merging was the last option before liquidation. We and directors before us, including Leon Wiegard, had been fighting for many years to keep the club afloat. We had activated all sorts of initatives, many out of left field, such as the Ahern loan, to keep the club going.

We had got to the stage where we believed we had almost exhausted all options, and as directors, we took the view that we were duty bound to preserve what we could of Fitzroy, and if that meant merging, it had to be done. We knew we could expect little or no assistance from the AFL.

The directors, quite wrongly as it turned out, took the view that Melbourne Football Club would be the best club to merge with. The colours of the two clubs were similar, Melbourne did

CHAPTER 5

not have a social club and we did and, if necessary, we thought we could live with the name the 'Melbourne Lions' because 'Melbourne' was a generic name rather than a suburban name. As well, we knew Melbourne was keen to talk. Melbourne was also secure at the MCG which was, at that time, easily the preferred ground. With the approval of the Board I first met with Ian Ridley (Melbourne president) and Noel McMahon (Melbourne vice-president) at Noel's city office. We discussed preliminary matters and on August 1, 1994 I drove to Ian's home for further discussions. By this time the financial situation at Fitzroy had become critical.

At the conclusion at the meeting with Ian, we had an 'in principle' tentative agreement, and we decided to go to the AFL Commission to see what help the Commission would give us if we merged. What was informally agreed upon was that a company named Melbourne Football Club – Fitzroy Football Club Pty Ltd, operating as the 'Melbourne Lions,' would play in the AFL. The jumpers needed little alteration but would essentially be a combination of the two. It was a fairly similar arrangement to the abortive Melbourne-Hawks attempt in 1996.

Rumours must have been spreading concerning Melbourne and Fitzroy because on August 2 I was rung by Hawthorn president, Geoff Lord, who wanted an opportunity to speak to us. I agreed and an appointment was made for Thursday, August 4. Coincidentally, on August 1, I had received a call from North Melbourne chairman Ron Casey arranging to have lunch with him at the Victoria Club on Friday, August 5. I met with Geoff Lord and John Lauritz, Hawthorn's CEO, at my chambers as arranged. The idea of the Hawthorn Lions was canvassed pretty extensively, but at that stage, Fitzroy had the 'in principle' agreement with Melbourne Football Club.

On the Friday morning we met the AFL Commission. We detailed the points that we had agreed upon and asked them what help they would give us. The Commission seemed very keen on the proposal although Ross Oakley raised doubts about the viability of the enterprise on the basis that the image of both clubs was so different – the 'silvertails and the workers' as somebody put it, Melbourne of course, being the silvertails. The AFL Commission agreed to get back to us quickly concerning what it could offer the two clubs. John Winneke told me, 'I don't think you will be too disappointed in what we can do for you.'

Later that day I met Ron Casey for lunch at the Victoria Club. He was with North Melbourne vice-chairman Peter De Rauch and chief executive officer Ken Montgomery. The dining venue had to be changed very quickly because when we arrived at the Victoria Club we found that John Lauritz, the Hawthorn CEO, and a number of the Hawthorn coterie group, the Confreres, were lunching at the time. We all made a hasty retreat to the hotel next door. Because we had been so far down the track with Melbourne – including the meeting at the AFL Commission that morning – we told the North Melbourne people that we were already committed to another club. They guessed it was Melbourne and argued that North Melbourne was a much better joint venture partner than Melbourne. We ended a very pleasant luncheon by saying that we'd be interested in talking with North Melbourne if our arrangement with the 'other club' did not eventuate.

At the conclusion of the AFL Commission meeting on the Friday morning, we stressed the need for confidentiality, mentioning that we had experienced some unfortunate episodes in the past concerning confidential information we had made available to the AFL. What a waste of words! The full story of the proposal, in minute detail including accurate pictures of the new jumper, were printed in Monday's edition of the *Herald Sun*. The report was so accurate it was almost as if a reporter had been hiding under the AFL Commission's table. To compound matters, Geoff Lord, at the Hawthorn chairman's luncheon on August 7, said that Ian Ridley had told him during a phone call that Melbourne had been having discussions with Fitzroy. Geoff always claimed that he was speaking 'tongue in cheek' when he made this

CHAPTER 5

comment, and that he had no real information to base it on.

Anyway, the proposed merger turned out to be a disaster. Sections of the press scuttled it from the start. For some reason the same press who had been urging us to merge for years now turned on us. Mike Sheahan wrote an article urging Fitzroy to 'Come Clean' complaining we were not informing the public (that is the press) of what we were doing. For some reason, whilst we were being accused of being somehow involved in underhand activities, Melbourne almost completely escaped any criticism whatsoever. An objective reader of the papers at the time could have been forgiven for thinking that we were merging with ourselves!

Merge plan set to fail

Daryl Timms
Herald Sun
18/8/94

In the days following the public disclosure of our intentions, Ian Ridley kept telling me that the Melbourne people he was speaking to were reacting quite positively to the proposal. However, this did not reflect the general feeling at Melbourne. As Ross Oakley so correctly anticipated, the Melbourne people thought they were way above us. Our supporters did not like them much either. On Thursday, Ian told me that although everyone was very positive about the merge there was no way the Board would accept the Fitzroy name being incorporated into the corporate name. To the Fitzroy directors that signified an attitude which was going to lead to bigger problems. The Fitzroy name was not going to be preserved with the team name, Melbourne Lions, and it did not appear to us to be too much to ask that it be preserved in the corporate name.

Realising our mistake in targetting Melbourne Football Club the directors passed a motion quite early in the piece which effectively put an end to that venture.

I rang Ron Casey on Thursday, August 12, to tell him that the other club had backed out on a key issue and asked him if North Melbourne had a proposal to put to us. Ron said that his key people were in Perth but they would get back to us. However, by this time it was probably too late to organise a merger before the next season with anyone else, so the Fitzroy directors set about trying to rebuild the club from the wreckage.

At this time Brisbane Bears made another public bid for Fitzroy. I recall saying at the next chairmans luncheon, somewhat annoyed, that if we had to merge, Brisbane would be the last option.

Brisbane's bid got some support in the press notably from Gerard Healy and Mike Sheahan, who was a continuing advocate for this union.

Home base, bigger board and Lions name

FRESH BEARS OFFER

Mike Sheahan
Herald Sun
11/8/94

This time Lions, seize the Brisbane option
Gerard Healy
Herald Sun
13/8/94

In a belated attempt to bring about some resolution between Melbourne and Fitzroy, John Winneke[6] organised a meeting between himself, Ross Oakley, myself and Ian Ridley in John's chambers in William Street in an attempt to mediate an agreement.

---

6. John Winneke was then a leading Queen's Counsel. He is now president of the Court of Appeal.

CHAPTER 5

At that meeting Ian was adamant the Melbourne people would not in any circumstances incorporate the Fitzroy name into the corporate body. Ross Oakley, stated that he did not believe that our request was unreasonable. The meeting ended without any resolution and that was the end of it.

Our decision to seek a merge with Melbourne instead of North Melbourne was a bad error of judgment. We were swayed by the similarity in jumpers and we thought we could live with the name Melbourne Lions. We were keen to preserve a local identity, that is the 'Melbourne Lions' as distinct from say, 'Perth Lions.' The two clubs were not harmonious and when push came to shove, the proposal had no chance. Hawthorn and Melbourne were much more compatible, although one could be excused for taking a different view in late 1996.

As the ashes of the failed merged attempt were cooling, more turmoil followed. Robert Shaw quit in a blaze of publicity – and we were in the process of losing Paul Roos, our captain and champion, although we did not know it at the time.

Fitzroy's coaches during my time on the board were a hugely different mixture of personalities and abilities. The longest serving was Robert Shaw, a creative and individual character who had a fierce determination to be successful. Under Robert's coaching there were some spectacular highs and equally devastating lows. The final ledger shows ladder positions of 13th (1991), 10th (1992) and 11th (1993), which was not a reflection of his enthusiasm and commitment. He, as with all the recent coaches at Fitzroy, suffered from a lack of senior players able to provide leadership and serve as role models for the younger ones on and off the field.

Shaw was particularly frustrated by the continual player drain. It was under him that Alastair Lynch moved to Brisbane. During this time, Shaw made the following observations about his current crop of Fitzroy players in a memo prepared for the board:

'(if) I could not see real improvement in the development of the team, then I would give every consideration to giving

someone else an opportunity... the loss of important players due to draft concessions was a harrowing experience... Considering this year's team could develop into a beauty, the thoughts of not coaching all of them would be extremely frustrating. My main area of concern is that just as we look like building a team we lose players to rules etc. We are continually in a state of re-building! I am very upset with Lynch – had he stayed Fitzroy would be on top of the ladder.'

Under Shaw there was considerable change in our playing personnel. Some were caused by AFL rules and financial inducements, others by poor trading choices and personality clashes. During his time however Shaw generated enthusiasm and discipline among the players, writing at one stage, 'It is an exciting place to be at present and a good environment in which to develop one's character.'

All these pressures contributed to his decision to leave the club. The board approached Shaw in mid-1994 about his future, following reports that he had had offers from an intermediary to take on the coaching position at Fremantle. The record shows however, that his next appointment was to be with the Adelaide Crows for 1995-1996.

His final months at Fitzroy caused some considerable concern to the board and to the football department. Shaw's statement six weeks from the completion of the season that he had lost the 'fire in his belly' placed the board in a difficult position – do we continue with someone who has lost interest? Should a new person be blooded to see out the remainder of the season? How will the players react? The debate among us was intense and it was one of the few times the board was split. Fuel was added to the debate by the fact that Shaw had been off-work for a number of days during this time – with the football department covering his absence. In the washup we decided to allow Shaw to see out the remainder of the season.

CHAPTER 5

Shaw gave a lot to Fitzroy. His efforts to assist the marketing of the club through business lunches at the hotel were a source of great merriment and a means to some useful fund raising.

As we contemplated our future, we had no banker, no coach, little sponsorship and our team had been decimated. However, we never underestimated the size of the hearts of the Fitzroy supporters and it was that, more than anything, that kept us going.

After Robert Shaw resigned, I received a phone call from Bernie Quinlan. He wanted to know if the coaching position was still vacant. I told him it was. Bernie wanted to talk to me about it and he made an appointment to see me at work. I must say, during the meeting I had with Bernie, he impressed me with his observations and ideas about the players and the club. The match committee was at the time considering prospective coaches but the directors strongly favoured appointing Bernie for a number of reasons.

'Superboot' as he was known, was a respected TV commentator. Bernie had won a Brownlow Medal and was a genuine Fitzroy hero. From the moment he was appointed at Fitzroy everyone's spirits rose enormously. His appointment was publicly regarded as a coup for the club. It was largely as a result of his appointment as coach that the club re-energised itself after the abortive attempted merger between Fitzroy and Melbourne and keep going. The board was delighted that such a champion player had offered to take on the challenge of coaching his former club at such a difficult time.

It is true to say, however, that there were some immediate reservations expressed by our football department, current and former teammates about his lack of experience in relation to coaching in general and to his ability to manage a position of such responsibility. This aspect was particularly noticeable when the search for personnel to support him began. To maximise the marketing opportunities of Bernie's appointment, a conscious decision was made to seek out former Fitzroy players to take up various positions in the club.

In the end Michael Conlan, one of our former favourite players, took the position of chairman of the match committee, Leon Harris served as reserves coach, Grant Lawrie worked as skills coach and Ross Thornton filled the position of team manager. Allan McConnell continued as assistant coach and ran our player development program. The only 'non-Fitzroy' member of the coaching staff was Warren Jones, the former Carlton stalwart who was now our specialist ruck coach. Mick Conlon resigned his position before the season started, but the others worked with great enthusiasm and dedication throughout what was to be a most difficult season. With Conlon's early departure Grant Lawrie took on the position as chairman of selectors (and later the position of reserves coach).

Our difficulties in finding a banker was the catalyst that would lead to a complex relationship with a tiny nation in the middle of the Pacific Ocean. Earlier in 1994 I had a phone call from George Coates, a former Fitzroy president, mentioning a person called Kinza Clodumar – and how he might be interested in doing something with Fitzroy. Kinza was the mover and shaker and the personal financial adviser to the President of the Republic of Nauru. I thought the idea was so fanciful that I put it out of my mind until September, when I was holidaying with my family in northern NSW. When I say holidaying, most of the time seemed to be spent at or near a phone. John Birt was reporting almost daily of knock-back after knock-back from the traditional lending institutions. We were running out of time very quickly to find a banker to replace the now AFL forbidden Bernie Ahern loan. John did say, however, that he was optimistic about the possibility of Nauru backing us after having had a meeting with a person called Kinza Clodumar.

I found it difficult to believe that anything would come of this development but on my return to Melbourne John told me that a deal was almost done! I arranged to meet Kinza and his solicitor, Graham Sherry, at the Flemington races where the Government of Nauru was sponsoring an early two-year old race. We met and

CHAPTER 5

it was only when Kinza confirmed that the Nauru Insurance Agency was prepared to lend us money that I dared to believe it!

And so the deal was done. The Nauru Insurance Company would lend Fitzroy Football Club $1.2 million over seven years. There were a number of conditions, of course, but it was a fantastic break for the club. No more would Fitzroy have to rely on the AFL's yearly redirection of our dividend or rely on a bank from year to year for our funding. All we had to do was to remain solvent.

SPORT

Lions land seven-year, $3m lifeline

Michael Davis and **Grantley Bernard**
The Australian
10/94

Once again Fitzroy had escaped the noose! A condition of the loan was that a representative of the Nauru Insurance Company would sit on the board. On November 16, 1994 we elected Kinza Clodumar, a very fine gentleman, as our tenth board member.

With funding secured and a new coach, we commenced an early membership drive, which was very successful. Once again we returned a profit for the year and as far as we were concerned we were back in business.

At the end of 1994 it seemed the Fitzroy Football Club had turned the corner.

Chapter 6

The start of 1995 was particularly hectic but as always the pre-season was filled with optimism. The hotel was running at a healthy profit and a number of other fund raising initiatives had been devised.

However, money was still a problem. Not only were our revenues significantly below other clubs, but the costs of putting a team on the field were spiraling upwards. The most significant cost increase was ballooning player payment increases which were brought about by market forces and a new agreement between the AFL and the Players' Association. Although revenue to the AFL was increasing dramatically, the league's dividends increased only marginally. A huge amount of money was going into the development of football in NSW and Queensland. The AFL pursued a policy of aggressive debt reduction, which significantly reduced the amount of money available to clubs through their annual dividend.

One of the initiatives we pursued at Fitzroy involved the Aboriginal community, as, historically, Fitzroy probably had a larger Aboriginal support in Melbourne than any other club. Pastor Doug Nicholls who played during the thirties and forties was one of our champions. Later, he became Governor of South Australia, the first Aborigine to hold such an honour anywhere in Australia. Alf Bamblett, well known Koori leader, was a staunch Fitzroy supporter. Daryl Pearce, then the executive director of the powerful Northern Land Council in Darwin, was a good friend of Alf's.

We organised a meeting between Alf, Daryl and myself as early as 1994, at the Fitzroy Club Hotel, with the view to try to develop something between Fitzroy and the Aboriginal Community. This was something that was close to my heart as a result of my own involvement over a long period of time with Aboriginal legal aid services since the early seventies. In these years I appeared as junior

CHAPTER 6

counsel in the first murder trial in Victoria to be handled by the newly formed Aboriginal Legal Service, and worked for thirteen months as a solicitor with the Northern Australian Aboriginal Legal Aid Service (NAALAS) in Darwin in 1977-78. One of my most vivid recollections is appearing in the first court sitting ever held at Oenpelli, an aboriginal community in Arnhem land. It was a beautiful day and the court sat outside – I suspect I may have been the first lawyer in Australia to appear in court wearing a white floppy towelling hat! After I returned to Victoria I continued practising in the Northern Territory for Aboriginal organisations and appeared for the families of a number of indigenous people at the Royal Commission into Aboriginal Deaths in Custody.

The idea discussed with Daryl and Alf was that Fitzroy would receive sponsorship from the Aboriginal community in return for heavy involvement of Fitzroy footballers in those communities. The deal would also include the training and development of Aboriginal footballers at Fitzroy. The seed of the idea grew very slowly but in early 1995, Daryl Pearce put a proposal to CRA (Rio Tinto Limited) whereby, in return for significant sponsorship of around a million dollars per year, Fitzroy would provide a host of services to the Aboriginal communities including regular football clinics. Furthermore, we would host Aboriginal players during our pre-season, although we could not place them onto our player list except through the draft system. CRA turned the proposal down – an attitude I still believe was extremely short-sighted. CRA had a number of huge mineral deposits on traditional Aboriginal land, and the proposed sponsorship would have been a small price to pay for such beneficial public relations.

One of the reasons given by CRA for rejecting our proposal was that it was heavily involved in Northern Queensland which was essentially a rugby area.[7]

---

7. Recently the AFL and Rio Tinto Limited (formerly CRA) announced an aboriginal development program which bares remarkable similarity to the one that was put on our behalf.

FITZROY

I recall the same near-sighted attitude displayed by BHP when I was working with Aboriginal Legal Aid in Darwin. One of the problems at that time was that there was very little for the young people to do on Groote Eyelandt. Unlike at some other Aboriginal communities, there were hardly any sporting facilities available. BHP operated a large manganese mine at Groote Eylandt – a small island east of the mainland in the Gulf of Carpentaria. There are two major Aboriginal communities on Groote Eylandt, at Umbakumba and Angurugu. At the time, BHP was experiencing a huge problem with Aboriginal youth – very heavy and expensive machinery would be taken for a bit of a spin as an escapade which would often end up with the vehicles badly damaged. Sometimes the repair bill would run into hundreds of thousands of dollars. I suggested that BHP might like to build a few sports facilities on the Aboriginal settlements. This was met with a flat refusal, BHP claiming it couldn't afford it. With the machinery and resources at its disposal, it would have cost BHP a pittance to level a couple of playing areas and to build a few basic facilities.

While the Fitzroy-CRA idea hit a dead end, we felt we might have more luck with Melbourne builder Bruno Grollo. Our potential connection with Grollo started with one of our closest supporters, pharmacist Warren O'Neale. Warren was a founding member of the Fitzroy Foundation. On a number of occasions when the club was under financial pressure, he rang me and offered financial assistance.

Contrary to what many of our members and most of the public believed, the Republic of Nauru was not a sponsor of the Fitzroy Football Club. What Nauru had done was to provide a seven year loan which replaced the Westpac loan and the subsequent Bernie Ahern loan. We had been seeking ways of involving the people of Nauru in the football club in a way which could benefit both of us. Warren put a proposal to Kinza Clodumar – our board member and special adviser to the President of the Republic of Nauru – which involved a significant saving on the provision of medical supplies to Nauru. Another of our board members, John Pettinella,

CHAPTER 6

a large market gardener, floated a proposal which he believed would have enabled the people of Nauru to save a substantial amount on the provision of fresh fruit and vegetables. Neither of these two proposals were taken up by Nauru. It was also Warren O'Neale's idea to link Bruno Grollo with Nauru.

At that time, Nauru owned a number of large building sites in Melbourne and in Sydney. It had recently bought – and commenced to redevelop – the Southern Cross Hotel on the corner of Bourke and Exhibitions Streets in Melbourne. It had acquired the huge Queen Victoria site and also the Carlton and United Brewery site in Carlton. Apart from the Crown Casino construction, Warren believed that Grollo's company (Grocon) did not have one single large contract in Melbourne or in Sydney. Warren O'Neale was instrumental in introducing Bruno Grollo to Kinza Clodumar.

As a result of this, a relationship developed in which Grollo became the preferred builder for the brewery site, a project with occupancy and finance almost assured. Planning approval was given for the go ahead in December, 1995. Unfortunately, as we will see later, politics in the Republic of Nauru later intervened in a very dramatic way. At that time, however, the Grollo-Nauru relationship looked promising for Fitzroy.

Another initiative involved increasing our membership base and our sponsorship potential. North Melbourne were already planning to expand into Sydney and other clubs were considering playing AFL games elsewhere. In January, 1995, I submitted a proposal to the Fitzroy board compiled by Ron Cahill[8], Chief Magistrate from the ACT, pushing for an AFL team in Canberra. A few years earlier a similar Tasmanian experiment had been abandoned, partly because of lack of support from the Tasmanian government, but also because the experiment was poorly prepared and implemented. Accommodation and travel costs were actually taken out of Fitzroy's gate receipts!

---

8. Ron Cahill a devout Collingwood Supporter was the leader of the 'AFL for Canberra' organisation.

Lion hiccup on Tassie

Daryl Timms
Herald Sun
20/8/92

Canberra had been itching for some years to have a team of its own playing in the AFL. Until the mid-eighties, Australian Rules football was the predominant code of football played in the ACT. However, after the success of the Canberra Raiders in the National Rugby League competition, support for the Australian code dwindled. In early 1995, the Fitzroy board decided that it would put its toe in the water by playing a premiership match in Canberra. Consequently the scheduled Fitzroy-West Coast match in Round 10 was transferred to Canberra. This was the first time a premiership match was ever played in Canberra and it generated a great amount of interest. Although the team was not playing well, on the day it put up a spirited show against the more than competent Eagles. With the crowd very much behind Fitzroy, the match was in the balance until well into the final quarter before the Eagles prevailed. The experiment was regarded as a great success by everybody, including the AFL – so we thought.

On June 16, 1995, a story by Malcolm Conn in *The Australian* headed 'Fitzroy's Canberra Fixtures Hailed by Collins' reported that the AFL supported Fitzroy's move to play four matches in Canberra next season. Conn quoted Collins as tentatively backing a joint venture between Fitzroy and the Canberra Raiders.

Fitzroy's Canberra fixtures hailed by Collins

Malcolm Conn
The Australian
16/6/95

CHAPTER 6

Conn's article read:

> 'The Australian Football League yesterday supported Fitzroy's move to play four matches in Canberra next season as part of a joint venture with Canberra Raiders. The positive response from AFL Football Operations Manager, Ian Collins, was prompted by the relative success of Fitzroy's hastily arranged match against West Coast at Bruce Stadium last month. 'We'll look at anything that is presented to us and we did want to play that game in Canberra,' Collins said yesterday of the Lion's transferred Round 9 match. 'We supported them to promote the game to ensure it did get a response. I think Fitzroy were happy with what transpired out of that hence they are now talking to the Raiders about how they may put a package together for next year ... the current confusion in the Rugby League community between the Australian Rugby League and the Super League competition gives a window of opportunity for the co-location agreements.'

After the match, discussions were held between Fitzroy, 'AFL for Canberra,' and the ACT Football League (ACTAFL). These negotiations were proceeding with the apparent blessing of the AFL. However, I had cautioned our directors and general manager, John Birt, against becoming too optimistic about the proposal. By then, I was so cynical about what I perceived as the AFL's attitude to Fitzroy – and its desire for a second team in Adelaide – that I feared that the AFL would appreciate only too well that the Canberra initiative was a lifeline for Fitzroy, and would, when a decision had to be made, ditch the idea.

My cynicism was well-founded. In the previous year both Ross Oakley and Graeme Samuel had been quoted regarding the 'benefits' of the AFL's Five Year Plan, which involved eliminating a Melbourne club. Oakley in the *Herald-Sun* on February 20, 1994 stated that losing a small club would actually 'have a positive impact on the revenue of the clubs.' Samuel was quoted by Stephen Linnell in The Age of July 22, 1994 as saying that 'if one of the weaker-supported clubs merged or dropped out, that would free up around $2 million for expenditure on promoting the game... without affecting the existence of the other clubs.' Our problem was the fact that we were the smallest club.

League chief leans on Lions

Stephen Linnell
The Age
3/5/95

We believed that our members would support a dilution of Fitzroy's presence in Melbourne as an alternative to merger or relocation. We would maintain our administration headquarters and training headquarters in Melbourne but were prepared to play up to seven premiership home games in Canberra. At board level, we agreed in principle that as long as we played half our games in Victoria, we could play the majority of the remainder in Canberra and the others interstate. In this way we would not be worse off than interstate clubs playing only half of their games in their home city.

Canberra, unlike Tasmania, was prepared to guarantee us a minimum of $350,000 for the four games. We indicated to them that, if necessary, we were prepared to play more matches – provided at least eleven were in Victoria.

There were great advantages in this for Fitzroy, benefits which were obviously understood by the AFL. There were strong corporate sponsorship possibilities in Canberra and substantial membership opportunities. The Canberra Raiders were playing at Bruce Stadium, where Fitzroy proposed to play. With two different clubs and codes playing, Canberra was prepared to develop the stadium into a first-class venue. We believed we could have made at least an extra $1 million dollars per year. Right up until the last moment the AFL appeared to support us.

CHAPTER 6

On Monday, August 28, out of the blue, Ian Collins rang me and told me that the AFL Commission had knocked back our application to play four games in Canberra. He said this was as a result of the Tasmanian experience. I asked him when the Commission meeting was held which made the decision, and he told me, 'Friday'. I asked Collins to set out the reasons for the knock back in writing, which he agreed to do.

Straight after I had hung up, I rang AFL commissioner Ron Evans (managing director of Spotless Services). I had previously spoken to Ron about our Canberra proposal and he seemed quite supportive. When I now spoke to him, I did not mention, at first, my conversation with Collins, and just asked 'What went wrong with Canberra?' This question was greeted with silence. I repeated the question, 'What went wrong with Canberra?' It was quite obvious from his answer that he had difficulty in picking up what I was talking about. I then said, 'Ian Collins has just told me that our application to play four games in Canberra has been refused.' Evans said something about him thinking that I was referring to our 'confidential conversation.' I could not recall any conversation with Ron which I understood to be confidential. Very quickly Ron said, 'Let me check my notes and I will get back to you.'

Sometime later in the afternoon Evans rang me back. He said that if we would play a 'majority of home games' up in Canberra the AFL might look at it. This was interesting because at the Fitzroy – Geelong game at Western Oval (just nine days earlier) Ross Oakley was a guest of the club along with Colin Carter, another AFL commissioner. I had asked Ross about our application. He said it hadn't been discussed at recent board meetings, they just had a couple of queries on it. There was no hint that there was any problem.

I subsequently received a letter from Collins setting out reasons for our rejection. The letter, dated 29 August 1995 was addressed to John Birt. It read:

'Please be advised that the AFL Commission, at its meeting on Friday, 25 August 1995, considered the request of the Fitzroy Football Club to play four (4) home games at Bruce Stadium, and other benefits to be underwritten by the AFL.

It was decided not to approve the request based on the assumption that unless most of Fitzroy's home games were played in Canberra and there was a substantial reduction in the Club's requirements for effecting such a transfer, it would not be a credible exercise in the Canberra market, as it would not appear to be of a permanent nature, but more of a temporary situation, especially with the hindsight of a similar unsuccessful venture in Hobart and the playing of one (1) game in Canberra in 1995.'

What Collins meant was a mystery to us. There was no underwriting that we were aware of that was requested from the AFL. We asked that the matches be televised and we assumed the AFL would pay airfares and accommodation for the matches, as it did with all other interstate matches, but, apart from that, there was no underwriting needed.

In light of the AFL's subsequent decision to allow North Melbourne to test the Sydney market by playing a handful of home games there the reasons given by Collins are hard to understand. Furthermore we were given no opportunity to negotiate or compromise on any of the AFL's supposed concerns.

Later on Ross Oakley was asked on air why the AFL had knocked back our application to play in Canberra. The reason he gave was the AFL was not going to send 'their worst product' up to Canberra. This was completely different to the garbled reasons given by Collins.

CHAPTER 6

Fitzroy would have been prepared to play seven games in Canberra, certainly enough to make it worthwhile for the club to go up there. If necessary, we would have looked at more. Further submissions were made to the AFL along these lines but it refused point blank to look at any proposal.

An official request was made by the 'AFL for Canberra' organisation to meet with representatives from the Fitzroy Football Club, ACTAFL (AFL for Canberra), the Ainslie Football Club, and the ACT chief minister to attempt to sort out a deal with the League Commission. All of these parties were keen to bring AFL football to Canberra.

The request bore no fruit at all.

On November 7, 1995, I received a letter from Ron Cahill stating that he had endeavoured, without success, to make contact with Ian Collins and that he would continue his efforts to contact AFL commissioners Colin Carter and Ron Evans. Finally, in a letter received in February 1996, Ron Cahill wrote to me, stating in part '… it seems that from your end, the AFL have indicated a completely negative attitude to any Canberra proposal for the Fitzroy Football Club. On February 21st, Ross Oakley was in Canberra to launch the program for the Ansett Cup Game. He clearly indicated to me then that AFL wouldn't support any initiative for Fitzroy to play games in the ACT in the immediate future.' In view of that, Cahill stated that they would be forced to look elsewhere.

On November 21, 1995, one of the less well – known AFL commissioners came to see me in my chambers. He admitted to me that the main reason our Canberra proposal got knocked back was that the AFL Commission wanted Port Adelaide in the competition – and therefore wanted to keep pressure on Fitzroy to merge.

The AFL's determination to bring Port Adelaide into the competition – at the expense of an AFL presence in Canberra – may have lost forever an opportunity to establish AFL football in the country's capital. The time was ripe for picking then as rugby league was in turmoil.

During 1995 there also seemed to be almost continual crisis on the field. The appointment of Bernie Quinlan as coach was seen as a boost for the club, but cracks started to become apparent in the football department shortly before the Ansett Cup games commenced early in the year. The board began receiving reports that Bernie's planning was below par and he was not utilising the professional advice that surrounded him. In a huge gain for the club, Doug Hawkins was signed by Fitzroy for 1995 after his sacking by Footscray. He was extremely popular with most AFL supporters and had a following among the younger supporters in general. Doug would have a very good year with Fitzroy and provide leadership both on and off the field. Brad Boyd, despite his youth, served effectively as captain. It was our view that the input of people of this calibre should have been used. Bernie, however, tended to keep his own counsel and make his own decisions.

Bernie's early efforts had been relatively well coordinated and he achieved some of the club's early objectives to be 'bigger, stronger and leaner.' The priorities in relation to player development were weight training, strength maintenance and weight skin-fold monitoring – all positive objectives but unfortunately were not linked with the overall development of the team.

Fitzroy's young player list required patience and understanding. We felt that perhaps Bernie could have more closely monitored the progress of injured players such as Brad Boyd, Jason Baldwin, Jeremy Guard and Mark Zanotti in these early months, a situation that did not improve as the year unfolded. Some injured players had the perception that they were no longer wanted.

As the year went on, the board became concerned about some of the information it was receiving. We were told that there was little evidence of planning in relation to skill-development and pre-match preparation. There were few written reports on

CHAPTER 6

opposition players, video analysis or detailed game plans. Few tactical moves were being made during games.

A modern professional coach is responsible for hundreds of minute decisions. The entire team relies on his organisational expertise, and when this planning does not eventuate, problems soon surface. One example was Bernie's attitude to certain exercises. Bernie – a remarkably gifted athlete and still a very fit person – took the view that if he could do something then everyone else could. Unfortunately that wasn't always the case. The board received a detailed letter from one of our doctors setting out his concerns. The board was so troubled by the situation that it obtained written advice from a barrister, Doc O'Callaghan, setting out that the directors – as well as the coach – could be personally liable if a player was injured by inappropriate exercises. We took steps to ensure the situation improved. The board gave Bernie a copy of this advice.[9]

Bernie's lack of coaching and training experience was reflected in his communication with the team. Motivation skills were not his strength – the basic message conveyed was to constantly urge the players 'to play with passion' and 'have a go.' Players felt disappointed over the lack of meaningful individual feedback, such as reasons for non-selection. The result was continuous approaches to match committee members and football staff by frustrated players.

The matter came to a head after Round 16 on July 22 when we played Essendon at the MCG. We had on at least two occasions prior to that invited Bernie to attend board meetings where we expressed concern at aspects of his coaching. We stressed that we were not criticising him but that we were trying to assist him in improving the performance of the team. We reiterated that he had very good people around him.

However, Bernie had taken the view that a number of people

---

9. The club had already received a writ from a player who claimed he was injured in the late 80s as a result of inappropriate exercises. This action was later settled out of court.

were trying to undermine him. He therefore would not discuss things fully with the match committee. We were told that he was getting a lot of advice from Don Scott, the former Hawthorn star who was then a television commentator. After the Essendon game, in view of the fact that Bernie had accused a number of the match committee of having a different agenda, I convened a meeting of senior players in my chambers along with football directors Colin Hobbs and David McMahon.

There were two areas of concern amongst the players. One was that the only game plan that Bernie had was 'kick the ball to the hot spot.' The 'hot spot' was round about centre half forward. The players said that every other team knew our game plan and had extra players waiting there. The other matter of concern was that Bernie would allow handball only to be directed in an arc in front of the players. That is, there was no handball allowed over the head or sideways to players running past. After the Essendon game, the players had watched a replay and pointed out to Bernie that a number of the Essendon goals came through handballs directed into Bernie's forbidden zone. Such feedback made no difference.

After we spoke to the players we called Bernie in and told him that a number of senior players had commented about those two aspects of his coaching in particular. We stressed that everyone was trying to help him and advised him to communicate with the senior players and take on board their concerns. However, the information we got back from the players indicated that Bernie's main actions centred on trying to find out which players had been 'disloyal' to him, rather than availing himself of the assistance available to him.

The board decided to stick with Bernie as there were only six more games for the year. However these games seemed like a whole season. In the fourth last game, against Sydney on August 13 our team was in disarray. Tony Lockett kicked 16 goals and at one stage looked like breaking every record in the book. We were told that players were making their own changes on the field. In fact, Mark

CHAPTER 6

Zanotti raced down on his own to pick up Tony Lockett in an effort to stem the avalanche. Our match committee reported back to us that Bernie just watched the proceedings as if transfixed. Sponsors were walking out of the function rooms before half time and members and supporters were complaining bitterly.

The match committee had been recommending very strongly for some time that Bernie be removed. The board – minus Elaine Findlay and Kinza Clodumar – met after the Sydney game and finally took the view that, apart from our contractual duty to Bernie, we had duties to our players, coaching staff, supporters, members and sponsors. We were particularly conscious of our duty to the players, many of whom were just embarking on an AFL career and whose weekly performances were central to our success or failure and to their future as AFL footballers. Despite the fact that we knew that we would be blasted by the press and many supporters for sacking Bernie Quinlan, a Fitzroy icon, we unanimously agreed to terminate his services. That decision was recommended by our chief executive officer, our football manager, and all of the match committee.

Three weeks earlier in my chambers I had suggested to Bernie that he might like to consider standing down. He said he would never resign. He now told John Birt the same thing – and John then terminated his services.

We were widely criticised, of course, not least of all by Bernie. The media questioned why there was a need for such action with only three games to go, unaware of the chaos within the team and at the club. Needless to say the decision was not taken lightly nor without a great deal of distress. The situation was simply that the players had lost confidence completely in him and were playing as such.

Bernie Quinlan's firing, we believed, was necessary, but the sacking of a popular coach further enhanced the perception of a club in crisis in the minds of observers unaware of the situation as we saw it. Fitzroy supporters will remember Bernie as 'superboot', one of our greatest players ever – and probably the best kick AFL football had ever seen. While his tenure as a coach was not a success, Bernie tried to help the club when it was in need.

The club was fortunate that assistant coach Allan McConnell was prepared to take on the senior position for the remaining matches in 1995. His elevation immediately bore fruit. We led with a minute to go before half time against Geelong at the Western Oval, although we ended up being beaten by four goals. The next week against St Kilda we were beaten by a few points before succumbing to North Melbourne by a larger margin at Optus Oval in the last game. Even though we did not win any of our last three games, the improvement in the side was remarkable. Alan's subsequent experience at Geelong in senior coaching roles has confirmed his skill and abilities in dealing with young players and his sound tactical knowledge of the game. His integrity was perhaps never more apparent than during our coaching upheaval in the following year. Yet again, Alan provided continuity and consistency for the club by stepping in to see out the remainder of the season.

We knew the 1996 season would be a difficult test of leadership, and we wanted to avoid the difficulties created by a lack of experience, so an exhaustive process was undertaken to ensure that the next coach we appointed was the best qualified coach available.

The coaching sub-committee interviewed a number of prospective coaches, including Rodney Eade, Jeff Gieschen, Terry Wallace, Alan McConnell and former Fitzroy champion John Murphy. Applications were also received from a number of other former players and football personalities.

The preferred option as Bernie Quinlan's replacement was Rodney Eade, who had just completed his time as coach of the North Melbourne Reserves – Rodney was most impressive and would have been a terrific acquisition to the Club. Unfortunately, we were not in a position to finalise financial arrangements with Rodney because of the uncertainty surrounding Fitzroy's future

CHAPTER 6

and eventually the Sydney Swans secured his services.

The delay in appointment of a coach was due to the financial difficulties the club was having at the time – until we were sure of the direction in which we wanted to go in 1996, that is, whether or not Fitzroy would be forced to merge, we were in no position to appoint him or, indeed, any other football or staff member.

In the end, Michael Nunan was appointed. Michael had been a very successful coach in the South Australian National Football League (SANFL) and generally speaking his engagement was seen by the media and Fitzroy supporters in a positive light.

He wanted the job badly, and presented submissions detailing some interesting theories in relation to the way the game was to be played. He introduced new training drills and new match play strategies that gave some direction and structure to the players. The fact that Alan McConnell was prepared to continue as assistant coach was also encouraging.

Michael Nunan was determined to do it his way. For the first time Fitzroy Football Club had no chairman of selectors. Michael and the match committee took on this responsibility. Player rules were tightened, training was planned, match days significantly altered as supporters and directors were restricted from access to the rooms. These approaches were welcomed by the board – it was pleasing to see some regimentation and control being reintroduced to the football department and we briefly allowed ourselves a moment or two of optimism. The player drain had eased somewhat in the last year. Other than the loss of Paul Roos, Jim Wynd and Mathew Armstrong, the list had stayed reasonably intact.

Unfortunately, the performance on the field did not improve. Colin Hobbs and I met with Michael Nunan early in the season after we had just received another hiding. The dialogue between coach and board had so far been minimal at best. We asked the coach if there was anything which could be done to improve match day results, and were staggered to be told, in effect, that 'If we wanted to win matches we had the wrong person as coach.' Michael said that he had taken the job on the basis of a two or three year plan, after which time we would see the fruits of his coaching.

Michael took the view that it was difficult to teach the older players because they were set in their ways and he was concentrating on bringing the younger players along. We later asked Michael to comment upon the status of the club. We received a page and a half memo outlining his dissatisfaction with the players on our list, the training venue, our social club, management structure, long term planning and business structure.

The eventual merger between the Nauruan appointed administrator and Brisbane resulted in Michael Nunan tending his resignation. The only other correspondence received from Michael was a solicitor's letter requesting that his payments for coaching be finalised. Michael, like Bernie before him, had certainly inherited a very tough situation which, unfortunately, ended on a sour note.

In some ways the financial difficulties Fitzroy faced by late 1995 made our on-field performance almost incidental to our survival. The board had taken the view that playing performance was cyclic and that our 'turn' would come. If all things had remained equal this may have occurred.

Chapter 7

About halfway through 1995, after reviewing financial projections the directors of Fitzroy concluded that it needed at least an extra $500,000 income to operate and another $500,000 to acquire quality players to bring our team up to standard. The board decided that unless it could obtain the extra finance, of $1,000,000, it would actively seek a merger partner.

All the Fitzroy directors who had fought so hard to preserve the club felt sick in the stomach at this prospect. But morale at that stage, I believe, was low throughout the club and even at the board table. We were not playing well, sponsors were dropping off and new ones were becoming increasingly harder to get, and the new AFL player rules further depleted our player strength.

During 1994, Fitzroy had walked part of the way down the aisle with Melbourne until a premature and inevitable leak followed by very negative publicity ensured that it was torpedoed. After word got out, it became apparent that the two clubs were not a congenial mix. I recall leaving the MCG after Fitzroy had thrashed the Demons in the late eighties and a Melbourne supporter calling out, 'They'll be happy in the slums tonight!'

North Melbourne had also pursued us in 1994, but when it entered the scene we were too far down the track with Melbourne. By 1996, most of the directors felt North Melbourne offered a partnership with much better prospects for success. Both clubs had a similar historical and sociological background and, more importantly, I believe both clubs needed each other to survive in the new national competition. The improved amenities at the MCG, including the recently constructed Great Southern Stand, had made watching football at other venues second rate by comparison. There was never any serious thought of merging with a club that did not play at the MCG – here, too, North was a perfect match. At this time Colonial Stadium was not even an idea.

FITZROY

One of our directors, David McMahon, initially favoured Collingwood. David was in fairly constant communication – in an informal way – with Collingwood's football manager, Graeme Allan. Collingwood's initial offer was 'Collingwood-Fitzroy Magpies' with a recognition of Fitzroy colours in the guernsey. As time went by and we ignored the overtures, the offer was continually improved. Collingwood was the best supported AFL club in Australia. Despite only one premiership in the last thirty-six years, the club enjoys enormous support right around Australia. When Collingwood is playing winning football, it can almost guarantee a full house at the MCG. David argued that a merger with Collingwood would guarantee we would be around forever. If we merged with a weaker club and that club folded, Fitzroy could cease to exist.

The view of most of the board, and David in the end, was that whatever the arrangement, Collingwood's sheer weight of numbers would overwhelm us. Collingwood should have been the last club to have to look for a merger. But a series of property investments, in a falling market, coupled with a lack of performance on the field, had placed them under an enormous amount of financial pressure.

In September 1995, North Melbourne made a written proposal to Fitzroy to enter merger discussions. The board appointed vice-chairman Elaine Findlay and board member Robert Johnstone to meet with them.

At our board meeting of September 20, 1995, the directors discussed our financial situation. Our Nauru representative Kinza Clodumar was in attendance on that occasion. He seemed surprised and disappointed when we indicated that unless we received a substantial injection of cash, we would look to merge. He made the comment that Nauru was with us for the 'long haul.' Kinza mentioned his discussions with Bruno Grollo, stating that he believed that Grollo would be the preferred builder for the brewery site complex. He also requested that the club prepare a report for

CHAPTER 7

him as to why we required increased finance in 1996. He wanted it by Friday September 22, and this was done.

We had put a proposal to Kinza for $500,000 sponsorship to be provided by the Republic of Nauru in conjunction with $500,000 sponsorship from Grollo. The indications from Kinza were that this would be looked upon favourably. However, negotiations were protracted.

On October 3, 1995, Kinza faxed to John Birt a lengthy letter suggesting that Fitzroy Football Club should look at a possible merger with Geelong Football Club. Nauru and Geelong historically had a long association. Indeed, if newspaper reports are correct, it seemed that Geelong was a little miffed when Nauru came to our aid in 1994. A detailed response to this letter was prepared by Colin Hobbs. His reply set out our options and made the point that the Geelong merger would present some practical difficulties and could be viewed by some as a relocation. The letter concluded that we felt that Fitzroy had a long-term future but that we would not be able to turn our fortunes around in twelve months. We believed, however, that huge progress could be made over the next two or three years.

Kinza replied in a letter dated October 4, 1995, on Republic of Nauru letterhead, informing us that cabinet had taken the decision (subject to Nauru Insurance Corporation's consent) that financial assistance be given to Fitzroy Football Club for an amount of up to $500,000. Nauru certainly appeared to be with us for the 'long haul.'

Kinza was back in Nauru during the course of these negotiations. Despite the indication given in the letter, the board was still not prepared to appoint Michael Nunan, who had accepted the coaching position subject to approval, until the loan was clearly and unconditionally ratified. A board meeting was scheduled at the Fitzroy Club Hotel for October 10. During the day – and while the board meeting was in progress – I attempted on a number of occasions to contact Kinza by telephone in Nauru without success.

At this stage, word had got out concerning Michael Nunan's pending appointment as coach and we were told during our board meeting that television cameras were waiting downstairs. The meeting continued into the night and at regular intervals, I attempted to contact Kinza at his office, at home and other venues in Nauru. Finally I succeeded at ten o'clock our time. Kinza and I discussed the chances of Bruno Grollo providing a further $500,000.

Kinza confirmed that Grollo was to be the preferred builder, which, as I understand it, meant that he did not have to put in a tender, and that the brewery site was certain to go ahead. Grollo had told him that if he (Grollo) did participate in a joint venture with Nauru, in the spirit of the arrangement, he would provide $500,000 worth of sponsorship to Fitzroy. There was no suggestion of any impropriety in the arrangement. Kinza and I had discussed the position he was in as chairman of Nauru Insurance Corporation and a director of Fitzroy Football Club. It was stressed to him – and he well knew already – that as far as his directorship of Nauru Insurance Corporation was concerned his sole duty was to the company. Kinza is a very astute and worldly person. He was fully aware of his duties as director of both companies.

During the conversation I had with Kinza on the night of October 10th, during our board meeting, Kinza said that Nauru Insurance Corporation was prepared to lend $500,000 to Fitzroy and that was with the confidence that Grollo would match it. At that time, the contracts for the brewery site were anticipated to be ready for signing in early 1996. I told Kinza that if Nauru was confident enough to put up another half a million on that basis, we would be prepared to accept it on the same basis. If the arrangement had been for a $500,000 loan only with no prospect of increased sponsorship, however, I believe the directors may have immediately pursued the merger option.

After I finished this conversation with Kinza, I returned to the board meeting, which was still in progress. We thereupon formally

CHAPTER 7

appointed Michael Nunan and the appointment was then announced to the press.

Later, on October 12, John Birt received an official letter which read:

> 'The Board of the Nauru Insurance Corporation met today and resolved that a second tranche 'B' totalling $500,000 be loaned to F.F.C. due for payment in December, 1995 under similar terms and conditions as per tranche 'A' (the previous loan). I would be grateful for the results of the raffle drawn on October 9, 1995, so that I may inform those who bought tickets at Nauru and Melbourne office. I await your reply.'
>
> Yours sincerely
> Kinza Clodumar

FITZROY

Four days later we received a second official letter, signed by Kinza as chairman of the Nauru Insurance Corporation. Kinza wrote:

'Dear John, thank you for your letter on 3 October 1995, offering your views on the various issues relating to the Club. (This was the letter drafted by Colin Hobbs)

Regarding your request of financial assistance of $500,000 in December 1995, I am glad to inform that the Board has adopted a resolution on 12 October 1995, of approving the loan at terms and conditions following the existing loan agreement between Fitzroy Football Club and Nauru Insurance Corporation (Vic) Pty Ltd.

The Board has also noted that the balance $500,000 of the total fund requirement of $1 million would be arranged from a separate source during the course of 1996.'

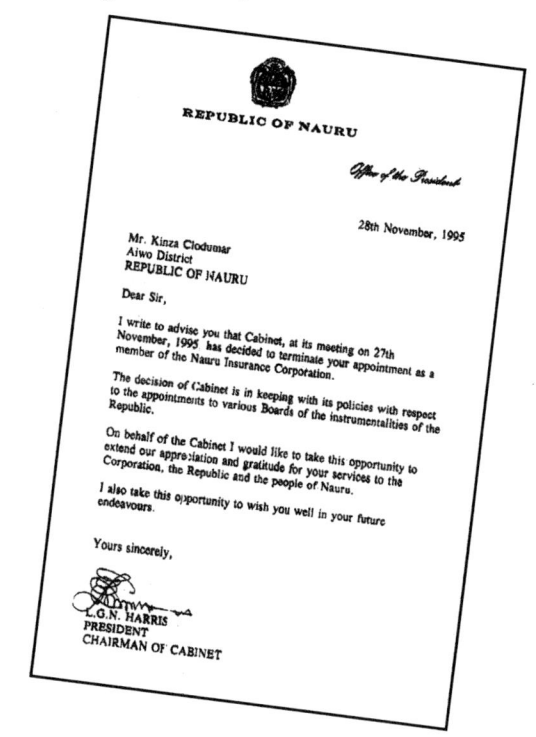

> **REPUBLIC OF NAURU**
>
> *Office of the President*
>
> 28th November, 1995
>
> Mr. Kinza Clodumar
> Aiwo District
> REPUBLIC OF NAURU
>
> Dear Sir,
>
> I write to advise you that Cabinet, at its meeting on 27th November, 1995 has decided to terminate your appointment as a member of the Nauru Insurance Corporation.
>
> The decision of Cabinet is in keeping with its policies with respect to the appointments to various Boards of the instrumentalities of the Republic.
>
> On behalf of the Cabinet I would like to take this opportunity to extend our appreciation and gratitude for your services to the Corporation, the Republic and the people of Nauru.
>
> I also take this opportunity to wish you well in your future endeavours.
>
> Yours sincerely,
>
> L.G.N. HARRIS
> PRESIDENT
> CHAIRMAN OF CABINET

CHAPTER 7

Our subsequent legal advice was that our acceptance of this offer constituted a legal binding contract. Between then and late November of 1995, I was in constant communication with Kinza by telephone, and there was no hint of any problem with the loan.

Wednesday, November 28, 1995 was a fateful day in the history of the Republic of Nauru – and for the Fitzroy Football Club as well. On that day general elections were held in Nauru. Kinza Clodumar stood and was successfully elected. Kinza's 'party' was also successful but only by one seat. It was explained to me that there are no political parties in Nauru as we know them . Candidates do not stand for a particular party. However, alliances among groups with common ideals are formed. The president is then elected by the whole parliament. In Nauru there were two main opposing groups. Unfortunately for us, after the elections, one of Kinza's party defected to the opposing alliance and Kinza and his 'party' immediately lost power. Politics in Nauru had apparently been fairly acrimonious in the years leading up to the election and the new government was determined, I was told later, to go on a witchhunt. All property contracts were put on hold worldwide while an international accountancy firm performed an audit on every building project that Nauru was involved in. The brewery site development was frozen.

On December 3, 1995, Kinza sent us the alarming news that his appointment as a member of the Nauru Insurance Corporation was terminated, and suggested that I contact the general manager of Nauru Insurance Corporation, Mr. S C Mallick, concerning 'our outstanding matters.'

FITZROY

A letter was sent to us which read:

3th December, 1995.

Mr John Birt
General Manager
Fitzroy Football Club
2 Charles Street
Northcote Vic 3070

Dear John,
Since the change of Government on Wednesday November 22 the new government of the Hon. Lagumot Harris M.P. as President had decided on a new policy of terminating appointments to the various Boards of the instrumentalities of government.

Hence I attach a copy of the notice dated 28/11/95 but received by me in the afternoon of December 1, 1995.

I suggest that you contact the General manager of Nauru Insurance Corp. Mr.S.C. Mallick on phone 555 4020 or fax 444 3731 to ascertain the new Chairman and members of the board. I would advise that your best bet would be to contact the G.M. on all outstanding matters.

I wish to take this opportunity to thank you, the Chairman Mr Dyson Hore-Lacy and the members of the Board for the wonderful relationship we have developed over the years and for the opportunity to work with you all for the Fitzroy Football Club. It has been a wonderful experience for me and one that I shall cherish.

My activities will now be curtailed as I have a constituency to look after but I look forward to meeting you all when next in Melbourne.'

I immediately had a sick feeling in my stomach, realising what may happen as a result of his message. There was no turning back now. Negotiating a merger would be a painstaking exercise which would take time, time which we did not have.

We needed $500,000 before Christmas for player payments. After we received Kinza's letters I rang him and he told me he believed there was no need for any concern, that the obligation would be met. After speaking to Mr. Mallick, however, I got the

CHAPTER 7

opposite impression – that the obligation was not going to be met. I therefore wrote a letter on December 5 to Dr David Audi Dabwido, the new chairman of the Nauru Insurance Corporation, setting out the history of the matter and concluding with:

> '...in the meantime, however, I am duty bound to inform you that any failure to honour our agreement will leave our club in serious jeopardy and threaten the repayment of the original loan. Furthermore, the money is needed to pay the players before the 20 December 1995. We are continuing to receive memberships for next year and a number of sponsorships have been put in place. Not only would our inability to keep trading be an acute embarrassment to both of us, but the damage to the club would be immeasurable.'

I subsequently spoke to Mr. Mallick by telephone and he said that he did not think that the Nauru Insurance Corporation Board really understood the ramifications of their failure to advance the money. With his concurrence, I wrote a much stronger letter on December 11. It read in part:

> '...you will see from the documents that the Nauru Insurance Corporation has agreed to lend us the extra $500,000. It is quite clear. As a precaution, we have had legal advice from Dr Peter Buchanan QC, that the contract is binding. If the contract is not honoured and the club falls over as a result of your breach, Dr Buchanan has advised us that your company would be liable for damages totalling many millions of dollars.'

The correspondence had the desired result. On December 19, 1995, the new chairman, Dr David Audi Dabwido, wrote to me stating that the loan request from the club for a further amount of $500,000 had been considered by the Board of Nauru Insurance Corporation, which had resolved that the loan amount be dispersed by two instalments under similar terms and conditions as the first loan agreement. The first instalment of $200,000 was to be advanced as soon as the loan agreement was drawn up and the remaining $300,000 would be advanced during the first fortnight of April 1996. By return fax, I accepted its new offer. I wrote: 'Our directors are grateful for the honourable matter with which you have dealt with us and the courtesy and assistance provided by Mr. Mallick. We understand that none of us live in easy times. We hope our relationship can develop to our mutual benefit.'

Dr David Audi Dabwido, as chance would have it, was coming to Melbourne over Christmas. As a matter of courtesy, I rang Graham Sherry, the solicitor who had acted for Nauru Insurance Corporation in the past, to make sure that he knew was aware of the history of what had happened. I was not sure as to whether the new government had retained his services. After Dr Audi Dabwido arrived in Melbourne, he met with Sherry. Sherry then spoke to me on the telephone and told me that he believed that I had bullied the Nauruan people. He implied that the Nauruan people were unsophisticated. I did not agree! Kinza Clodumar was a very astute person, blessed with an abundance of common sense, and when I subsequently met Dr Audi Dabwido, it emerged that not only was he a Doctor of Divinity, but a Doctor of Medicine who had obtained his degree at Melbourne University. He was over sixty years old and had worked for a long time as a doctor in Papua New Guinea.

Sherry told me that he had advised his clients that it was unlawful for a company to lend money to an insolvent company. He claimed that Fitzroy was insolvent because we could not pay our players. I said that the company wasn't insolvent and the only reason we might not be able to pay our players was because of the Nauru Insurance Corporation's breach of its contract.

By agreement with Sherry, I got in touch with Dr Audi Dabwido. In conversations with me by phone, he mentioned nothing about Fitzroy trading whilst insolvent – or anything like it. He did indicate however that the Nauru Insurance Corporation was going to reconsider its decision to lend Fitzroy the money. I rang Sherry back and I told him that Dr Audi Dabwido had said nothing to me

CHAPTER 7

about Fitzroy trading while insolvent but he (Dr Audi Dabwido) seemed to think that the Nauru Insurance Corporation had the complete discretion to review its decision. Sherry said he would speak to him.

In the meantime, Fitzroy had to find the money to pay players. Other clubs were regularly behind in player payments and it did not attract so much as a raised eyebrow. But with Fitzroy it was different. We knew if word got out that the players were not paid according to their contracts, we would be murdered in the press.

It was quite obvious to the directors that no money would be forthcoming from Nauru before Christmas. Substantial player payments were due in late December. The only way we could find money was from ourselves. If we did not, the repercussions were unthinkable. Consequently, seven of us (the directors) agreed to lend the club a total of $235,000. For some of us, the provision of this money created real difficulties. I know a number of the directors, if not all, had to borrow the money to be able to forward it to the club. The money was secured, like other loans to the club, with a wobbly third debenture against Bondborough Pty Ltd, the company which ran the Fitzroy Club Hotel. The reason it was wobbly was that $650,000 had already been borrowed against a hotel lease which at its last valuation was $750,000.

On December 23, 1995, the directors met at the Fitzroy Football Club Hotel. At this time the directors were meeting about every second day. It was a breakfast session and we worked right throughout the day. We went through the budget item by item and knocked off approximately $300,000 of next year's expenditure. Without the $500,000 from Nauru – and with the prospect of the other $500,000 not forthcoming – we had to take desperate measures.

Once again, we approached another Christmas with our backs to the wall, wondering how long the Fitzroy Football Club could continue. The $235,000 would be sufficient to pay the players as long as all cheques were not collected and presented before

Christmas! We knew on past performances that it was most unlikely that everyone would present their cheques straight away, and this in fact proved to be correct. We barely scraped by.

I arranged to meet Dr Audi Dabwido face to face at Islander House on Wellington Parade, East Melbourne, on Boxing Day, December 26. We had a very friendly and open meeting which included detailed discussions concerning Fitzroy's future. I produced cash projections and a letter signed by all the directors stating that we were of the view that the club was solvent. We left with Dr Audi Dabwido saying that he would go back to his board for a decision.

On January 12, 1996, from Graham Sherry of Baker and MacKenzie, we received the following:

> 'Dear Mr. Hore-Lacy
>
> Re: Nauru Insurance Corporation Pty Ltd
>
> As you know, we act for the above company. Our client has instructed us to notify you that it will not advance the amount of $500,000 to the Fitzroy Football Club. All further communications regarding this matter should be addressed to our office...'

Our worst fears were realised. We knew we could take action against Nauru Insurance Corporation for breach of contract, but from what we had heard, it was possible that the company was insolvent in any event. As well, it would take so long for any action to be processed through the courts that any legal resolution in the short term would be impossible: we did not have the luxury of being able to wait for a long term determination.

What made matters worse was that after a conversation with one of the partners of Alex Robertson and Associates, the estate agents handling the Nauru Queen Victoria property deal, it became quite clear that there was no likelihood of the brewery site development going ahead in the near future. Everything was ready to go but Nauru, who we were told had had a relatively small stake

CHAPTER 7

in the development at this stage, was paralysed. The projected date for the signing of the development contracts went from January to February and then from February to April and then from April to 'who knows when.'

Bruno Grollo's $500,000 sponsorship came very much into focus. After conferring with his legal advisers, in early 1996, Bruno confirmed his sponsorship obligation to Fitzroy Football Club upon the signing of the contract for the Queen Victoria project.

Fitzroy's position was further worsened by the decision of our major sponsor, Quit, to cut down heavily on our sponsorship to only $125,000 for the year. This compared to the minimum $400,000 that most other clubs received. Furthermore, we did not have a 'back of the guernsey' sponsor. We searched everywhere for sponsorship in an attempt to increase our revenue. Over fifty of Australia's largest companies were approached with proposals being submitted in late 1995 and early 1996. The only significant success we had was with Clipsal, a South Australian company which made electrical fittings and who became our back of the jumper sponsor. Although the sponsorship of that company was much appreciated, it was still less than six figures.

We could not obtain a major sponsor and were forced to retain Quit for their bargain basement price. The directors had thought of going public in our quest for a major sponsor, but concluded that this would only fuel speculation concerning our future and that it would be best to stick to traditional methods.

During early 1996, we approached Bruno Grollo for sponsorship on a different basis. Warren O'Neale was in constant communication with him and he put a proposal to Bruno for a three year sponsorship agreement totalling $2 million per year. For that sort of money Grollo would obviously have to have some fairly large concessions, such as naming rights. The Grollo Lions (similar to the 'Camry Crows') was mentioned. With a sponsorship of that magnitude, we believed we could get the club off the ground.

In the end, while expressing differing amounts of interest at different stages – ranging from very enthusiastic to very unenthusiastic – Bruno Grollo decided against the proposal. In fact, we were told that his company surveyed the public concerning the popularity of the Fitzroy Football Club as thoroughly as he did concerning building the world's tallest building. Bruno was under a lot of pressure at the time as he had been committed for trial for alleged tax offences and for alleged attempted bribery. Bruno was subsequently found not guilty by a jury of the attempted bribery case after a trial lasting 12 months. The remaining charge is pending.

We believed that a major sponsorship of Fitzroy Football Club would have been a fantastic public relations opportunity for Bruno. This was particularly important as his first trial was getting closer. We believed his assistance would not hurt as far as his perception by the community was concerned. Unfortunately, Bruno did not see it this way and our last real hope for avoiding a merger faded dramatically.

When Kinza Clodumar first came on the Board, a proxy was appointed to represent Nauru when Kinza could not attend board meetings. The person so appointed was Robert Johnstone – a senior executive with McDonald's. When Peter Mitchell resigned from the Board during 1995, Robert was appointed as a director in his own right. During late 1995 and early 1996, McDonald's was negotiating a very large sponsorship deal with the AFL which subsequently came to fruition.

With a financial crisis looming the Fitzroy directors canvassed the various possibilities open to Fitzroy. It was obvious that without the Nauru funding, on our projections, we could not make it to the end of the year. We made the unpalatable decision that if the AFL would fund us through to the end of the season we would agree to attempt to arrange a merger to take place at that time.

Robert was a very passionate Fitzroy supporter and also a corporate person. He had personally been conducting negotiations with Ross Oakley over the sponsorship from McDonald's and the Fitzroy directors asked Robert to raise the possibility with Ross, of

CHAPTER 7

the AFL underwriting Fitzroy for the rest of the year on the basis that Fitzroy would merge if it could not repay the money at the end of the year. We made it clear, however, that we would not give an unequivocal undertaking to merge because our legal advice was that in order to do that, we would need to amend the memorandum and articles of association which would need the consent of seventy-five per cent of our members and shareholders. Furthermore, I had often publicly stated that I and the directors would never merge the club without first going to the members and shareholders.

Robert contacted the AFL and later reported back to us a positive reaction from that source.

We were, of course, suspicious because positive reactions from the AFL had usually turned into disasters for us. I recall going to an AFL meeting of all the club delegates in early 1996 where Wayne Jackson – now chief executive officer of the AFL – told me how well disposed the AFL was to Fitzroy and how it would do anything to help us. At this very time, the AFL had served one of their notorious solvency notices on us! This was the second time in consecutive years we had received one, forcing us to prove to the satisfaction of the AFL that the club would be solvent for the next twelve months after the request was made – with no rights of appeal.

As a result of Robert's contact with Ross Oakley, an independent solicitor, Michael O'Bryan, was nominated by AFL commissioner Graham Samuel to draw up the necessary documents.

The deal that Fitzroy proposed was that the club would be underwritten to the tune of a maximum of $750,000 during the 1996 season – and we were prepared to reduce this amount if necessary. The $750,000 was the maximum sum we believed would be needed. $400,000 was our actual projected figure. If the amount advanced to Fitzroy was not paid back by October 31, 1996, we said we would agree to an AFL appointed administrator moving in. Furthermore, we were prepared to agree that if at the end of the year, we could not satisfy the AFL that we would be solvent for the next twelve months, the AFL could move an administrator into the club under their solvency rules. We were prepared to extend this period for two years if necessary.

At a meeting at McDonald's, in early 1996 before the Premiership season started, attended by Michael O'Bryan, Ross Oakley, Graham Samuel, Ron Evans, Robert Johnstone, Elaine Findlay and myself, it quickly became apparent that the AFL would not give any assistance unless we could guarantee a merger. Samuel claimed that another White Knight might come along and save the club and they would be left without a merger! The league seemed to fear our survival more than our demise. Samuel was making all the running – as he had in almost every meeting that I attended.

We said we could not guarantee a merger because our legal advice was that we could not effect one without changing our articles of association, and we could only do that by getting 75% of our members and shareholders to agree. The AFL wanted us to do that straight away. That is, to convene a meeting of Fitzroy members and shareholders and to change our articles of association to allow Fitzroy to merge. We pointed out to them that it would be a disaster if we did that before the season closed let alone before the season had started. It would have an impact on our funding, on our playing performance, and on the general morale of the club and end in disaster. The AFL did not seem to be too concerned about that. They just wanted a guaranteed merger.

Our proposal was designed to buy time to allow us to merge in such a way as to get the best possible deal for the club. We offered to use our best endeavours to bring about that merger. O'Bryan, who handled the drawing of the contract and the discussions very professionally, had drawn a draft contract ready to be signed. Oakley said he would take our proposal back to the Commission and let us know. All we were proposing was that the AFL fund us through the season and then we would look for a merger. We did not know precisely what the AFL had in mind at that stage but we were soon to find out.

Ross Oakley rang me late on Friday afternoon, April 5, 1996.

CHAPTER 7

He told me the full Commission had met and discussed our submissions. The problem he said was maintaining consistency with their 'five year plan.' That is, the AFL did not want to act as our banker. This was hard to understand. All the AFL had to do was advance our dividend by some months and we would have seen out the year. I pointed this out to Oakley. But he said the AFL could not pay us our dividend. Again this was difficult to swallow. In the skirmish we had with the AFL and Westpac some three years before, Jeff Browne told me that the AFL's legal advice was that we were entitled, as a matter of law, to a dividend once we had played our first premiership game.

I asked Oakley what was going to happen with the solvency notice that the AFL had served on us in mid-January. He told me that Kevin Lehman, the AFL finance manager, had written a letter to us requiring more information concerning our finances. Oakley said that the AFL was looking for a guaranteed merger. I replied once again that this was not possible because our memorandum of articles, which legally governed the situation, would not allow us to do it. I recall getting particularly annoyed with Oakley at that point and I finished the conversation by telling him that they had better 'batten down the hatches. This would be a Centenary Year to remember.'

By now we were desperate for funding. On April 9, I rang Mark Robertson from Alex Robertson & Company regarding the brewery site development. He said there was a 60% chance that Grollo would be the preferred builder and that he had heard that Nauru was receiving a large amount of money at the end of the month. The timetable, however, was now July for the signing of the necessary documents.

FITZROY

On April 9, 1996, I received a phone call from Jeff Browne. He set out quite specifically what the AFL Commission had decided. This was:

1. The AFL would not go ahead with our proposal.
2. If our current licence were handed back, the AFL would grant a new licence until the end of the year to a new entity known as the Fitzroy Lions Pty Ltd.
3. The shares in this new company would be owned by the AFL. The board would comprise Fitzroy directors and AFL people. It would have a majority of Fitzroy directors. The powers of the directors would be limited in respect of financial decisions. The football operations would continue.
4. The AFL would appoint an interim general manager – and it was Roger Hampson, the former Essendon general manager, it had in mind, we understood.
5. The charter of the new entity was to trade as successfully as it could for the rest of the year. All sponsor rights would be assigned to the new entity. The AFL would underwrite costs. The objectives were to:
    a) trade through the year; and
    b) complete a successful merger.

The board would decide who the merger partner would be and the AFL would 'assist.' If the merger was not completed by the end of October that would be the end of the road for the club. An indemnity for the trading company Fitzroy Lions Pty Ltd – for the debts incurred by the new trading company – would be given by the AFL. The old company would wear its own debts. Nauru would not get paid but the AFL would pay any debts that involved personal responsibility for the Fitzroy directors. The hotel would be treated as a separate entity.

CHAPTER 7

I asked Jeff to put this proposal in writing for the board.

On April 10, 1996 I received the first draft proposal from Jeff Browne. It was a three page document which reflected what Jeff had told me. The last paragraph read:

> 4. *'The AFL and the Lions would take no position in relation to the future of Fitzroy Football Club which would either be liquidated voluntarily, by a creditor or may be placed into receivership by Nauru, they being the only secured creditor.'*

I was outraged by this proposal – as were my fellow directors when they heard about it. The plan was simply to transfer our licence to a new company, and the creditors, apart from the tax office, would be left lamenting.

The AFL had performed a similar manoeuvre with the Sydney Swans some years before. The Swans owed Hambros, a finance company, $3,000,000. I was told that the AFL simply transferred the AFL licence to compete in the AFL competition to a new company and Hambros received a $3,000,000 'haircut'. It sued the AFL which later settled the court case for $1,000,000. An AFL official proudly told me later, 'The Swans did not miss a training run.'

Without a licence to compete in the AFL Fitzroy's creditors – including Nauru – would have most likely received nothing.

I took the AFL's written proposal to Peter Buchanan, QC. He believed that it was political dynamite for the AFL. He was of the view however that because the document did not specifically set out that all the Fitzroy creditors would be dumped this needed to be confirmed with Jeff Browne.

I rang Jeff and asked him to spell out exactly what the proposal meant. He said that it meant that whatever happened to the Fitzroy Football Club was entirely a matter for Fitzroy's directors. The AFL did not propose to make money available from the merger monies for the creditors. The extent of the support for the old company's debts would be $650,000 to pay off the tax liability. I asked him what would happen to the old company (Fitzroy Football Club Ltd). He said he thought that it would have to be liquidated. He said that he suspected that Nauru would be unhappy with the situation and would take control of the company by appointing a receiver. This conversation confirmed unequivocally what the AFL proposed as far as Fitzroy's creditors were concerned.

By now, we had our backs hard up against the wall.

On February 21, 1996 Noel Gordon had rung to say that Brisbane was still interested in merging with Fitzroy and he promised on this occasion not to go public with any discussions. In late March, I believe the day after the Centenary Ball, Noel Gordon and Andrew Ireland visited me in my chambers to discuss the Brisbane-Fitzroy merger proposal. A number of issues were canvassed and later I received a letter formally setting out Brisbane's interest. We were at this stage still hopeful of snaring Bruno Grollo's sponsorship, and John Birt was working on a RACV proposal involving two million dollars worth of sponsorship. Our very last option, if the worst came to the worst, was the AFL's.

I called a board meeting in my chambers on April 11, 1996. I thought I would break the news to Kinza Clodumar gently. He was unaware of developments, having missed a number of recent board meetings. I took the view that, as Kinza was a director, regardless of any immorality involved in not telling him, I was duty bound to inform him of the AFL's proposal. Later, before the board meeting, I arranged to have lunch with Kinza. There I told him of the AFL's proposal. He was shocked.

During the board meeting we discussed in detail what our options were. Kinza asked if he could borrow the AFL's draft proposal to show it to Ruben Khun, the Minister for Finance for the Republic of Nauru, who happened to be in Melbourne at that time. I agreed, and the board meeting broke up at about eight o'clock that night.

Two days later, Kinza and I met with the minister at the Downtowner Motel in Carlton. There the matter was discussed

CHAPTER 7

and we parted on the basis that I would put a proposal to Mr. Khun early next week concerning further finance from Nauru.

On Sunday, April 14 the Fitzroy directors had another board meeting at McDonald's administration headquarters in Victoria Street, Collingwood. I was then formally authorised by the directors to put two proposals to Nauru. The two proposals in effect would have achieved the same result. They involved advancing to Fitzroy the $500,000 necessary to see us through the year and in return we would promise to pay them back out of the AFL inducement monies ($6,000,000) if we were forced to merge. We set out these proposals in detail and they were forwarded to the minister on the following Monday. Kinza was extremely confident that the Government of Nauru would agree to one of our proposals.

As the days went by after April 15 we waited to hear back from Nauru. We waited and waited. To this day we haven't had a reply – or any other communication – from Nauru about the proposals.

At around about this time more rumours started circulating in the press concerning the future of Fitzroy. This was nothing new. In the past whenever the AFL knew that we were experiencing difficulty, it was only a matter of time before it would reach the press. Back in late January, Tony Jones from Channel Nine rang to say that a friend had heard from someone very reliable that we would not be fielding a team during the current year. This was only two days after receiving the letter from the AFL requesting financial information pursuant to the solvency rule! This conversation occurred shortly after my request to Oakley for an advance payment (by about two weeks) of $100,000 of our AFL dividend. The AFL would not agree to this although Oakley did agree to advance $60,000. My request must have set alarm bells ringing.

On April 24, Daryl Timms of the *Herald Sun* rang me saying, 'As I understand it, Fitzroy has to present something to its members at its annual general meeting.' This was obviously a reference to the AFL's proposal set out in Jeff Browne's letter. The AFL expected us to pull the plug on the club at the coming annual general meeting which was set down for Monday April 29.

Nearly every week *The Footy Show* featured a rumour that Fitzroy was on the brink. Indeed Barry Breen, the general manager of the Tasmanian Football League, appeared on that program in April stating that he had heard that Fitzroy had only ten days left in business. Coincidentally, that day he had been in a meeting with the AFL concerning the proposal for a team from Tasmania to play in the AFL or some other Victorian competition.

In the meantime, we were still hopeful, buoyed by Kinza's optimism of a positive response from Nauru. We had to have fallback positions, however, and as a consequence, we continued negotiations with the AFL's solicitor right up until shortly before our AGM which was held on Monday April 29.

Not coincidently, on April 24 we received the third of three proposals from the AFL. This was similar to the other two but with some refinements. This was the one which was expected to be a knock-out blow.

It stated:

> 'the AFL assistance package, being the first revised draft proposal with the amendments referred to in this note (the final AFL assistance package) will be withdrawn at:
>
> a) 5.00 p.m. on Friday April 26, 1996 if not accepted by each and all of the Fitzroy Directors by that time.
>
> b) on 30 April 1996 if:
>
>   i) the current licence is not surrendered and;
>
>   ii) the final AFL assistance package is not unconditionally accepted by the requisite majority of Fitzroy members at the annual general meeting on the 29 April 1996;
>
>   iii) at any other time if the final AFL assistance package is not able to be fully implemented other than as a result of any matter within the direct control of the AFL .'

CHAPTER 7

What the AFL proposed was that at the AGM we would throw up our hands and say 'sorry, we can't trade any more, we are insolvent' and then surrender the licence and adopt the AFL's scheme. We had to unequivocally accept the deal before 5pm on Friday before the AGM otherwise the offer would be withdrawn. This was designed to put enormous pressure on the Fitzroy directors.

The Fitzroy directors took the view that a merger with Brisbane would be preferable to the AFL's devious proposal. With $6,000,000 on the table for two clubs to merge, we believed there would be plenty of money available to pay all creditors.

With AFL pressure on us we begin talking in earnest with Brisbane Bears when I met with Andrew Ireland (Brisbane CEO) and Noel Gordon in my chambers in Lonsdale Street. This was during the weeks leading up to the AGM.

In that meeting, Gordon told me that Terry O'Connor, the AFL commissioner, was very supportive of Brisbane and Gordon believed that O'Connor would support them in their proposals. I discussed the merger possibility on the basis that all of Fitzroy's creditors were to be paid – though I would not have minded if Nauru had taken a reduction in view of the fact that I believed that it was their blatant breach of contract which had put us in the situation we were in.

Noel Gordon went from our meeting to meet with Ross Oakley. Later I received a detailed letter from the Bears which was, in effect, almost identical in some respects to the AFL draft proposal we had earlier received from Jeff Browne. In other words a new company was to be formed, the licence would be transferred to the new company and Fitzroy's creditors including Nauru would get nothing.

I rang Noel and told him that we did not want to be party to the AFL's dubious scheme. Noel appeared to be embarrassed and said that it was the scheme put to him by Ross Oakley. In his following letter, dated April 26, Noel said, 'You and your Board should be assured that the action proposed in the first paragraph of my letter was one which the AFL recommended and, as a result of our meeting with the AFL, we decided to adopt. This course of action is not identical to our proposal. However, you should understand that what we are trying to achieve with your assistance, is the position that the Brisbane Bears Football Club Limited and the Fitzroy Football Club Limited merge.....'

The 'action proposed' that was referred to in Noel Gordon's letter was the termination of the Fitzroy Football Club Ltd licence and the issuing of a new licence to a different entity.

At this time the trading position of the club was a concern for the directors as far as personal responsibility was concerned. If we permitted the club to trade whilst insolvent we would be committing offences under Company law. All Fitzroy directors had received very close advice on a number of occasions during the year from Dr Peter Buchanan QC and from Dean McVeigh, a partner and solvency expert from Melbourne accountants Horwath and Horwath, the same firm in which finance director John Stewart was a partner. We also had advice from Bruce Curl, a partner in Williams Winter and Higgs. We had to meet player payments by mid-May and our financial projections showed a progressively worse situation in the months of June and July.

We had available to us the AFL option, the Brisbane option and the possibility of the Nauru help. It was in the context of this situation and acting on the best advice available, that the directors took the view that the company was not insolvent. However, as a precaution, the directors had instructed the Fitzroy Football Club administration not to enter into any new contracts. Furthermore, the directors had decided that the club could not incur any further debts. A small overdraft offered by St George Bank was refused for this reason.

D-Day, Friday, April 26 – came and went. We did not respond to the AFL's threat. They thought they had us over a barrel. They were fully aware of our financial situation and I believe they took

CHAPTER 7

the view that we could not trade on. At this stage, I personally believed that our best bet was Nauru. If the worst came to the worst, we would take to the streets for the money. I believe all directors felt the same way as I did. In any event we would never surrender the club's licence without giving an opportunity to the members and shareholders to do something about it.

It was in this environment that the annual general meeting was held. It was scheduled for 7.00 p.m. on April 29, 1996. The air was thick with anticipation by the press. At Fitzroy we had little doubt that it was AFL leaks that had been fuelling the media focus on our financial situation. Before the AGM started, all the directors met at the Victorian Commercial Teachers' Association (VCTA) building in Hotham Street, Collingwood. There I read to the directors what I proposed to say, and our finance director, John Stewart, did the same concerning his financial report. When we arrived at the AGM at the Fitzroy Town Hall we found that the press had surrounded the place. By arrangement I entered through one of the rear doors – but the television cameras were there as well.

I began my address, after welcoming our supporters, members and sponsors, by saying, 'For those who have come to feed off our dead body, you are going to be hugely disappointed. Fitzroy lives. To those members of the press, and I am not referring to all of them, who have come along to witness Fitzroy's demise, I apologise.'

Later I added, 'I have publicly stated often enough that the directors of the Fitzroy Football Club would not enter into a binding agreement to merge without going to the members and shareholders first. As an added comfort our legal advice is that we cannot do that in any event without a change to our memorandum and articles of association, which requires the consent of 75% of our members and shareholders. So no one has to worry about a decision being made over which they have no input or control.'

John Stewart also spoke and cast a fairly gloomy picture. John told the meeting, 'Our total revenue for the year was some $4.07 million as compared to approximately $4 million in the preceding year. When you consider that in excess of 50% of this operating revenue is required to be expended in player and football staff payments, it is obvious the problem we are facing is in deriving sufficient revenue to compete with all other clubs. Press reports indicate that most other AFL clubs are earning revenue between $7 and $12 million. That simple analogy indicates to you the continual problems that we are faced with.'

Likewise, I announced that: 'The stark fact is that, under present AFL policy, it is becoming increasingly difficult to compete financially with the millionaires of AFL football. We are a million dollars down on gate receipts and a million dollars down on memberships compared to some clubs. I believe a similar position relates to sponsorship..... What the club needs is a person or organisation who is prepared to give long term and substantial financial support to the club to give us a chance to develop to the extent that we need to. We have been trying our utmost to secure that assistance and, although we have come close, we have had no success to date in that respect. I, and the other directors of the Fitzroy Football Club believe that we would be negligent as a board to fail to explore other options especially if the situation becomes one in which the continued existence of the club is threatened. To that extent we have now, and have been for some years, looking at what is available. We have not come to any agreement with an AFL club or any other club for that matter, to date...'

I then went on to add, 'In a little while I will permit questions, but please don't ask me about details of any discussions we may have had. You will appreciate that this is a public forum.' Question time did in fact contain a number of questions from members about merging. I recall one which led to an answer by me which canvassed the pros and cons of a merger with a Melbourne-based club compared to an interstate club.

As time passed after the AGM and we heard no news from Mr.

CHAPTER 7

Khun, Nauru's minister for finance, we decided that we best start canvassing the Brisbane option with our senior supporters and coterie members as being the next best option. Meetings were arranged for May 5 at the VCTA building in Collingwood. The first meeting consisted of myself, Elaine Findlay, John Petinella and Colin Hobbs representing the board, while Phil Taylor, Arthur Hobson, Warren O'Neale and Alan Drummond represented the coteries and the Fitzroy Foundation. Straight after that meeting, on the same morning, we held another one. This consisted of a number of our key supporters, among them Des Whittingslow, Eddie Hart, Tom Reynolds (Minister for Sport, Youth and Recreation and our number one ticket holder), John Riordan, Bill Stephen, Ray Slocum, Norm Brown, Nancye Cain, Barbara Hardy, Noel Beaton and Ray Paton. Once we explained the history of our problems and the choices we had, everyone, I believe, was unanimous in the fact that we had no alternative but to merge. Most believed a merger with a Melbourne club would be preferable to a merger with Brisbane although some, including Tom Reynolds, expressed a preference for Brisbane. At that stage, the Brisbane option was the only option being discussed as it was the only option on the table.

In February, the board had authorised me to discuss merger possibilities.

The year before (1995) we had brief discussions with North Melbourne but after we were guaranteed the additional Nauru loan, with the probability of increased sponsorship, we decided against going down that path. In early 1996 I had rung Ron Casey on a number of occasions, asking him if North Melbourne was interested in talking. Ron said it was but there was always some reason why the timing was not right. At the meeting on May 5 in Collingwood Warren O'Neale asked if he could approach North Melbourne. We said 'certainly'. The next day I received a phone call from him saying that a meeting had been arranged at his home that night! Ron Casey, North Melbourne president, and Peter De

Rauch, its vice-president, would be attending.

Warren was one of our keenest supporters. At about 7.30 p.m. that evening I went to visit him at his home in Kooyong. When I arrived Casey and De Rauch were not yet there. A short time later they arrived and the four of us Ron, Peter, Warren and myself sat down to discuss the matter in Warren's study.

At the meeting various options were discussed. Both clubs agreed that they wanted to merge. Both clubs said that they believed that the only successful way of doing it, to carry supporters of both clubs, would be to do it on an equal basis. On that particular night, the only agreement we came to was to take the matter further.

On March 6 the board had resolved that 'Dyson Hore-Lacy, Elaine Findlay and Robert Johnstone be empowered to enter into any agreement that they deemed necessary in the interests of the Fitzroy Football Club provided that no agreement shall be entered into which irrevocably commits the Fitzroy Football Club to cease operating in the AFL past the 1996 season.'

At this stage, I was getting a little impatient. I did not want to get too far down the track with the Bears and suddenly switch horses in mid-stream. On Wednesday, May 8, David Dunn, Brisbane's solicitor, rang me at home in a state of agitation saying that he had heard that we were talking to North Melbourne. I did not deny it, reiterating what I had said earlier to Noel Gordon and Andrew Ireland and that was that we could not put all our eggs in one basket and we reserved our right to talk to other people. But I did tell him we would not keep them waiting for an inordinate amount of time. Fitzroy had to act quickly in any case.

A further meeting with North Melbourne was arranged for Thursday afternoon on May 9 again at Warren O'Neale's home. On this occasion, after about half an hour, Elaine Findlay and I were becoming quite depressed as North kept probing us concerning our financial situation. I remember at one stage saying, 'Look, is there any point in continuing our discussions?' Ron Casey just looked at me and said 'No, no, we'll keep going.' The discussion went for some hours – and eventually culminated in a

CHAPTER 7

momentous handshake 'agreement' for Fitzroy and North Melbourne to merge.

The name was to be the Fitzroy – North Melbourne Kangaroos. The colours were to contain the colours of both clubs in approximately equal proportions. A new song was to be composed. Board membership would be equal. I recall us all shaking hands before we left Warren's that night.

Another meeting was arranged for Saturday afternoon, at which time lawyers from North Melbourne and Fitzroy would attend and formalise our 'agreement.' On that Saturday, Fitzroy was playing a centenary re-enactment game against Carlton at Princes Park and North Melbourne was playing West Coast at Perth on the Sunday. Saturday afternoon was the most convenient time to hold the meeting, and in view of the importance of it, I arranged for Elaine Findlay, as vice chairperson, to fly the flag for me at the Centenary Game at Optus oval.

In the meantime a further meeting had been arranged with Brisbane and its solicitor for Friday, May 10. We decided to attend the meeting as there had been no absolute finality with North Melbourne and we wanted board approval before we decided irrevocably to go with North Melbourne.

We met at the Collins Street offices of Brisbane solicitor's, Blake Dawson Waldron. Noel Gordon, Andrew Ireland and Alan Piper from the Bears were present, as were David Dunn and Arthur Aposs from Blake Dawson Waldron. Elaine Findlay, Colin Hobbs and I represented Fitzroy. The meeting was quite cordial. In addition to what Brisbane had offered before, they indicated that they would put $150,000 towards paying out our shareholders and also secure the money lent on the Fitzroy Club Hotel.

Essentially the proposal by Brisbane involved the name (Brisbane Lions), colours (predominantly Fitzroy colours), directors (two or three from Fitzroy) and venue – at least six games in Melbourne. In addition there would be coterie rights and membership rights to the games played in Melbourne. Questions concerning the transfer of the licence were not discussed. We told them that we would let them know on Monday, May 13. We then organised a board meeting for early that Monday morning.

In the meantime, Ron Casey and Greg Miller had gone to the AFL on Thursday, May 9, to make enquiries about player lists and the like for the proposed merger. Of course, in accordance with invariable custom, the story was broken in huge print in *The Sunday Age* on May 12. A two page feature article appeared, written by Rohan Connolly, concerning the Fitzroy-North Melbourne merger. In the article it was mentioned that Greg Miller and Ron Casey had been to see Ross Oakley. Ron Casey told me that no one else at North Melbourne apart from himself and Greg Miller knew that they had been to see Oakley. They had not even told us.

Lions close to merger
Rohan Connolly
Sunday Age
12/5/96

On Saturday, May 11, the day of the Fitzroy Carlton centenary game we once again met at Warren O'Neale's place. On this occasion, in addition to the people who had attended before, were Bruce Curl and John McArdle, our solicitors from Williams Winter & Higgs, and Tony Darvall and Carl Thompson, from North Melbourne's lawyers, Corrs Chambers Westgarth.

The involvement of legal experts was crucial from this point on. The legal mechanics involved in bringing about a merger were very complicated due to the fact that the two clubs had quite different ownership and corporate structures.

North Melbourne was a company which was technically privately owned. Although it had members, the members had no say in the election of office bearers.

In the early stages of our negotiations, we believed that there were about two and a half million North Melbourne shares floating

CHAPTER 7

around. Fitzroy was a company limited by guarantee and there was a limited shareholding attached to it. There had been about 575,000 shares issued in 1986. These shares had voting rights attached. However, the voting rights were limited, pursuant to the memorandum and articles of association. At least three of the ten Fitzroy board members had to be elected by ordinary members only. As far as shareholders were concerned, they were entitled to *one* vote per share provided that no single shareholder was entitled to more than 5% of the issued shares as far as voting rights were concerned. It would be fair to say that Fitzroy was halfway between North Melbourne's position of being privately owned and the clubs which have no shareholding and are completely controlled by ordinary members.

At the meeting on May 11 we discussed various methods of amalgamating the two companies. After a while, all the lawyers went into a huddle in a separate room and when they came out they were of the view that the only way the merge could be legally effected was by a scheme of arrangement. This meant, in effect, that the two clubs would apply to the Supreme Court which would merge the two clubs at corporate level. It would be a lengthy and messy business and the lawyers were of the view that if a merger was to be implemented for the 1997 season application would have to be made within a month or so to the Supreme Court. There was also concern expressed that Carlton Football Club, which owned 20% of the North Melbourne shares, might somehow attempt to block the deal, thereby delaying the proposed supreme court action.

One of the advantages of merging with North Melbourne in the first place was because it did not have to go to its members to implement a merger agreement. We were confident that our members and shareholders would, once faced with the reality of the situation, support a reasonable merger. With North Melbourne most of the shares were held by directors and North believed that it had control of the necessary 75% required to implement the deal.

FITZROY

At about 4pm on Saturday 11 May an 'agreement' was reached between North Melbourne and Fitzroy and we dictated it to Carl Thompson, North Melbourne's solicitor, who wrote it out.

One possible stumbling block in our negotiations with North Melbourne was that we had to be certain that the $6 million AFL inducement was still available for a merger.

The original merger option – including the $6 million dollar inducement – was officially open only until October 31, 1995. It was common belief that it would still be available but we needed that assurance from the AFL. Jeff Browne was rung on the Saturday afternoon and later on that evening he attended Warren O'Neale's house after the football. Later Jeff told me that he was happy when he saw the terms of the agreement. He believed it would work and I believe he genuinely supported it.

On the previous Saturday night (May 11) at seven o'clock, Jeff Browne rang to tell me that the AFL had agreed to make the $6 million available. He rang Peter De Rauch with the same news.

The document Carl Thompson recorded was titled 'Heads of Agreement dated 11 May 1996 between Fitzroy Football Club Limited FFC and North Melbourne Football Club Limited NMC.'

The document read:

'whereas Fitzroy Football Club (FFC) and North Melbourne Club (NMC) are desirous in merging their operations and wish to record the terms of the proposed merger:

1. These Heads of Agreement have been negotiated in good faith and are not binding upon the parties. Each party will use their bona fide reasonable endeavours to complete the transactions and actions contemplated herein as expeditiously as possible.
2. The FFC and NMC will merge by whatever legally appropriate method into a new corporation (or other appropriate entity).
3. The name of the new club shall be Fitzroy-North Melbourne Kangaroos.
4. The new club will have a new club jumper which substantially incorporates the present colours of FFC and NMC in a style which is appropriate to the 1990's which will create an effective merchandising.

CHAPTER 7

5. The new club will have a board of 12 directors with six persons nominated by each of the present boards of the parties. The Board of 12 shall include the chairman.
6. The first chairman (who has been chosen by lot) shall be a former NMC director and the chairman shall have a casting vote.
7. In the event that the inaugural chairman retires within 2 years of his appointment, the new chairman shall be appointed by those members of the Board nominated by NMC.
8. The parties will use their best endeavours to implement the merger including (without limitation), executing any necessary documents convening any necessary meetings and taking all necessary legal action.
9. The parties will constitute a joint committee comprising not less than 4 persons being 2 nominees from each party, to oversee implementation of the merger.
10. All staff appointments by the new club will be made by the Board of the new club and will be made on merit.
11. The parties will keep this agreement and its contents confidential (save for communication with advisers and the Australian Football League) and no public announcements will be made by one party without the prior consent of the other party.
12. The provisions of clauses 5, 6 and 7 will operate for four years from the date hereof. Thereafter appointments to the Board will be made by shareholders of the new club.
13. Each party will give the other party an opportunity to conduct a reasonable level of diligence and will make available such records and will give such access as is necessary to facilitate diligence by the other party.
14. The constitution of the new club will enshrine the provisions of clauses 3 and 4 so that they can only be amended by approval of 90% of shareholders.
15. The parties will use their best endeavours to have a binding agreement executed within three weeks of the date hereof and the parties will, at that time, make a joint announcement of the proposed merger.

It was signed by me, Ron Casey, Peter De Rauch, Warren O'Neale and later on that evening by Elaine Findlay.

FITZROY

After the agreement was signed, we shook hands all around and then opened up a bottle of wine. I recall Peter De Rauch saying, 'Relax, all your worries are over' and we listened to the last portion of the Fitzroy-Carlton game. Famous last words!

During our discussions on the Thursday night, one of the sticking points was the appointment of the first chairman. North Melbourne insisted it be a North Melbourne appointee, arguing that North Melbourne had a much more significant shareholding than Fitzroy. All agreed the chairman would have a casting vote, as in the usual situation, but we could not have cared less who was chairman – it was the last thing I wanted. In fact my thoughts at the time were that I would fill the vice-chairman's position, and after the new entity got off the ground I would quietly disappear from AFL Football.

Whilst we were debating the point, I asked somebody to give me a coin. A twenty cent piece was passed to me and I flicked it in the air, caught it, turned it over placed in on the back of my left hand and covered it with the palm of my right hand. I said to Ron Casey 'Call.' Ron was a little startled. I just said 'Call.' He said 'Tails.' I lifted my right hand in such a way that only I could see the coin. 'You win Ron, you're first chairman', I said as I showed him the coin.

It was agreed Fitzroy would nominate the vice-chairman. I do not believe I have ever disclosed to anyone what I would have done had the coin come up heads. As to the choice of the name, we told North that they could have their pick – North Melbourne-Fitzroy Lions or Fitzroy-North Melbourne Kangaroos. This was in accordance with the AFL merger guidelines and we believed that the club that had the first name should have to sacrifice its logo. This was later to cause a huge problem. When the merger proposal became known publicly, all the football experts assumed that North Melbourne would get the first name, the logo and just about everything else including the colours. Consequently when it became known that Fitzroy had the first name, certain sections

CHAPTER 7

of the press criticised it on the basis that North Melbourne, being in an apparently superior position to Fitzroy, should have the larger share of any merger apportionment.

This expectation that North would end up with almost everything caused unhappiness among many North Melbourne supporters when the terms of the agreement were finally revealed.

On Saturday, May 11, I suggested strongly that we make a public announcement as soon as possible, but North Melbourne were very much against this. They saw themselves as a genuine premiership chance (with more than a little justification as it turned out!), and did not want to disclose our deal for as long as possible. From past experience we knew very well that once the AFL knew about the proposal it would be in the public arena within 48 hours. This proved to be true. Unfortunately, we were bound by the confidentiality clause in the agreement and could not make any public comment without North Melbourne's permission. At that time, I had a new silent number at home which was almost unknown to the press. When the story broke in *The Sunday Age* on May 12, I was unavailable for comment. The press caught up with Ron Casey at Subiaco Oval in Perth that afternoon but were unable to contact me. Ron denied the story.

Naturally, on Monday the newspapers were bursting with the news.

On Tuesday morning I rang Peter De Rauch, telling him we had to make a public statement. I said that we should talk to the players and staff as soon as possible. He agreed but said that he would have to canvas the matter with his board first. Peter and I were in constant contact. We had agreed that whatever happened we would keep in contact and keep talking because we knew there would be difficult times ahead.

On Monday morning, May 13, the directors held a board meeting at the Fitzroy Club Hotel. I had informed certain directors of what was happening but at the Board meeting we told the full board (plus our CEO, John Birt, who had not been privy to the discussions) the full details of what had passed and the 'agreement' that had been signed with North Melbourne. The directors were unanimous in their view that the North Melbourne proposal was far preferable to the Brisbane proposal.

At this meeting, the directors formally appointed Colin Hobbs to replace Robert Johnstone on the 'merger' sub-committee and the directors endorsed the action taken by myself and Elaine Findlay. Unfortunately, Robert Johnstone had been defeated by Greg Basto at the election held at the annual general meeting on April 29.

The board further authorised the sub-committee to take the necessary action to finalise the proposal to merge the two clubs, namely Fitzroy and North Melbourne. Up until now, the sub committee had limited authority. The board also agreed further that I be authorised to advise Brisbane that a proposal to merge with Brisbane was rejected.

When I returned to chambers after the Board meeting I rang David Dunn and advised him that the Brisbane offer had been rejected. I said I was sorry I could not really elaborate but that Fitzroy was going in a different direction. He sounded extremely disappointed. On that Monday I asked John Birt to talk to the staff and tell them what we proposed to do although, acting in accordance with the terms of our agreement, I asked him not to disclose which club we were considering merging with but he could say that it was a Melbourne club. At that stage, what we were publicly saying was only that we were working towards a merger – which was true as the document we signed was not legally binding and there was much to be done before the joint venture was completed.

On Tuesday I heard that the staff were not entirely happy with the news that had been conveyed to them, and, after speaking with Michael Nunan, I addressed them on Wednesday and attempted to ease their understandable concerns. At this time, I had not addressed the players. I was very keen to do so, but I was not allowed

CHAPTER 7

to by North Melbourne until I had approval from their board. When I addressed the administration, I told them most of the details including the fact that staff would be selected on merit. I also said that I would do all I could for them as far as future employment was concerned; all existing employment entitlements would be met. It was my intention not to mention the name of the partner club as I had no clearance from North Melbourne to do so. However, I am told that I accidentally mentioned North Melbourne by name, although it would probably have been obvious in any event.

The North Melbourne board meeting was held at the North Melbourne Social Club sometime that same Wednesday afternoon, May 15. At this time North Melbourne were still in public denial mode. Somehow the press found out about the board meeting and the North Melbourne directors were put under siege. They apparently waited and waited but the press would not go away, and in the end they emerged to face the music. A sheepish Greg Miller admitted for the first time that North Melbourne were having discussions with Fitzroy, and they produced Wayne Carey, who mumbled something about winning the premiership. The prior agreement had been that both clubs would speak to the players at exactly the same time, for obvious reasons. However, North Melbourne were caught on the hop, and because of the pressure they were under, Greg Miller addressed the players that night. This left me out on a limb. I had canvassed with Michael Nunan the best time to talk to the players. On the Wednesday there were different people training at different venues and Michael felt the next full night of training (Thursday) would be a more appropriate time to address them.

The North–Lions *merger*

Merger on agenda

Bruce Matthews
Herald Sun
16/5/96

TALKS ARE ON

Herald Sun
16/5/96

Roos: We're talking

Fans can have say

By SCOTT GULLAN and DARYL TIMMS

But Roos deny deal done

Scott Gullan and Daryl Timms
Herald Sun
16/5/96

Hard to imagine no Roys

Finance probes

Terry Brown

I addressed the players on the Thursday night, one day later than North Melbourne's squad heard the news. David McMahon and Colin Hobbs accompanied me to our training complex at Coburg. We waited until training had concluded. Once again the press were waiting in droves outside the Coburg Football Ground. All staff, match committee, coaches and players were present at the meeting.

CHAPTER 7

I went into the history of what had happened in considerable detail including the crucial Nauru let down. I told them we were working towards an equal merger, where the best list would be selected from both clubs and that all staff would be selected on merit. I said I would do my best for them. I recall saying that it would not necessarily be the best players who would go across, but that the new entity would want a balanced list, taking into account such things as age and potential. I specifically mentioned that North Melbourne was the club we were talking to, as by that time North Melbourne had admitted it.

IT'S A DEAL

Mike Sheahan
and **Daryl Timms**
Herald Sun
15/5/96

North, Roys to merge

The Heads of Agreement we signed with North Melbourne was not legally binding and we knew there was a long way to go. We also knew obstacles would be put in our way by some in the media and by others who may have wished a different scenario. Fitzroy continuing in its own right was still an option, but the board had decided that we were no longer interested in band-aid measures. It would have needed a huge injection of funds which would have enabled us to rebuild the club rather than struggle from hand to mouth, year to year. To that extent, we did not burn our bridges behind us completely.

On May 17, 1996, I met with people connected with the Reidy Lake Golf Park project near Geelong. They put forward a proposal to us which they claimed could have brought in millions of dollars for the club. I was sceptical. The people involved claimed to be Collingwood supporters but Collingwood had knocked their proposal back and so had Geelong and I knew how much Collingwood needed the money.

On Tuesday afternoon, May 21, at the offices of Williams Winter & Higgs, we had a meeting with the lawyers representing Fitzroy, North Melbourne and the AFL. In attendance were myself and Peter De Rauch, with Jeff Browne representing the AFL. Also present were Bruce Curl and John McArdle (both representing Fitzroy), and Richard Lustig, from Corrs, representing North Melbourne.

By this time the North Melbourne lawyers had cooled on the idea of a scheme of arrangement and they suggested that North Melbourne keep its existing company and make necessary changes to that company structure and memorandum and articles of association to incorporate Fitzroy. North Melbourne would continue with its licence and Fitzroy would surrender its licence – although we would have preferred it if both existing licences had been surrendered and a new one issued. North Melbourne were against this last mentioned proposal because, it claimed, there were certain clauses in contracts of key players which may have allowed them to go to other clubs in the event of North Melbourne changing their corporate structure. In particular they expressed concern about Wayne Carey's contract.

The North Melbourne proposal could not be regarded as a merger in a corporate sense – but their explanation and reasoning was acceptable to us and we did not think that it made any practical difference.

For a number of days thereafter we had regular meetings with the lawyers and different draft agreements were prepared. During our discussions we made an interesting discovery – in addition to their three million ordinary shares, North Melbourne had 60,000 B class shares with 75 voting rights per share.

Add this to the one vote per share for the ordinary shares and it could readily be seen that the North Melbourne voting rights amounted to 7,500,000. Our initial 'heads of agreement' specified that it would take 90% of the total shareholding of both clubs to change key parts of the agreement (name, colours etc). We thought

CHAPTER 7

this would be safe as there were 570,000 shares held by Fitzroy shareholders. The 'heads of agreement' provided that new shares were to be issued to those shareholders one for one with the North Melbourne shares. The B class shares had not been mentioned at our earlier meeting and their disclosure made us realise that North Melbourne was in a position to obtain more than 90% of the vote with ease.

Elaine Findlay, Colin Hobbs and I were becoming increasingly suspicious about North Melbourne's bona fides. We trusted Peter De Rauch and Ron Casey, with whom we did the initial deal, but we were concerned that new spokesmen were entering into discussions as time progressed who may not have shared the same spirit of trust that, we felt, existed between us and Peter and Ron. Shortly after the merger discussions were first leaked to the media, Ron Casey became ill and he was confined to bed at hospital for some weeks. As Ron's influence and control diminished, other people, far less capable, we believed, started entering the picture.

At North Melbourne's chairman's luncheon on Saturday, May 18, Mark Dawson – a North Melbourne director and chairman of selectors – had grabbed the microphone and defiantly announced, 'We will still be North Melbourne, we will still be the Kangaroos, Denis Pagan will still be coach and Wayne Carey will still be captain.' This may have been how things would have turned out but what was said gave a very misleading impression and only fuelled the common belief that our agreement with North Melbourne was a take-over rather than a merger.

Roos won't risk losing stars over merger

Stephen Linnell
and Len Johnson
The Age
17/5/96

Carey worry on merger

Stephen Linnell
The Age
16/5/96

In relation to the press, we had decided that we would say nothing until we had something significant to say. We wanted to wait until the ink was dry on the agreement before we made any public comment. We regarded this as being very important because we knew that once the detail of the merger became known, supporters of both clubs would object. This was especially the case with North Melbourne because its supporters, fuelled by press speculation, believed that it would get the major share of the deal. I had told our players that we would keep them informed if anything significant happened. At that stage, the plan was to go to the members and shareholders for approval once final agreement was reached. We had made it clear to the AFL, Brisbane, and North Melbourne that we could not merge without the consent of the members and shareholders.

One of our problems was that we were relying on the AFL for finance. We did not need extra money as such, but we needed the early advancement of the AFL periodic dividends which would normally be paid.

In a spirit of cooperation, the AFL indicated (through Jeff Browne) that it would finance us sufficiently to allow North Melbourne and Fitzroy to complete the merger. When the deal was done, the $6 million AFL inducement would become available to the merged entity. We had about $100,000 of player payments to meet at the end of May. We had about $300,000 due to us from the AFL on the 15 June and we requested a two week advancement. We never believed that this would be a problem, as negotiations with North Melbourne were being facilitated by Jeff Browne acting for the AFL.

CHAPTER 7

During discussions I had with Jeff, however, he indicated that the AFL wanted to be certain that Fitzroy would merge. This was the same hard line that the AFL had been running all year. Jeff Browne told us the AFL was unwilling to advance any money unless the merger was guaranteed. I reiterated – once again – that I could not legally guarantee it because we had to get the consent of our members and shareholders first.

I told Jeff Browne that I had no doubt that the Fitzroy members and shareholders would support the deal and, if necessary, I believed that we would be able to get sufficient proxies for the required 75% approval by members and shareholders. After my initial conversation with Jeff nothing more was said about it, and in view of our continuing amicable discussions with the league, as time went by I believed that the AFL were no longer insisting on those proxies.

On May 20, we met with our major shareholders at the VCTA building in Collingwood, the alternative venue organised by Colin Hobbs. On occasions, the press would be waiting in ambush for us at our regular meeting place, the Fitzroy Club Hotel. Elaine, Colin and I spoke to the shareholders at that meeting and explained to them in great detail the club's predicament and the events leading up to it. Most of those in attendance indicated support for what we were doing with North Melbourne.

After our meeting with shareholders I informed Jeff Browne of what had transpired. Jeff asked me if I had obtained the necessary proxies. I asked him if it was really necessary and he replied that his client – the AFL – insisted on it. Without the proxies we would not get the money needed to pay players and staff. Consequently we had to organise another meeting very quickly with shareholders to obtain the required proxies. This time, however, we decided to expand the invitees to include all shareholders who had 200 or more shares rather than just the major ones.

We believed that almost all our members and shareholders eventually would support us in what we were doing once they knew the true and full story.

In the Fitzroy Football Club Ltd. Memorandum and Articles there was a form set out for proxy voting. Peter Buchanan QC drafted a proxy form which was slightly different but more appropriate. Although it was expressed to be 'irrevocable,' Peter said that in fact legally it wasn't. It was thought the insertion of the word 'irrevocable' might impress the AFL!

Meanwhile, negative Fitzroy stories concerning club finances commenced. On May 21, 1996, Stephen Linnell published a story in *The Age* under heading '10 Day Deadline for Lions' which read, 'Fitzroy has a deadline of Friday week to merge or the AFL will take over the administration of the embattled club. The Lions will be unable to meet a large portion of their monthly player payments believed to be as much as $100,000 – when they fall due on the 31 May 1996…'

3AW, who had my home telephone number, rang me very early on the morning of May 21 and read parts of the article to me. I did an interview with the 3AW Breakfast show, and then rang 3UZ. Later I did an interview with Peter Couchman on 3LO and I also did a piece for ABC News. At the time I did the interviews, I had not read the full article. Nor had the full article been read to me but key parts had been. During my interviews I denied essentially two things:

1. That players would not be paid; and
2. That an administrator would be moved into the club.

I did not deny that Fitzroy was in financial trouble. Fitzroy's finances had been well documented for some time. We were extremely confident in the outcome of the merger discussions, especially as the AFL seemed to be cooperating. We were close to a final agreement with North Melbourne. Furthermore, we had back-up funding if absolutely necessary. Ross Oakley denied *The Age* story on 3AW that day as well.

Peter De Rauch and Warren O'Neale had generously indicated a week or so earlier that, if needed, they may fund Fitzroy for the

CHAPTER 7

rest of the season to give us an opportunity to complete the merge. A former AFL president, Geoff Lord, had rung me indicating that he may support us to get through the season if required. In other words, there were a number of possibilities for raising the $100,000 short of having an administrator appointed. All we had to do with North Melbourne, we believed, was settle the Nauru debt, but we did not believe that would be a problem. Peter De Rauch had said on a number of occasions that, if necessary, we would pay Nauru out in full, 'Even if we had to put them on the drip feed.'

As an added protection, there were a number of legal formalities, such as giving fourteen days notice, which the AFL had to comply with under our licence agreement before it could move an administrator in.

The expanded meeting with shareholders was held on Tuesday, May 28. At that meeting I repeated what I had said earlier, explaining exactly what had happened to the club in recent times and why. The narration included the Nauru saga and what I could say about the Fitzroy-North Melbourne deal. Most of the same people who were present the week before were present at this meeting. I told them why I needed the proxies. I also told them that if they got legal advice it would probably be that the proxies, although expressed to be irrevocable, were in fact not. In other words I was making certain they understood that if they wished to change their mind they were able to do so.

At the end of the meeting – also attended by Elaine Findlay and John Birt – I fielded a number of questions. At the conclusion I asked for people to indicate whether they would support the directors. The vast majority indicated they would.

The AFL had for months been hassling us, requesting information regarding the solvency of the club pursuant to their unique solvency rules. But it never occurred to us that the Australian Securities Commission (ASC), the national corporate watchdog, would get involved.

On May 6 the ASC raided our auditors, KPMG, under a warrant

for 'suspect trading whilst insolvent.' The investigation was for allegedly contravening sections of the Corporations Law between 1993 and 1996. I was told the investigators also wanted to interview Kevin Lehman, the AFL's finance manager. When I heard of the raid, I rang Mr McLeod of the ASC immediately. I tried to assure him that there was nothing untoward. I asked him if there had been a complaint or was the investigation self-generated. He said that there were a number of reasons for the investigation but he would not say whether they were acting on a complaint or acting on information.

The next day, I went to speak to the ASC alone. We went into a room with a long boardroom table. I sat on one side. I related to them what had happened and what we were doing and that we were in the process of merging and explained what options we had. They appeared to be satisfied. Later Elaine Findlay, John Stewart, Kevin Ryan and I met formally with ASC investigators Peter Hyland and Richard Coburn where we answered all their questions[10]. At the meeting they indicated there had been a complaint made but would not say by whom.

At around the time of the ASC raid, a number of directors had notices served on them for non-payment of group tax owed by the club. I personally received a notice claiming liability by way of penalty of $214,506.79, and the others received claims for similar substantial amounts.

The club – and its directors – were under increasing pressure from a number of sources. Now board members appeared to be the target of multiple government agencies, accompanied by raids like a scene out of 'The French Connection'. Who were these people under investigation? Loyal, hardworking directors, acting in an honorary capacity, doing their best to keep a football club afloat at considerable personal cost to themselves and their families.

---

10. No further action was taken by the ASC as far as we are aware.

CHAPTER 7

At the expanded shareholders meeting on Tuesday May 28, I asked members not to talk to the press when they left. Someone left the meeting early, came back in and said that the television cameras were waiting outside. Elaine Findlay and I were the last to leave. Jim Wilson from Channel 7 was waiting for us and although I said nothing, the meeting was widely reported in the papers the next day including pictures of me getting into my car saying 'No comment.'

When Elaine counted the proxies the next day, we had about 70% of the issued shareholdings in all, and we believed that had we needed to use these proxies, we had more than the 75% needed. Bearing in mind we only required 75% of the votes of people who actually voted. Thinking we needed only 50% of the vote, a newspaper reported that we had received 51% and that became the accepted figure by the press.

Negative Fitzroy stories began to appear in the newspapers regularly. We believed that someone from the Brisbane Bears had leaked details of our finances to Stephen Linnell of *The Age*, which they had been advised of during our discussions with Brisbane.

Now threat of finance probe
Stephen Linnell
The Age

Merger mind games can shred a flag
Patrick Smith
The Age

Share bid by Roys fans
Stephen Reilly
The Age

Ex-Lion hits out at his old club
Anthony Mithin
The Age

187

In *The Sunday Age* on May 19 under the heading, 'Reported and Missing in Action,' Patrick Smith wrote, 'Both administrations stand guilty of misleading their supporters by denying that talks were in progress. For Hore-Lacy to address the players for the first time about the issue on Thursday night is to treat them with contempt.' The next day, in *The Age*, under the heading 'When Fact Merges with Fiction,' Smith added 'However, we advise against believing any thing football administrators say in the hot bed, that is, merger negotiations.'

No one from Fitzroy had denied merger talks. Only three of our board members, I believe, were aware of our discussions with North Melbourne at the time. John Birt, when asked, said, 'It's the first I have heard of it,' and he was right. He had not heard of it.

I believe the increasing venom shown by some sections of the press was because we did not tell them everything we were doing in relation to the merger, step by step.

The word 'missing' in the headline above referred to the fact that I was not at the Fitzroy-Carlton Centenary Game. I was, in fact, at Warren O'Neale's house formalising the deal.

In fact, everything had finally been revealed in the article appearing in *The Sunday Age* by Rohan Connolly on Sunday, May 12.

On May 30, 1996, under the headline 'Clubs Have No Right to Mislead, Misrepresent,' Patrick Smith accused me of misleading the members. This article is the subject of a defamation action brought by myself against Patrick Smith and *The Age* newspaper. The action has not finalised and I am, at this stage unable to comment further on it.

Not to be outdone by *The Age,* the *Herald Sun* published a story on Friday May 13, 1996 under the heading 'Key Lion Hits Out.' The article referred to Greg Basto, who had been elected to the Fitzroy board at the recent AGM. He had achieved a deal of popularity with the rank and file supporters as a result of the 'Dollar

CHAPTER 7

a Day' campaign in 1994, which became a significant source of income for the club. Basto had, I believe, campaigned for the board position against Robert Johnstone for some time. Unfortunately the directors did not move quickly enough to try to block him. At the last moment the directors and I distributed pamphlets strongly supporting Robert Johnstone but it was too late. Basto emphasised in his campaigning how much he supported me. He supported me to the hilt – so he said – and was going to get the club money… investigate the finances… examine the performance of all directors, all the catchy promises calculated to appeal to the uninformed. The end result was that I got about 98% of the vote and Basto narrowly defeated Robert for the second position.

SPORT

❝ The directors are like rats deserting a sinking ship ❞   ❝ They're all looking after themselves by merging the club ❞

Key Lion hits out

Herald Sun
31/5/96

Right from the start his involvement on the board created problems. Unfortunately, Greg passed away in 1998 and has no opportunity to refute what I say. However, the whole story is not complete without accurate comments, which I attempt to record with some moderation – and with the knowledge that the other directors shared my views.

Basto commenced every board meeting by asking, 'Is the club solvent'? He explained that the ASC had advised him to do this. This led us to suspect that it may have been as a result of an approach by him to the ASC which prompted the raid on May 6. His manner was confrontational and insulting. Without knowing much about the club finances, he set his mind against merging with anyone. He had the simple idea that he could get one thousand people to donate $1000 to Fitzroy and he would get $1 million that way. In the blink of an eye we could multiply this by 5 and end up with $5 million. At one board meeting, he was so insulting to some of the other directors that I had to abandon the meeting. I believe I said words to the effect that I would speak to directors in private. It became almost impossible to hold a board meeting with Greg present. He went on a one-person campaign against the direction the other directors were heading. He started collecting money to save the club. The directors were so concerned about this that we later felt obliged to put an advertisement in the paper stating that no single Fitzroy director had authority to receive money on behalf of the club.

When Basto found out that we were discussing merger, he went on radio attacking me and the board and organised a rally at our home game against Melbourne. He was to speak at half time in the reserves but no one turned up to hear him so he delayed his speech until half time in the seniors.

The *Herald Sun* article reporting his comments featured a photograph of me and contained a number of defamatory allegations against me and the other directors. The two worst two were that, 'The directors are like rats deserting a sinking ship,' and, 'They're all looking after themselves by merging the club.' I have never known a group of people to be more angry than the directors were at Basto's allegations. Instructions to issue a writ on Basto and *The Herald Sun* for defamation was given within hours of the article appearing.

I will not comment on the wild and unfounded allegations in detail except to say the defamation action was settled in mid-1999, after Greg's death, and whilst the details of the settlement must remain confidential, I can say that the directors, including myself, were well satisfied with the outcome. The *Herald Sun* – in June 1999 — published an apology acknowledging that the allegations were entirely without foundation.

CHAPTER 7

> **Fitzroy Football Club**
>
> On May 31, 1996 the *Herald Sun* published an article under the headline "Key Lion hits out".
> The article quoted a Fitzroy Football Club director, Greg Basto, accusing chairman Dyson Hore-Lacy and co-directors of acting in their own interests rather than in the interests of the club in their attempt to bring about a merger between Fitzroy Football Club and another AFL club.
> The *Herald Sun* never intended to endorse these comments and accepts that they were without foundation. The *Herald Sun* apologises to Dyson Hore-Lacy and the other directors and their families for any hurt they suffered as a result of the article.
>
> Herald Sun
> 25/6/96

I believe the directors of Fitzroy did more than anyone could ever ask for the football club. Whilst this book is not intended to be a justification of our actions it is fair to point out that most of the director's lent money or gave sponsorship to the club over the years. Most of the directors incurred personal liability for taxation debts and had been working under threat of legal action from the AFL and other sources for years, not to mention the ASC investigation.

Chapter 8

Brisbane's reaction to the North Melbourne-Fitzroy merge announcement was to plead its cause through sympathetic reporters in the press.

Members still have say over deal
MERGER SNAG
Daryl Timms and
Michael Horan
Herald Sun
25/6/96

Roys fans 'silenced'
Daryl Timms
Herald Sun
30/5/96

Both North Melbourne and Fitzroy sent explanatory letters to their members. I asked to be allowed to mention details of the provisional agreement in my letter to members. North Melbourne would not permit it. It was almost universally accepted by the general public that Fitzroy was going to get the bum end of the deal, despite my continued public claims that the arrangement was equal. North Melbourne-Fitzroy Kangaroos was the name generally accepted by the press as the proposed name of the new entity.

CHAPTER 8

The letter I sent to the members read:

Dear Member/Shareholder,
It may be that in the next month or so the Fitzroy members/shareholders will be asked to give their approval to a joint venture with the North Melbourne Football Club.
...
There is no doubt that the AFL policy and philosophy is directed towards the reduction of the number of Melbourne clubs.
...
The directors believe that the overwhelming majority of our members/shareholders would rather us merge with a Melbourne club than an interstate club. Brisbane is, once again, campaigning through the press, with the assistance of 'on side' reporters, to merge with us. Whilst the Brisbane offer has some superficial attractions, the directors have formed the view that the North Melbourne proposal is far superior.
...
The directors believe that North Melbourne is probably the most progressive club in the competition. North Melbourne and Fitzroy have strong similarities historically, geographically and culturally. We believe that the union of the two clubs will not only keep the identity of both clubs, but will lead to the development of a very strong club that will never again be under threat.
...
Yours sincerely,

Dyson Hore-Lacy
(Chairman – Fitzroy Football Club Ltd)

In late May 1996, Mike Sheahan published an article which, for the first time, set out key details of the merger. In particular the article referred, to the real proposed name, Fitzroy-North Melbourne Kangaroos. After the Sheahan article came out, North Melbourne supporters and people in the media who had predicted that we would get very little out of the deal started to kick up a fuss about the Fitzroy name being mentioned first. *Footy Show* comedian and North Melbourne supporter, Trevor Marmalade, being part of a show that had fired cheap shots at Fitzroy all year was outraged that North Melbourne was going to merge with us. Malcolm Blight, former North Melbourne champion footballer, Brownlow Medallist and coach, was publicly condemnatory of Fitzroy having the first name. Everybody in Melbourne seemed to support mergers – unless it involved their club, at the mere hint of which they were up in arms!

Roys tell: Why Roo bid's better
Mike Sheahan
Herald Sun
29/5/96

On Friday, June 14, Elaine Findlay and I attended a meeting with Ron Casey, Peter De Rauch, Greg Miller and Ken Montgomery at Arden Street. At this meeting we came to a final agreement concerning shareholdings, how long the agreement would last, and the circumstances in which key conditions could be changed. A draft document recording our completed agreement was delivered to my home on that Friday night after it had been drawn up by the lawyers.

The next day, all the directors except for Greg Basto had lunch at David McMahon's spacious home in Templestowe where Elaine, Colin and I wished to informally canvas the views of the others. Whilst we were there we went through the draft document in detail. There were a few minor queries but all the directors were, in the circumstances, extremely happy with the deal.

On June 18 I attended a meeting with Graham Sherry, the solicitor acting for Nauru, at the offices of Baker and McKenzie. Sherry, now sits on the AFL Tribunal. The offices of Baker and McKenzie were situated high in the Rialto Building with a beautiful view over the city. The purpose of this meeting was to try to settle

CHAPTER 8

the Nauru debt. Sometime into the meeting we were joined by a litigation solicitor with Baker and McKenzie. An offer of $350,000 had been earlier made to Nauru on the advice of all the legal people. Sherry wondered – with some justification – why the secured creditor, Nauru Insurance Corporation, should take less than 100 cents in the dollar when the other creditors would end up getting paid in full.

I told Graham that we would pay them $550,000 out of the merger money and that I believed we may be able to get the AFL to put in another $200,000 making a total of $750,000. The amount of $550,000 was all I was authorised to offer Nauru by North Melbourne. I told Graham that we would not be able to merge if we had to pay Nauru Insurance Corporation more than that amount.

This was the case. North Melbourne wanted as much money as it could get out of the deal, which was understandable, and what had to be paid to Nauru would obviously effect the final balance available to the merged entity. We owed Nauru $1.25 million plus a small amount of interest. Our accounting advice was that if we paid them $1 million dollars immediately that would be the equivalent of meeting our obligations under the contract in full. I allowed Sherry to talk with John Stewart, one of our finance directors, concerning our finances. Nothing definite was determined at that meeting. Graham said he would get instructions from his client as to how much money it was prepared to accept. While Sherry sought these instructions, I asked Jeff Browne to see if the AFL would throw in the extra $200,000.

Some time later, we received a letter from Baker & McKenzie saying, in effect, that Nauru would only accept repayment of the total amount including interest.

I went straight from the meeting at Sherry's Office to a meeting which had been arranged between North Melbourne and Fitzroy at Corrs Chambers Westgarth (solicitors) to finally execute the agreed merger agreement document. However, when I got there,

I was told that the meeting had been cancelled.

When I got back to chambers I rang Greg Miller from North Melbourne and asked what the problem was. He said that they had something that they wanted to discuss with us and wanted to meet us later that day. I asked them to tell me over the phone but he was not prepared to do so. Obviously there was a serious problem. That afternoon I met Elaine at the North Melbourne Social Club car park and we joined a meeting with Peter De Rauch, Mark Dawson and Greg Miller. Ron Casey was not there, as he was recuperating in Queensland.

Greg Miller started the meeting by talking about the importance of the name to the North Melbourne supporters and how many members were opposed to it. I cut him short and said 'Okay, cut the crap, what's the bottom line.' He said that the merger wouldn't go ahead unless it was called the North Melbourne-Fitzroy Kangaroos and that was final.

I felt like walking out. They had to have the name first. They had to have the logo. They had to have the home ground and they would eventually have the coach, the captain and everything else which was important to them. However, as a compromise they did say that they may agree to put the Lion logo on the jumper. We told them that we were not going to change the agreement that we had. All the work we had put in looked like being for nothing. We knew that Fitzroy supporters and the world would see such an arrangement merely as a take-over, more than a merger. More importantly, this brought the Brisbane Lions offer back into focus. By comparison it was not so unattractive as it looked previously. Elaine and I left the meeting feeling extremely depressed.

On Thursday, June 20, we had a board meeting at the Fitzroy Club Hotel administration office. The new North Melbourne proposal was discussed in detail and rejected. Whilst we were there however, Bill Atherton, Peter De Rauch's friend and accountant, faxed us another suggestion from North Melbourne.

Peter De Rauch, I am sure, was upset at the turn of events.

CHAPTER 8

When our board rejected the North Melbourne-Fitzroy Kangaroos it resolved, however, that it may accept a number of alternatives: Fitzroy-North Melbourne Kangaroos and North Melbourne-Fitzroy Lions would have been considered. So would have North Melbourne-Fitzroy United. During discussions, the possibility of North-Fitzroy Kangaroos was raised and the consensus was that we could probably live with that.

A further meeting with North Melbourne was organised for Sunday, June 23. I did not see any point in attending. Peter De Rauch, Greg Miller, Elaine Findlay, Mark Dawson, Warren O'Neale and Colin Hobbs met at Warren O'Neale's home. North Melbourne would not give any ground at all, except as a trade off, Peter De Rauch suggested a corporate logo consisting of a lion and a kangaroo standing holding a football be developed.

The next day I decided to ring the Brisbane solicitor, David Dunn. I told him that I was considering recommending to the board that I put the choice between North Melbourne and Brisbane to the members. I had received a lot of correspondence from members supporting both North Melbourne and Brisbane, however, I believed that most who supported Brisbane believed the joint venture with North Melbourne was more of a takeover. I suggested that if Brisbane was interested, it could put its best offer to us. Next day Dunn rang back and said Brisbane would make an offer but it would not be binding and – for some reason I could never understand – he said that Brisbane was not keen for us to go to the members. I said the only thing that was contemplated at this stage was to give the members a vote on the best deal. Brisbane had been publicly suggesting that I was the one who favoured North Melbourne and that most of the other directors and members preferred Brisbane. I told David Dunn we were not interested in anything other than what I was proposing to him.

Meanwhile North Melbourne was refusing to budge and time was passing.

On Tuesday morning, June 25, I rang Browne and told him what happened with North Melbourne and that we were at a stand-off. He said that we were getting off the rails and said that something had to be done to get it back on. He arranged a dinner between Peter De Rauch, himself and myself that night at Zio Joe's restaurant in East Melbourne.

Over dinner the matter was discussed in detail. When the compromise came, it came very quickly. Jeff Browne was the note taker and facilitator. We agreed on:

1. North-Fitzroy Kangaroos. (The Melbourne part of the North Melbourne had been taken out)

2. The logo for merchandising was to be a kangaroo and lion holding a football together in a shield.

3. As a concession for the dilution of the name the jumper was to incorporate a small gold lion on the left breast.

4. The agreement was to be for at least 20 years.

5. In all other respects the agreement was to stay as was negotiated on the May 11. A rough diagram was drawn of the logo and both Peter and I signed it.

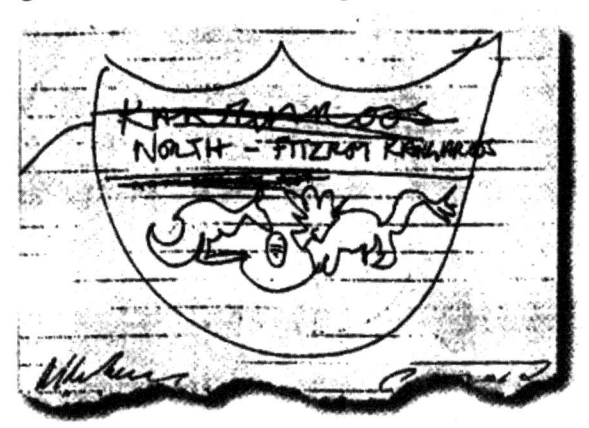

CHAPTER 8

Finally, after nine weeks of negotiating the only problem left – we thought – was settling the Nauru debt, and we did not think this would be difficult.

Time was dragging on. Nauru had extracted an undertaking from the AFL that the AFL would not pay Fitzroy any part of its dividend without giving 48 hours notice. The club was choking to death through lack of money and we were tired of the procrastination. We instructed Jeff Browne to send a letter to Nauru's solicitors giving them 48 hours notice of their intention to send us our dividend which was due. The club could not operate without it.

In return, we received a letter from Baker & McKenzie demanding repayment of their debt before noon Friday, June 28 – or it would send in an administrator. None of the legal advisers thought that Nauru would proceed with their threat to do this. We were told that commercially, it would be the best thing that could happen, as in those circumstances, Nauru would end up with nothing. As a precaution, Jeff Browne faxed Nauru's solicitors a letter to say that the $6 million dollar merger package was no longer open to Fitzroy. This way, it was thought, that Nauru would end up with nothing if it moved in an administrator and therefore would not carry out its threat.

Nevertheless, we were still keen to come to an amicable arrangement with Nauru.

On Wednesday night, June 26, less than 48 hours before Nauru's deadline, I rang Nauru's solicitor Sherry and offered him $550,000 plus $100,000 to be paid over the next two years. This was as much as I was authorised by North Melbourne to offer. This offer was rejected.

On Thursday I spoke to Sherry again and said that I could possibly get them $750,000 by the end of August. He said Browne had already offered that and he had rejected it. I asked him how much he wanted. He said $750,000 by the end of August, and $100,000 in three successive years. Sherry said he had already conveyed this to Browne. I was surprised by this as no one had informed me that Browne was negotiating with Nauru and I certainly did not know that this offer had been made. I suggested $750,000 by the end of August plus $100,000 in the following year. Sherry replied, 'Not enough.' I said I would get instructions for $750,000 by the end of August plus $100,000 a year for two years. I said I would move heaven and earth to get instructions to offer that amount, and he said he would get back to me. To let me know what his client's attitude was to that.

Some time later, Graham Sherry rang me and said he would accept this but with an extra $50,000 in the third year. I told Sherry that I would get further instructions and get back to him. On Friday morning, June 28, I tried to contact Peter De Rauch, but I was told that he was in transit on the way to Western Australia, as North Melbourne was playing the Eagles in Perth. He was booked into the Hyatt and I rang there on a number of occasions leaving messages for him to ring me.

At about 4.00pm I received a phone call from the Fitzroy office informing me that an administrator, Michael Brennan, appointed by Nauru had arrived and was in the waiting area. I said do not do anything yet. I would get back to them as quickly as possible. Finally I managed to contact De Rauch in Perth. Although the administrator was by this time at the club, as yet no damage had been done.

I told Peter I could settle with Nauru for $750,000 by the end of August plus $100,000 for the next two years and $50,000 in the third year. Peter said that was too much. He said Graeme Samuel had rung him from Sydney airport and said that the merger deal would eventually go through on the terms we had negotiated with North Melbourne – but only if North held out against Nauru. If that happened Nauru would get nothing and there would be an extra million dollars available for the merging entities. Peter said North Melbourne were not going any higher than the $550,000 and I was told to withdraw any higher offer I had made to them. I

CHAPTER 8

told De Rauch that this was a huge mistake – and that if North Melbourne put their faith in the AFL, the whole thing would end up in a disaster.

During a number of conversations I had earlier with Sherry on that Friday afternoon, I pleaded with him to accept the $750,000 that Browne had offered them. This was before De Rauch told me to withdraw that offer and to stick with the $550,000. I told him that the AFL would eventually fix them up. I had previously shown Sherry the Brisbane draft proposal whereby it was proposed that Nauru would end up with nothing, and told him, 'You can see what they're trying to do to you!' (referring to the transfer of the licence to the new company) When I rang Sherry back after my conversation with De Rauch, and said I had to withdraw the offer, Sherry said they were going to conduct a press conference at 5:00 p.m. and blow the AFL out of the water.

Of course, all hell broke loose when the administrator officially moved in.

That Friday night going home I heard extravagant claims on the car radio by the administrator, Michael Brennan, regarding Fitzroy's finances. I rang radio station 3AW that night and did an interview and then rang the three major papers and answered questions. John Stewart, our finance director and a leading accountant also rang – we told anyone who would listen what the true situation was.

Brennan was claiming that the debt was $4.5 million dollars! In fact it was about $2.7 million. What he was doing was projecting what our debt would be at the end of the year totally ignoring our future income – including any AFL distribution. This did not paint a true picture.

On the Saturday morning, the appointment of the administrator was headlines. According to all the papers Fitzroy was finished. On that Saturday morning I again rang Peter De Rauch in Perth. I said that the situation was a disaster. I asked him not to go the AFL's way, and rang Graham Sherry at home. I told Graham I would try to get $550,000 by the end of August and $150,000 in the following twelve months and $100,000 in the year after that. This was structured a little bit differently but $50,000 less than Sherry wanted the day before. Sherry said he would recommend it to his client. Finally, there was some movement.

I rang De Rauch. He said that it sounded okay, but that he could not do anything until the Monday when he would canvass the matter with his board. I said, 'I don't believe that. Everyone is putting pressure on us, it's about time we put some pressure on North Melbourne.' I warned him that if he went the AFL way, not only would North Melbourne be getting a shell of a football club, but no director (including myself) would support a new club formed that way. I rang Ron Casey and told him the same thing. I gave him half an hour to accept the deal that Sherry had indicated that he was prepared to accept. Ron rang back and said that North Melbourne could not do anything in half an hour, but they would meet over the weekend. I wanted a quick answer as I wanted to announce the settlement at our chairman's lunch, which I had the unenviable task of hosting. I could never fully understand why North Melbourne's decision making had to be so laborious.

With the benefit of hindsight, it is my very firm belief that North Melbourne may well have been deliberately prevaricating at this stage. They had accepted the AFL's assurance that the AFL would pick up Fitzroy at the end of the year bringing with it the benefit of an extra million dollars. In my conversation with Casey on the Saturday – when I told him that Nauru would accept $550,000 plus $150,000 in the next year and $100,000 in the year after – he asked, 'Why wouldn't they accept that yesterday?' I replied, 'They might have, but you (North Melbourne) wouldn't let us put the offer.' I could not help wondering just how much information Ron was getting at that stage.

On that Saturday, June 29, I did a number of press interviews. I said I was extremely confident that the North-Fitzroy merger would go ahead as planned and I was extremely confident that

CHAPTER 8

Fitzroy would play out the rest of the season. I knew how much it would cost the AFL in money and credibility if Fitzroy stopped playing and I was also, I suppose, relying to some extent on what Peter De Rauch had told me of his conversation with Samuel. Past experience should have taught me to be more guarded.

The next day (Sunday) we arranged an informal emergency meeting at the Victorian Commercial Teacher's Association offices in Hotham Street, Collingwood. In attendance was Robert Johnstone who, although not now a director, was one of the major investors in the Fitzroy Club Hotel. Along with other directors, apart from Greg Basto, we discussed the situation at length. Finally we agreed that we would, if necessary, raise the balance of the money amongst ourselves to pay Nauru an amount that was necessary above the $550,000 that North Melbourne was always prepared (until Friday June 28), to put in. I rang Ron Casey at home to tell him that Fitzroy would make up any shortfall and he seemed to be quite satisfied with this arrangement.

Meanwhile, some of our other AFL 'brother' clubs, Essendon and Richmond in particular, were starting to make noises like 'Why should Fitzroy be bailed out? How much is it going to cost the other clubs?'

An AFL Commission meeting was scheduled for Monday night, July 1, to discuss the crisis. I had not intended to attend but at about 4:30 p.m. Jeff Browne rang and suggested I address the commissioners in person. I rang Ross Oakley, asked if I could attend the meeting and he said he would talk to the commissioners and ring me back. At 6:30, Ross rang back and told me that the Commission would see me. I shot down from work, and about an hour later I was called into the full Commission meeting. I was there for one hour.

I commenced my address by speaking of the hardship North Melbourne and Fitzroy had endured to get to the stage of agreement on every major point. I also told them of all the hurdles put in our path despite the active encouragement of the AFL. I went through the details of the agreement including the sharing of the colours. At this point commissioner Terry O'Connor, former chairman of the West Coast Eagles interrupted and said, 'What's Fitzroy going to have, a little bit of red on the shorts?' There were a number of other questions and comments from the commissioners which gave me the impression that some if not most of them had not the faintest idea of what North Melbourne and Fitzroy had agreed upon or the history of the negotiations.

I found this bewildering as Ross Oakley and Jeff Browne had been aware of the essential details of the merge since early May. During the course of my address to the commissioners I mentioned what Peter De Rauch had told me, that is that Graeme Samuel had promised him that if North Melbourne pulled the plug on Nauru, Nauru would get nothing, North Melbourne would get a million dollars extra and the AFL Commission would deliver the North Melbourne-Fitzroy merger at the end of the season.

Samuel denied this from the outset. He said he did not ring De Rauch at all, but De Rauch rang him. He agreed that there was a conversation but maintained that De Rauch had, in fact, asked him if the commission would guarantee the Fitzroy-North Melbourne merger at the end of the season. Samuel said he had told De Rauch, 'Look, I am just one commissioner, I can't guarantee you anything at all.' Samuel said that Peter had asked him for an indication, but he replied that he couldn't give one. I said, 'All I can say is what Peter De Rauch told me on the Friday and that he (Peter) had confirmed this in a subsequent conversation on Sunday.'

Some months later, Peter told me that there was indeed another conversation on Friday night between Samuel and him after the initial one when Samuel had rung him from the Sydney airport, well after the administrator had moved in, and that Samuel had backed away a little from what he had earlier said, saying things such as he could not guarantee that the commission would deliver at the end of the year. However, Peter said that Samuel left him in

CHAPTER 8

no doubt that the AFL Commission would deliver the merger. Regardless of what the position was, Graeme Samuel was regarded as being easily the most influential commissioner, and anybody could be excused for treating an indication as something stronger.

I relayed the outcome of the negotiations to the commissioners and how we had settled on the name being 'North-Fitzroy.' I remember becoming quite emotional on a couple of occasions.

I told the commissioners that I believed North Melbourne were prepared to pay $550,000 to Nauru and that the Fitzroy directors would find the balance required to settle the Nauru debt.

During the meeting I got the feeling that O'Connor and Samuel were quite hostile to Fitzroy, but that Ross Oakley was supportive. I do not recall John Kennedy, the chairman, saying anything and hardly a word was spoken by Ron Evans or Wayne Jackson. Colin Carter asked some questions and seemed quite interested. Overall, I thought the vibes were bad, although it was impossible to read anyone apart from Oakley, Samuel and O'Connor.

As soon as I left the meeting, I tried ringing Peter De Rauch at home to get him to come in and address the commissioners. I spoke to his wife Patti and she told me that Peter was at the AFL offices. I looked out through the glass door in the foyer, which is where I was ringing from, and there was his large frame just standing there. I got the security man to open the door and let him in.

'We have lost this,' I said. 'Samuel denies the Perth conversation.' I said to him 'Do you want to merge or not?' Peter said yes, so I asked, 'Would you settle the Nauru debt for $550,000 to be taken out of the merger proceeds?' He said 'Yes, that's always been our position.' I said 'Okay, the Fitzroy directors will underwrite the rest, get in and tell them that.' Peter agreed. We walked from the front entrance down to where the commissioners were holding their meeting. I knocked, went in and said that Peter De Rauch happened to be there and that he will agree to Nauru being paid $550,000 out of the merger monies, and asked if they wanted to hear him. They said yes, so Peter went in and I went out. He was in there for twenty minutes to half an hour.

When he came out of the meeting he once again confirmed that North Melbourne were prepared to accept $550,000 out of the merger monies as the figure for the payment to Nauru with the remainder of the debt being paid out of hotel profits. Peter did not require any undertaking or commitment from the Fitzroy directors. He was smiling and made a circle with his thumb and forefinger indicating that everything was okay.

Later on that evening I went home and watched the television, waiting for some news. Robert Johnstone turned up on my doorstep with a bottle of Scotch and we had a quiet drink awaiting the verdict. Sometime after *Talking Footy* had finished at around midnight, Ross Oakley did a live interview, announcing that the Commission had decided that it would be a Fitzroy-North Melbourne merge and we would have five days to complete it. What a relief!

The next morning the *Herald Sun* headlines screamed 'Deadline. Merge by Friday noon or die – AFL', As usual, I did a number of radio interviews.

DEADLINE

Merge by Friday noon or die – AFL

Michael Horan and Daryl Timms
Herald Sun
2/7/96

Friday Lions' new D-Day

Stephen Linnel
The Age
2/7/96

CHAPTER 8

On that Tuesday morning, North Melbourne held another board meeting. One of the North Melbourne people rang me and told me that North Melbourne wanted to meet with me, Elaine and Colin Hobbs that afternoon. I said 'What about?' but he wouldn't tell me. I said, 'You're not going to back down on our agreement, are you?' but he only replied, 'We'll talk about it later.'

I straight away rang Jeff Browne. I said 'I have a gut feeling that North Melbourne are going to go back on their agreement.' Jeff said Greg Miller had already been to the AFL and the AFL told them 'No way.' Jeff suggested I ring Ross Oakley which is what I did. I told Ross about the phone call and that I had an uneasy feeling that North Melbourne was going to back down on our agreement. I said that we needed AFL assistance to make sure that they did not. Ross said, 'They have already contacted me, and I told them where to go.' Ross also said that a couple of commissioners had already rung North Melbourne to tell them that they had to stick to their agreement.

At 3:40 p.m. that afternoon Elaine, Colin, Warren O'Neale and myself met with Peter Johnstone (another North director), Peter De Rauch, Greg Miller and Mark Dawson at De Rauch's Brunswick offices. After waiting for Dawson and Johnstone for about an hour the meeting commenced. We discussed the agreement including questions relating to the staff and players. We also discussed the meeting which we had organised for later on that night with Nauru, plus what would happen with unsecured creditors of Fitzroy, etc. Nothing was said at that meeting at De Rauch's office to indicate that there were any problems or that North Melbourne wished to renege on any points of agreement. We arranged to meet at Mark Dawson's office later that evening to discuss in detail our tactics in relation to attempting to finalise settlement of the Nauru debt at the meeting scheduled for later on that evening.

At 6.30 p.m. we met at Dawson Consulting, Mark Dawson's business, near the Old Melbourne Hotel in North Melbourne.

Greg Miller, Ken Montgomery and Mark Dawson were there representing North Melbourne and Elaine, Colin and myself were representing Fitzroy. Neither Peter De Rauch nor Ron Casey attended. We commenced discussing what sort of arrangement we would offer Nauru.

During the discussions, which were quite amicable, there was a lull. Greg Miller discreetly beckoned me into another room. When we got inside, Greg said that because of the events of the weekend, the current Fitzroy board members were seen by the public to be 'tainted' and that North Melbourne, as a result, wanted fewer Fitzroy board members on the new board. I asked him how many. He said four, half the original number. Greg said to me that I should also reconsider my position as the vice-chairman of the new club for the same reason, that is, that my reputation had been tarnished, and suggested that I consider my position. My ears started burning.

After a pause to compose myself, I replied, 'As far as I'm concerned, I would welcome the opportunity to get out of football. I have only agreed to be part of the new entity because I thought it would help bring Fitzroy supporters on board and I am sure that most of our board members feel the same way. I cannot speak for other directors, but I can tell you one thing, there will be eight Fitzroy directors and there will be a Fitzroy vice-chairman.'

I was seething. Miller and I went back into the meeting. We sat down. I quietly relayed the conversation Greg and I had just had to the others. I could see the look of horror on Elaine's face. Colin was also shocked. Our meeting finished soon after.

As it turned out the Nauru meeting was called off that night because the Nauru delegation had only just arrived in Melbourne and wanted to rest.

I was floored. I felt like I had been hit in the back of the head by a sledgehammer. Looking back on it now, I wonder whether everything that happened between North Melbourne and Fitzroy during the negotiations was not orchestrated to some degree: the

CHAPTER 8

delays, the change in name, the reluctance to pay Nauru more than $550,000 and, finally, this belated attempt to take advantage of our present predicament. A predicament which was, we believed, largely brought on by North Melbourne's reluctance to pay Nauru any more than $550,000.

Next morning, Wednesday, July 3, before the rescheduled meeting with Nauru commenced, I rang Greg Miller. Referring to our conversation the night before, I asked whether the board situation was resolved. He said, 'Yes, we will be having eight Fitzroy directors and eight North Melbourne directors.' Then he added, 'none of the current board of directors will be serving on the board of the new entity'. I quickly said, 'I did not say that would happen, Greg! I can't speak for the other directors. They may or may not wish to be directors.'

I next asked Greg, 'Can you give an undertaking that the agreed position between North Melbourne and Fitzroy would not be changed?' Greg said he couldn't give that undertaking. I said, 'In view of what has happened I want you to undertake that there will be no more last minute changes, and I want your solicitors to give that undertaking as well.' Greg said 'I will have to get back to the board.' I said that I would give him a half an hour to get that undertaking. Greg never got back to me.

At this stage, it seemed quite apparent to Elaine, Colin and me that North Melbourne was going to try to maximise its position as much as possible without too much consideration for us. Whilst the AFL Commission decision to allow us to merge with North Melbourne was a victory for us, we knew the downside was that North Melbourne would see us as being in a corner and may take advantage of the Friday deadline and the fact that there was now no competition from Brisbane. I believe both Ron Casey and Peter De Rauch to be honourable men but we believed that their influence in the whole process had been substantially eroded. As negotiations progressed, Ron, mainly because of ill health, receded into the background as did Peter De Rauch to a lesser extent. In

FITZROY

their places came Mark Dawson and at the last minute, Peter Johstone. Greg Miller seemed to have assumed the leading role in our continuing negotiations.

That morning I spoke to Fitzroy coach Mike Nunan. I gave him my personal support as well as the support of the board and expressed our wish that he continue on as coach should the merger occur. I started to discuss the player lists but he did not want to discuss it at all. In fact, he did not want to discuss anything with me. He said he would sit down and talk to the new entity on Friday.

Later on Wednesday morning, Colin and myself, Peter Johnstone, Greg Miller and Dean McVeigh (the Horwath and Partners solvency expert) met in the offices of Baker and McKenzie. Nauru's solicitor Graham Sherry and Baker and McKenzie's litigation solicitor were also in attendance as well as the new chief executive officer of Nauru Insurance Corporation.

After amicable discussion Nauru indicated it would accept $550,000 paid before August 31, 1996, $350,000 paid before October 31, 1997 and the balance at the rate of $50,000 per year for three years paid by way of sponsorship and signage. A relationship was to develop between North Melbourne and Nauru which would involve visits to Nauru of high profile footballers and a whole host of similar benefits. During the meeting, Greg Miller was continually on the phone attempting to get some sort of authorisation to conclude the agreement. He was unsuccessful but we all left the meeting well satisfied that the great stumbling block, the Nauru debt, was settled. However, we were still concerned about North Melbourne's intentions as far as our 'agreement' was concerned.

A union with Brisbane on favourable terms appealed to many Fitzroy supporters more than being swallowed by a Melbourne club. We did not want to find on Friday, with the deadline approaching, that North Melbourne had backed down on key elements of its agreement and that Fitzroy ended up being merely absorbed into the North Melbourne Kangaroos.

CHAPTER 8

Later on that Wednesday afternoon John Stewart, one of our finance directors, rang. He said Brisbane had been in touch with him sounding him out about the possibility of a Fitzroy-Brisbane merger. John said he told them that there was no chance and that we had completed the deal with North Melbourne. Andrew Ireland, the Bears' chief executive officer, had worked in the past with John when Brisbane was checking our financial situation, and perhaps he saw a possible ally in John. John was loyal to the Fitzroy board, but as an accountant, was probably more concerned with the financial aspects of the merger than were some other directors.

After John told me of the approach, I relayed what had happened with North in the last 24 hours and said, 'Greg Miller had still not given any undertakings as far as our 'agreement' was concerned'. I told John to 'tell Brisbane the door is open half an inch.' Later we were told that, unbeknown to us, whilst this was going on, Brisbane had been heavily lobbying both Michael Brennan, the administrator and the AFL without our knowledge.

That evening, after work, I went around to Colin Hobbs' offices in Fitzroy and from there we went around the corner to Via Volaré in Brunswick Street, with Elaine, for something to eat. We learned that Greg Miller had stated on TV that if the new merged entity could not choose 54 people from the Fitzroy and North Melbourne list, there would be no merge.

This concerned us greatly. We rang John Stewart and told him to tell Brisbane to get ready to make their best offer in case the North Melbourne-Fitzroy deal fell over.

No one from North Melbourne had ever consulted us concerning their insistence on a 54 player list! Whilst the choice of 54 players was in accordance with the AFL stated policy on mergers issued the year before, a number of Melbourne-based clubs had been expressing disquiet about this aspect for sometime.

The larger clubs Essendon, Carlton and Collingwood and later Richmond, according to its own assessment, had long complained about their supposed subsidy of the smaller Melbourne clubs and had from to time to time urged merger on them. But when push came to shove, some of the larger clubs seemed more concerned about a new 'Super Club' forming which might turn out to be more powerful than their own. The attitude seemed to be, we want you to merge, as long as you do not become as strong as us!

No compromise say Roos
Stephen Linnell
The Age
4/7/96

Super team fears grow
Mike Sheahan
Herald Sun
3/7/97

Clubs have every right to be suspicious
Patrick Smith
Herald Sun
3/7/96

Merger in doubt as clubs hesitate
Stephen Linnell
The Age
3/7/96

MERGE DOUBT
Herald Sun
3/7/96

Clubs' warning to AFL

CHAPTER 8

Leon Daphne, the Richmond president, was at the forefront of the AFL resistance to the 54 player request. Leon had always reserved Richmond's position concerning benefits flowing to two AFL clubs which merged. He organised a meeting of AFL club presidents for Thursday afternoon, July 4, at Punt Road oval. As a matter of courtesy, Leon invited me to attend, although, since the administrator had assumed control, I had limited or no legal standing at Fitzroy.

Miller's 'no 54 players, no merge' comment, gave us even more reason to fear the worst as far as a North Melbourne-Fitzroy merge was concerned – or was it merely a bluff?

It was obvious to us that North Melbourne was running its own race at this stage. We could not understand why Miller insisted on an extra 10 players, bearing in mind the limitations of the salary cap, and bearing in mind it was our understanding that the list would have to be reduced to 44 in the following March, in any event. North Melbourne, it seemed to us, was playing a most dangerous game of brinkmanship.

Commencing Wednesday night, through the next day, Brisbane faxed renewed offers to Colin Hobbs' office which kept upping the offer. This included a new offer of fifty cents in the dollar for shareholders.

Next morning all the directors (with the exception of Greg Basto) met at the Victorian Commercial Teacher's Association headquarters for breakfast. This was D-Day. The presidents were to meet at 2:00 p.m. at Richmond and after that meeting, all going well, the AFL Commission would meet to sanction the merger. After we finished a breakfast of orange juice and toast, our finance directors, John Stewart and Kevin Ryan, went through all the figures and projections on a whiteboard which was set up in the boardroom.

We worked all through the morning and through lunch. We analysed both the North Melbourne offer and the Brisbane offer. At that stage, the Brisbane offer was substantially more than the

North Melbourne offer in monetary terms and that was something we had to consider. We were also company directors as well as football club directors and legally we would have had a lot of difficulty choosing a path which meant creditors would be paid less than if we chose the other path.

The directors, including John Stewart, were unanimous in their choice of North Melbourne over Brisbane as a merge partner but we obviously had to consider the financial aspects. In the end, we concluded that the North Melbourne offer would allow all creditors to be paid with a shortfall of only $100,000. Elaine and I, as directors of Bondborough Pty Ltd which held the hotel licence, agreed that this shortfall would be made up by the hotel forgoing $100,000 of the $550,000 debt the football club owed it. As Bondborough directors, we justified this on the basis that a Brisbane-Fitzroy merger would be such a disaster that the hotel may lose much more. This line of thinking proved to be correct as it eventually turned out – the hotel received only 27 cents in the dollar in the administrator's final wash up.

The hotel was becoming a key factor in the negotiations. Some months earlier I met with Bernie Ahern, our White Knight and a very astute businessman, to discuss concerns the directors had with the running of the hotel. We were not making as much money as we should have and there was no one on the board, since the retirement of publican Peter Mitchell, to keep an expert eye on the business.

Bernie took me to meet the 'Pokies King of Melbourne,' Bruce Mathieson. Initially, all we wanted was for Mathieson, with his vast expertise and resources, to help us with the running of the hotel. Bruce had his people look at the hotel and he concluded what we had always felt, that the hotel had excellent potential but it needed $1 million spent on it to turn it into a first rate venue. Mathieson and Bondborough entered an agreement whereby his group would refurnish the hotel and would run it for us. As part of the deal we did with Mathieson, we exercised an option to

CHAPTER 8

purchase the freehold on his behalf so that he now owned the freehold and we would agree to enter into a new lease for the expiration of our term (sixteen years). Projections from the Mathieson Group was that the new business would earn us approximately $500,000 per year.

Initially, the hotel formed no part of our discussions with North Melbourne but during the morning of July 4 we had inserted in our agreement with North Melbourne, with North Melbourne's consent, that any profits from the hotel could be used to pay off creditors of Fitzroy Football Club. During that Thursday morning we were in continual discussions with the North Melbourne solicitor handling the matter, Richard Lustig from Corrs Chambers.

On the morning of July 4 Footscray made an application in the Supreme Court for an injunction to stop Fitzroy from merging, claiming that it had an occupancy agreement with Fitzroy to play games for a number of years at the Whitten oval.

Although the application for an injunction failed, Footscray continued its action against Fitzroy (or the administrator of Fitzroy) and later settled out of court for an undisclosed amount.

Sometime during the morning of July 4, Jeff Browne rang. He said the AFL had canvassed the AFL clubs and there was no doubt that we would get rolled on our request for 54 players. He said we should drop it to 44. I conveyed this information to Ken Montgomery and Greg Miller. Later on that morning Jeff rang me and said that the North Melbourne-Fitzroy merger would be the only merger tabled for discussion that evening. If that merger was defeated it would give an opportunity to Brisbane to do something with Fitzroy on the Friday morning. Jeff suggested that we might like to take the Brisbane option now as, 'You wouldn't want to be seen as taking second best' in the event that the North Melbourne-Fitzroy merger was defeated. I told Jeff that we had settled with North Melbourne.

I then rang Greg Miller and asked him if his threat the night before concerning the 54 players was serious. Greg *ummed* and *aahhed* and really did not answer the question. I informed Greg of the information that had been passed on to me from Jeff Browne and advised him to lower his demands. This time, for the first time, I could detect some anxiety in the way Greg was talking. He told me that he had discovered that Brisbane was back in the game. From that point in time we settled the niggling bits of our negotiations with North Melbourne very quickly.

Although we had a provision in our 'original agreement' that the new jumper would combine the colours of both clubs we were told by one of our supporters, who claimed to have rung North Melbourne pretending to be a supporter, that he was told that Fitzroy representation on the jumper would be minor compared to North Melbourne's. I said to Greg that we wanted a stipulation in the final agreement that the colours of both clubs would be represented in approximate equal proportions. Greg said 'What, is this something new is it?' I said 'No Greg, it is within the spirit of what was initially agreed upon and what we were prepared to trust you on. In light of what has happened we want it in black and white.'

Greg agreed to the new provision without argument. Later on that morning Ken Montgomery, the former North Melbourne chief executive officer and current financial controller arrived at the VCTA offices to be on hand to assist with the final settlement of our agreement with North Melbourne which we wanted to complete (and which we in fact did complete) before the presidents meeting later on that day and before the AFL meeting. Ken is a gentleman and a thoroughly decent person. I said to him that our directors were extremely disappointed about recent events and that it may help if he said something to them. I was referring, of course, to Greg Miller's attempt to change the agreement. Ken agreed and addressed the Fitzroy directors who were present. He apologised for what had happened. He said all the North Melbourne directors were very decent people and they were just trying to do what was best for their club as they saw it.

CHAPTER 8

It was an extremely emotional moment, and largely because of Ken's sincerity I believe most of our directors, if not all, were prepared to put what had happened behind them. When final settlement of our agreement with North Melbourne was reached, it was almost 2.00pm. We now had a formal document, registering the proposed merger in fine detail – after almost two months of negotiations. All that was needed were signatures.

There was nothing more to do except to get the AFL club presidents' blessing, the AFL's blessing and to sign the agreement on Friday morning. The Nauru debt had been settled, we were told, and there were no more hurdles to jump.

Somebody organised some sandwiches for lunch. I had a quick bite and after grabbing Colin's mobile phone, I shot off down to Richmond Football Club offices where the AFL presidents meeting was to be held, with Colin driving. On the way one of our key supporters rang and offered to put in $250,000 himself to help with any financial shortfall if it was needed.

When we got to the Richmond Football Ground, the place, was under siege from reporters and photographers.

I finally found my way into the meeting room at which time proceedings were just about to commence. One of the issues that had surfaced in recent days, fuelled by the reported grumbling of some AFL clubs, was whether the AFL should use any money at all to pay Fitzroy creditors including Nauru. As soon as I arrived at the meeting I said to Dawson and Miller, 'You've got to up the financial offer to match Brisbane's.' I also told him that one of our supporters was prepared to throw in $250,000 to help bridge any gap if necessary.

Leon Daphne opened the proceedings and the presidents were then addressed by Michael Brennan, the administrator. He informed everybody of what he would do if the AFL just cut its losses with Fitzroy and left Nauru and other creditors lamenting. One of the courses he threatened was to sue the AFL for conspiracy! I believe this threat related to the previous plan, documented in writing, by the AFL to transfer Fitzroy's licence to a new company thereby leaving all creditors, including Nauru, lamenting.

After Brennan spoke, Ross Oakley addressed the gathering. He went through the facts and figures, including that the AFL would lose more financially if Fitzroy did not play out the rest of the season than if it was underwritten by the AFL for the remainder of the year. He also referred to the huge loss of credibility for the AFL during this, the Centenary Year, if Fitzroy folded halfway through the year. Oakley's strong recommendation was that the AFL support Fitzroy for the remainder of the season. When a vote was taken it was unanimous to keep Fitzroy playing for the rest of the year. We were over the first hurdle!

Then began the discussion concerning the Fitzroy-North Melbourne merger. Mark Dawson and Greg Miller were representing North Melbourne. The other clubs spoke against the new entity on the basis that they did not agree with North's demand for a list of 54 players. Brisbane's Noel Gordon spoke up, saying that it was prepared to take only 44 players. Gordon informed the presidents of some aspects of the Fitzroy-Brisbane proposal – but left out key elements. He said a number of Fitzroy directors favoured the Brisbane deal. When I was allowed to speak, I said that was totally untrue. I said the directors were unanimously behind the North Melbourne-Fitzroy deal. I said at some stage a director or directors had expressed a concern because the North Melbourne-Fitzroy deal may not have paid off all creditors, whereas the Brisbane deal may have appeared financially more favourable. But, apart from that, the directors were unanimously behind the North Melbourne proposal.

It had been a long day already, and I feel I did not do justice to the situation when I spoke.

Eventually a straw vote was taken. The vote was unanimous against the North Melbourne-Fitzroy merger except for North Melbourne's solitary vote in favour. Brennan, as Fitzroy's Nauru-appointed administrator, did not vote. Then, and only then, did

CHAPTER 8

Greg Miller say that he was prepared to reduce the player request from 54 to 44, the same as Brisbane. There was then some general discussion as to whether this would be acceptable, at which point, an AFL club director said 'Just a moment, you (North Melbourne) have had your turn, now we'll discuss the Brisbane-Fitzroy merger.'

This turn of events was our worst fear. Even though we had been told that only the North Melbourne-Fitzroy merge would be on the agenda, we understood how the AFL worked, and how quickly things could change in this sort of situation.

I was immediately fearful that there would be a vote taken then and there on Brisbane's offer, with Fitzroy thereby consigned to Queensland. At some stage St Kilda's president, Andrew Plympton, who I had always regarded as one of the more astute presidents, suggested that the question of which club Fitzroy merged with should be sorted out between the administrator and the AFL Commission. Most agreed with this suggestion and the meeting concluded. The presidents then meandered over to AFL headquarters at the MCG and I followed, one of the last to arrive. When I got there people were standing around in huddles. Ron Casey was there by the time I arrived. Noel Gordon from Brisbane was also there with Andrew Ireland and their solicitor, David Dunn.

Negotiations seemed to go for hours. I was approached by no one at all to canvass the views of either myself or the other Fitzroy directors. At some stage Ron Casey told me that North Melbourne had now matched Brisbane's financial offer. Before then, it was nearly a million dollars short. This fact would later assume great importance.

I got to work on the mobile phone and rang VCTA headquarters where the directors were waiting. I told them that the financial offers were now equal. I asked Elaine Findlay to confirm that the choice for North Melbourne was unanimous. This was done and conveyed to me. I went up to Ross Oakley and informed him of this. He did not seem to be interested at all. At this stage I may well have been an insect on the wall as far as anyone at AFL House was concerned. On that fateful evening, I do not recall ever feeling so irrelevant – nobody seemed at all interested in the views of the Fitzroy directors about the future of their club. It was quite obvious that a decision was going to be made solely on what the AFL considered to be in its best interests.

After what seemed like hours, the North Melbourne delegation was called into the AFL boardroom to receive the verdict from the commissioners. A short time later they came striding out.

I was standing on my own near the foyer and as the North Melbourne contingent swept past me heading for the exit doors. Ron just uttered the words 'We've lost.'

Ron Casey later told how, after the decision was made to merge Fitzroy and Brisbane, he asked John Kennedy why the AFL Commission had gone the way of Brisbane. John said, 'For strategic reasons, Ron.'

Casey thereupon withdrew from the race and the North Melbourne contingency left hurriedly. In hindsight, this was a tactical mistake. With North Melbourne having withdrawn, there remained, only one offer on the table and only one offer to go before the AFL presidents. Had North Melbourne stayed and put its case to the AFL Commission, it is conceivable although unlikely, that the club presidents would have backed North Melbourne. The meeting of AFL presidents was reconvened as soon as North Melbourne departed as under the Articles of Association of the AFL they had to sanction the merger deal. The only deal which was put to them was the Brisbane-Fitzroy proposal and that was, I am told, unanimously passed.

It was finished. After all our efforts, we were finished.

After the North Melbourne contingent left, I rang through and David McMahon and Colin Hobbs came down to the MCG to pick me up. To avoid the press I went a circuitous way to the members area where David finally found me. It was a forlorn trio which proceeded back to Collingwood.

We all went from there to the Office Inn Hotel where we

CHAPTER 8

watched the quartet of Oakley, Daphne, Gordon and Brennan giving a press conference, sitting side by side, and (it seemed to many Fitzroy supporters), gloating at Brisbane's triumph. Gordon was throwing his head back and laughing and saying things like, 'It's never over until the fat lady sings.' Certainly not with the AFL, I thought.

Later on, Gordon appeared on the Channel 9 *Footy Show*. In the space of about five minutes he single-handedly lost most of Fitzroy's supporters with what many thought were arrogant and insensitive comments. When asked about the approaching Fitzroy versus Bears' game, he declared, 'It'll be a percentage booster for Brisbane.' The Fitzroy supporters were devastated. Ron Casey was also devastated. He was interviewed in a live cross on the *Footy Show* and, given that he was not in the best of health anyway at that time, he looked terrible.

The Fitzroy directors hope that history remembers the deal done between the administrator, Michael Brennan, and the AFL on the night of July 4, 1996, as one of the most cynical and insensitive acts ever perpetrated in the history of sport. The decision was made with, it seems, little consideration at all given to the supporters and members of a club which moved the motion to form the VFL (the forerunner of the AFL) a century earlier, and a club which had won eight premierships. A founding member of the competition – and its supporters – was obliterated by the stroke of a corporately-driven pen. The motive, I suppose, was to give Brisbane a Melbourne supporter base, not to mention a boost of at least three million dollars. The roll call of AFL commissioners that evening was John Kennedy, Ross Oakley, Graeme Samuel, Ron Evans, Terry O'Connor, Colin Carter, Wayne Jackson and Ian Collins (who was a non-voting commissioner).

The AFL's decision on the Fitzroy-Brisbane-North Melbourne saga would eventually come home to haunt it in the form of the spectacularly unsuccessful (and harmful) Hawthorn – Melbourne merger attempt later on that year. In view of the way that the AFL

FITZROY

handled these two merger attempts it is difficult to see how any two Melbourne Clubs could ever succeed in merging in the future.

> **❛ We are delighted to announce ... a merger relationship with the Brisbane Football Club and the Fitzroy Football Club. ❜**
>
> Ross Oakley
> Chief Executive, AFL
> The Age
> 5/7/96

THE FITZROY CRISIS RESOLVED

AFL clubs ensure Brisbane coup

Grantley Bernard
The Australian
5/7/96

Lions for Brisbane in shotgun merger

Malcolm Conn
The Australian
5/7/96

WHAT SAID

So the clubs were worried about a North-Fitzroy super club, but didn't express the same dislike for a Brisbane-Fitzroy union. Strange.

Jokes leave sour taste

Mike Sheahan
Herald Sun
6/7/96

❛ What we needed were unequivocal assurances Fitzroy was a desired partner.
We said – edited by Mark Robinson

The Centenary Balls-up

Rohan Connolly
The Age
9/1996

Chapter 9

Early next morning, after a very poor night's sleep, I rang the 3AW breakfast show. Ross Stevenson put me on straight away and I delivered a monologue for about 10 minutes on the history leading up to the merger, and in particular the AFL's involvement. There was not one word of interruption.

Lions were 'shafted': Hore-Lacy

Stephen Linnell
The Age
6/7/96

I went into work and later on that day rang Rod Nicholson from *The Sunday Herald Sun* intending to give him the story leading up to the events of the previous day. He was not there, so I left a message. There was no reply. Later I rang again and left another message. Time was running out so I rang Rohan Connolly from *The Sunday Age* who, like Rod Nicholson, was a very well-respected journalist. Rohan was in the office and we arranged to meet on Saturday afternoon for the purpose of doing a story for the *Sunday Age*. Not all of the press had a negative attitude towards Fitzroy, there were some journalists who were very supportive of us.

On Saturday July 6, I went to the Fitzroy game at Optus Oval where we were playing Melbourne. I arrived unannounced at the 3LO broadcasting box at about 12:30 p.m. Ace caller and commentator Tim Lane, together with Peter Booth and others looked a little surprised to see me but they put me on. Whilst I was being interviewed Tim Lane had Graeme Samuel on another line.

He said 'Graeme, I have got Dyson Hore-Lacy here and you were not aware of that when you agreed to do the interview. If you both would like to be interviewed together I would be happy to do that, or if you would rather not, then in fairness to you, you don't have to.' Samuel declined. My microphone was switched off at the time and I simply said, 'Won't get into the witness box, eh?' This comment, I was told, actually found its way on to the airwaves.

After I completed the interview with Tim Lane and 3LO I went into the ground and watched the game from the outer until half time when I went down to *The Sunday Age* offices to be interviewed by Rohan Connolly.

Whilst I was at *The Sunday Age* I detailed to Rohan the proposal of the AFL to cut off Nauru, and all other creditors, by transferring the licence from one entity to another. Rohan had a *Sunday Age* journalist put what I had said to Oakley who was at the MCG watching the football. I was told that Oakley denied it, saying that the AFL always intended that Nauru be paid out of the proceeds of the merger monies. A very fine article appeared the next day in *The Sunday Age* setting out the history of what had occurred including the AFL's hand in it.

Secret Lions deal
Rohan Connolly
Sunday Age
7/7/96

Lions chief says it's time for the truth
When the dust settles it won't be pretty
Rohan Connolly
Sunday Age
7/7/96

AFL plan to abandon creditors
Rohan Connolly
Sunday Age
7/7/96

CHAPTER 9

Fitzroy people were devastated by what happened. Shortly after July 4 Brisbane organised a public meeting in the Dallas Brooks Hall in an attempt to sell the 'merger'. Hundreds of people turned up to hear a number of people speak in favour of the deal done by the administrator, the AFL and Brisbane. I did not attend but Colin Hobbs did. When Brisbane again falsely stated that some Fitzroy directors favoured the Brisbane option, Colin took the microphone to refute this. He said 'either name the directors or withdraw the allegation because it is nothing but a bloody lie'. There was no response. This comment of Colin's was given wide television coverage.

The meeting was rowdy with a vast majority of people expressing opposition to the deal that had been done. The pity of it all was that a number of Fitzroy stalwarts who did attend were clearly not aware of the true story of what had happened.

North were also stunned by the chain of events. On July 1, North Melbourne and Fitzroy had been told that they had until Friday, July 5 to merge. On Thursday, before the deadline, the AFL and the administrator merged Fitzroy with Brisbane. The Fitzroy directors could not take action on behalf of Fitzroy because once the administrator moved into the club, he assumed all the powers of the Fitzroy board.

North Melbourne was in a different position however. We attempted to convince the North Melbourne directors to take legal action under S.52 of The Trade Practices Act for alleged deceptive and misleading conduct.

BITTER ROOS
'We have no faith in AFL'

Daryl Timms
Herald Sun
5/7/96

FITZROY

Part of the agreement Brennan had signed with the AFL was that Fitzroy would not take legal action against the AFL – this is what has stopped Fitzroy suing the AFL to this day. North Melbourne were not in the same position, however, so a meeting was arranged in the chambers of Cliff Panham, QC for Monday, July 15.

Present were Ron Casey, Mark Dawson, Peter de Rauch and myself. Everything was canvassed and a written opinion was delivered later that day. North Melbourne, in the end, chose not to take legal action but requested substantial compensation from the AFL which, I was later told, was paid without argument.

Relations between the Fitzroy directors and Michael Brennan were very, very cool. Brennan was a key player in the merger with Brisbane which was contrary to the unanimous wishes of the Fitzroy directors, who had, after weeks of negotiations, come to a binding and satisfactory agreement with North Melbourne. An agreement which, we believed, would have seen Nauru satisfied and all creditors paid in full. Brennan was involved in a commercially pragmatic arrangement with the AFL which not only affected Fitzroy creditors but was we believed, contrary to the wishes and interests of the vast majority of Fitzroy members, shareholders and supporters.

Brennan arranged a meeting at the offices of Ernst and Young on Wednesday, July 10, 1996. Also present, apart from all of the Fitzroy directors, were a couple of Ernst and Young accountants: Greg Swan, a principal in Ernst and Young, and Mark Sheeds, an executive director of the corporate and solvency department.

We all assembled in one of the boardrooms. Brennan opened the meeting by saying he wanted to discuss items on a previously distributed agenda. He did not want the meeting to be an adversarial situation, but he said that he was 'here to stay.'

Speaking on behalf of the other directors (except Basto), I said we had all 'come to listen' and that was all.

Brennan said that they had formed an advisory committee of

CHAPTER 9

management with himself as chairman, an AFL commissioner, and John Birt, our former CEO, on it. He said they wanted the directors to be represented on the committee.

'Anyone interested in joining the advisory committee'? he asked. Silence.

He continued, 'I would now like a list of the people who would be interested in attending the chairman's lunch for away games.' Once again, silence.

Undeterred he continued, 'I would now like a list of directors interested in attending home games?' There was a silence for a while until Colin Hobbs, much to everyone's surprise, said 'Yes, I may very well be interested in that.'

Brennan jumped in, 'Well, we can put you down for chairman's lunches for home games, can we?'

'No, I did not say that,' said Colin mischievously, 'I may very well be attending home games, but I certainly won't be going to the lunches, I'll be in the outer.'

For a brief moment, I was tempted to feel sorry for our esteemed administrator.

He had not a clue who any of the directors were, apart from myself. He battled on, no doubt hoping to encourage someone to come on board. He said optimistically 'We already have a group of influential Fitzroy supporters who are interested in becoming part of the Brisbane Lions.' 'Who are they?' somebody asked, as we were not aware of anybody. 'Well, there is Arthur Wilson, George Coates, Laurie Serafini and David Lucas.' Laurie Serafini was a former star Fitzroy player, Arthur Wilson was a former football manager, George Coates had been a former Fitzroy president who had been lobbying on behalf of a Brisbane – Fitzroy merger for some years, and David Lucas was a director of the club some ten years previously.

'Brisbane is anxious to maintain and establish a supporter base in Melbourne, and I as the administrator will support them,' he droned on, adding, 'On Monday, when I took over, I told them that my position was completely independent of Brisbane.' Later, of course, Brennan would sue Elaine Findlay and me in the Supreme Court of Victoria for the lease of the Fitzroy Club Hotel – an action funded by the Brisbane Bears.

Hore-Lacy faces legal action over hotel lease

Malcolm Conn
The Australian
24/7/96

I then asked Brennan if in making his decision he took into account the enormous potential difference between going with the club with the support of all directors, compared to going with the club which had the support of no directors. He gave a non-committal reply. Brennan went on to say that a meeting of creditors would be held on July 25 and that he believed the merger would proceed as a matter of course.

We asked Brennan if it was legally possible to reverse the decision. He said he did not think so. He was going to execute the formal deed with Brisbane and the AFL on Friday, July 12. I asked him if he would defer signing any agreement until the following Monday. He said he would not.

I asked Brennan what would be the position if we found enough money to pay off all creditors 100 cents in the dollar (on July 5 a person from Adelaide had contacted us claiming to be a multi-millionaire offering to pay out all debts. In fact, it came to nothing but at the time we were ready to rely on any ray of hope).

Brennan said that that would not prevent him from signing the document.

Brennan continued, 'Would you be prepared to sign the Deed of Company Arrangement? It is usual for the directors to sign.' We asked him if we had a legal duty to sign. Brennan said no. All

CHAPTER 9

of us then said we would not sign.

Then Brennan raised the question of the hotel. By this time he knew that Elaine and I would not give up the hotel willingly. I had previously written to Brennan telling him that we had no intention of making the hotel part of the 'deal' that he had consummated with the AFL and Brisbane.

Brennan said that Brisbane was prepared to offer $500,000 with another $300,000 paid out of future profits. This offer was conditional upon Bondborough (who owned the hotel lease) letting go the $550,000 debt it was owed by the Fitzroy Football Club. 'It seems like a pretty good offer to me,' said Brennan.

Brennan could not have had much of an idea of the value of the hotel lease. He had not spoken to any valuer or analysed any of the financial figures. At that time we already had a substantially higher offer for the lease and we were later to sell it after fending off his hopelessly doomed court action.

Fitzroy hotel 'mystery' stumps Brennan

Greg Denham
The Age
2/7/96

Brennan went on to say that on his projections the unsecured creditors of Fitzroy Football Club would be paid 60 cents in the dollar. Fifteen months later, however, they were only paid 27 cents in the dollar. We pointed out that with the North Melbourne deal we believed that everyone would have been paid 100 cents in the dollar, but instead he chose to follow a path against the wishes of every director. Brennan did not respond. After some further inconsequential discussion the meeting concluded.

Next day I rang Brennan and said to him, 'Take note that I think it would be legally dangerous for you to enter into a binding agreement with the AFL and Brisbane when it is possible that creditors could be paid 100 cents in the dollar.' I asked Brennan for a copy of the agreement he proposed to sign with the AFL and Brisbane and he assured me that he would send it as soon as possible. This was done.

In fact we had no grand plan to take court action against Brennan. Our legal advice was that our options were extremely limited. We just hoped, if we kept enough pressure on Brennan, that he and the AFL would realise what a hopeless deal they had struck and would reconsider. That was wishful thinking. I was also still hopeful that something might come out of left field which would see the creditors paid 100c in the dollar, which would be an offer the administrator could not refuse, unless he was legally committed to the path he had taken.

On the night of July 15, 1996, I spoke at a supporters' rally organised by two of our keenest supporters, Shane Harrop and Janene Howells. Shirley Hardy-Rix was also involved in the organisation. Greg Miller, Colin Hobbs, Jan Wright and I spoke at the rally and I answered a number of questions. Most of the Fitzroy people, as always, were supportive, except for an abusive handful.

Meanwhile, back on the football field, the team played out the remainder of the year. Completely dispirited it lost every game by large margins.

Michael Nunan resigned as coach. Once again Alan McConnell took over in our hour of need. Part of the agreement struck between Brennan and the AFL was that Brisbane would take at least eight Fitzroy players. Matthew Primus refused to go and eventually finished up at Port Adelaide where he has become the star he was always going to be. Brad Boyd, Simon Hawking, Chris Johnson, Jarrod Molloy, Shane Clayton, Scott Bamford, Nick Carter and John Barker were the players who went to Brisbane. Only Jarrod Malloy and Chris Johnson remain.

Although Fitzroy did not win another game during 1996, large crowds came to farewell us.

The AFL called the new 'Brisbane Lions' a merger between

CHAPTER 9

two clubs, Brisbane Bears and Fitzroy, yet all the football world, it seemed, wanted to farewell Fitzroy. No one thought of farewelling the Brisbane Bears. This was for obvious reasons. Very few believed that what had happened constituted a true merger between the clubs. Another irony was that many more Fitzroy supporters turned up for the last half of the season than at any time whilst I was at Fitzroy. Most were brandishing brand new items of merchandise such as scarves and flags. I could not help thinking that if these people had been as supportive during the previous few years, we might not have been in the predicament we were.

Fitzroy played its last match at Fremantle. That club put on a very moving farewell. When the Fitzroy players left the field a number of them were in tears At a club function in the following week, many of them, if not most, had a tattoo of the Fitzroy lion emblazoned on some part of their body.

Chapter 10

The directors still had not given up hope that we might be able to undo the Fitzroy – Brisbane deal on financial grounds. As an administrator, Brennan's responsibility was to get the best possible deal for creditors. We hoped that he would be forced to accept a better deal for creditors once he realised how mistaken his calculations were.

On Tuesday, July 16, I asked Brennan to tell me exactly what the respective offers were. He said that North Melbourne offered $3.9 million for the creditors (including players). North Melbourne's original offer was for $2.9 million which, according to Brennan, only left $150,000 for unsecured creditors. Brennan said that North agreed to match Brisbane's offer by offering a further million dollars. Some $950,000 was to be for unsecured creditors and $50,000 for Brennan's costs. The North Melbourne offer now totalled $3.9 million.

The Brisbane offer was according to Brennan:

Nauru debt	–	$1,250,000
Liability for the players	–	$1,000,000
Unsecured creditors	–	$1,000,000
To Bondborough (for hotel lease)	–	$ 500,000
(out of future profits)		$ 300,000

This totalled $4.05 million.

The offer also included $300,000 for the administrator's expenses. According to North Melbourne, it was unaware of this item. This made the grand total $4,350,000.

However, Brennan's calculations included the hotel which formed, quite correctly, no part of North Melbourne's offer. Right from the start I had told the administrator that Fitzroy Football Club did not own the hotel lease; it was owned by Bondborough.

CHAPTER 10

Elaine Findlay and I were the sole two directors of Bondborough Pty Ltd, and owned between us four of the five shares. We had no intention of making the hotel part of the AFL and Brennan's deal. Furthermore, Brisbane would have been gaining an asset worth far more than what was offered. If the $800,000 for the hotel is deducted it reduces the Bear's offer to $3,550,000 – $350,000 short of the North Melbourne offer.

During one of my conversations with North Melbourne's Peter De Rauch in the weeks following the 'merger', I asked Peter what North Melbourne's final offer was and he told me. At that stage, I knew what the Brisbane offer was and it was apparent, on De Rauch's figures, that the North Melbourne offer was substantially higher. Greg Miller was later to sign a statutory declaration setting out the terms of what he claimed was North Melbourne's better offer.

I asked Peter if the North Melbourne offer was in writing. He said it was on a piece of paper which was given to Ian Collins, the football operations manager of the AFL. I asked Peter to retrieve the document. Later Peter got back to me saying that the AFL told him that it was lost! The North Melbourne offer was contained on a slip of paper which was handed to Brennan, who then gave it to the AFL.

This as well as other significant matters were raised at the creditors' meeting on July 25, 1996. This was to be a momentous day. If the creditors approved what Brennan proposed, that was effectively the end.

That meeting was tape recorded. I will set out some of the dialogue as it is instructive on a number of levels. The anger and emotion of many of those present almost jumps out of the transcript of the meeting.

Michael Brennan introduced himself as the administrator of the Fitzroy Football Club, Ltd, pursuant to the Corporations Law, appointed by the Nauru Insurance Corporation Pty Ltd on June 28, 1996. His role was to chair the meeting of creditors that would decide Fitzroy's fate. He said the creditors could either liquidate the club, execute a new deed of company arrangement or even end Brennan's administration and return the club to the control of the board.

Among those present at the meeting were various creditors and their representatives; I wanted to know why Ian Collins the AFL football operation manager and non-voting commissioner, and Andrew Ireland Brisbane's executive officer, were present. Brennan explained that the AFL was a creditor for 'unpaid transfer fees' and that earlier that same morning Nauru Insurance Corporation had 'assigned its debt' to the Brisbane Bears.

Next, Brennan acknowledged receipt of the Fitzroy board's official response to his appointment and financial report. Kevin Ryan's letter, on our behalf, pointed out that Brennan included future liabilities, such as player payments, in the balance sheet, but failed to include the coming AFL dividend of $1.3 million. Kevin's view of the club's financial position nominated a deficit of slightly over $2.8 million – so the non-inclusion of the AFL funds made quite a difference.

Brennan then dealt with the history leading up to his appointment. He began with the comment:

'This (his appointment) was not in any way caused by the Australian Football League and I understand that it was as much a surprise to them as it was to the general public.' He added that one of his first acts as administrator was to inform the AFL that, as he was personally responsible for incurring any future liabilities, he 'did not intend to field a team the next day as I had no way of paying the players or any of the costs.'

I objected to the portrayal of the AFL as innocent bystanders, almost victims. I said, 'This is not correct. The AFL were given the same notice by way of documentation that North Melbourne and Fitzroy were given and indeed before you were appointed, I understand, as a ploy the AFL withdrew the $6,000,000 offer for the first two clubs to merge.' I also recounted Peter de Rauch's

CHAPTER 10

claim that an AFL commissioner advised him not to settle with Nauru, saying the merger would be delivered without the need to pay them. I continued to point out the absurdity of Brennan's view that 'it was as much a surprise to them (AFL) as it was to the general public. They were parties, the AFL, to the negotiations from the word go with North Melbourne. They were parties to the negotiations with Nauru, to the offers that were made with Nauru. Their solicitors were privy and cognisant and indeed advising at all stages.'

Peter De Rauch disputed Brennan's claim that the North Melbourne offer was the same as the Brisbane offer. I asked if, having already spelled out the Brisbane offer in fine detail, he would be prepared to specify the North Melbourne offer made on July 4.

Brennan refused, saying only that it was a draft agreement accompanied by 'Words on a handwritten piece of paper which said to the effect, 'We will match the Brisbane offer to provide a million dollars to the unsecured creditors'.' When asked where this piece of paper was, Brennan said it was given to the AFL commissioners. I attempted to find out what had happened to this extremely important document. The following exchange occurred.

MR HORE-LACY: All right. You have spelt out the Brisbane offer in fine detail. Would you please spell out in detail the North Melbourne offer made to you on 4 July.

MR BRENNAN: I'm not able to do that, Dyson, because the North Melbourne offer made to me consisted of a draft agreement which specified a number of matters and words on a piece of paper handwritten which said to the effect, "We will match the Brisbane offer to provide a million dollars for the unsecured creditors."

MR HORE-LACY: Where's that piece of paper and where's the draft agreement?

MR BRENNAN: The draft agreement is in my files. The piece of paper was given to the AFL commissioners and the AFL commissioners returned to me only the successful offer.

235

MR HORE-LACY: Well, the AFL commissioners, they deny that they have got it. Ian Collins, I'm told, denies that he has got it; Ross Oakley denies that he has got it. Would it be all right to ask Ian Collins where that piece of paper is?

MR BRENNAN: Mr Collins, would you like to respond?

MR COLLINS: As far as I know, I don't know where the piece of paper is and it's as simple as that and that has been conveyed to Mr Casey the other day – exactly the same situation. The piece of paper obviously is of concern to North Melbourne and Fitzroy.

MR HORE-LACY: Sorry, I thought the AFL were claiming you had it but that's apparently not true. Is that right, Mr Collins?

MR COLLINS: I don't know. I don't know where the piece of paper is, Mr Hore-Lacy.

MR HORE-LACY: This is the North Melbourne offer, the crucial offer, you have lost it.

MR COLLINS: No, just get your facts right. I am not aware of where the piece of paper is.

MR HORE-LACY: Have you made inquiries?

MR COLLINS: No, I haven't made an inquiry.

MR HORE-LACY: Despite the fact that Ron Casey has been asking you for it.

MR BRENNAN: Dyson, we have made inquiries of Mr Lehman and Mr Collins and they have told us that they cannot find the piece of paper. But let me reiterate that at the Richmond meeting, at the AFL commission meeting, North confirmed to me that they would match the Brisbane offer. Now, I happen to be in the business of occasionally having to sell businesses to deal with matters. This was somewhat of an auction and there's an implication that I didn't accept the highest bid. It's an implication that I utterly refute.

MR HORE-LACY: Mr Brennan, Gregory Alan Miller has signed a statutory declaration which has been distributed to the creditors which says in effect that – and we know this is correct – the initial offer was $2.9 million. They then raised that offer by a

CHAPTER 10

million dollars. They were told that they needed to offer a million dollars to match the Brisbane offer and they then offered another million dollars. Is that correct?

MR BRENNAN: No, sir.

MR HORE-LACY: What's incorrect about that?

MR BRENNAN: At 2.30 p.m. in these offices on 4 July we discussed with the North Melbourne Football Club – Mr Casey and Mr Miller – the fact that we had received a better offer from Brisbane. It is true that they had been talking about offering $2.8 million as Fitzroy's share of the merger proceeds. We informed them that the Brisbane offer provided a pool of funds available to the unsecured creditors of a million dollars.

The North Melbourne people didn't respond. At approximately 4.45 p.m. at the Richmond meeting after the clubs indicated they would not favour a merger with North Melbourne – I suspect principally because of the player concessions sought – they advised the meeting that they would match the Brisbane offer in relation to player concessions and would match the Brisbane offer in relation to providing a pool of funds to the unsecured creditors.

I then attended a meeting at the commission where I was asked to report what had happened and what had transpired and what offers I had received. I was then asked by the AFL commission to go back to both Brisbane and North Melbourne and ask them, 'Is this your final and best offer?' Mr Oakley, I understand, also spoke with both Brisbane and North and reiterated the comments, 'Have you put in your final and best offer?'

MR HORE-LACY: The affidavit by Greg Miller states that at 5 p.m. on Thursday 4 July, Mr Casey signed on a club letterhead a new offer from the North Melbourne Football Club that to 'our best knowledge increased our offer to $3.9 million'. Are you saying that's incorrect?

MR BRENNAN: Yes.

MR HORE-LACY: All right. I have got a note of a conversation I had with you on Tuesday afternoon of 16 July where you said the

North Melbourne offer was $2.9 million. They then agreed to match the Brisbane offer to make available to unsecured creditors a further $1,000,000 taking it to $3.9 million. Now, do you deny that conversation with me?

MR BRENNAN: I can't recall the conversation, Dyson, but I can certainly state that virtually all of the words are what I believe to be the situation, other than taking it to $3.9 million.

MR HORE-LACY: That's perhaps going to be a matter for a civil court.[11] What do you believe the final offer was for North Melbourne then? What did it total? You have got the Brisbane offer set out in fine detail. What did the North Melbourne offer finally total?

MR BRENNAN: $2.8 million plus or – sorry –

MR HORE-LACY: $2.8 million plus what?

MR BRENNAN: Approximately $600,000.

MR HORE-LACY: That's what they offered, $2.8 million plus $600 thousand?

MR BRENNAN: No, that's not what they finally offered.

MR HORE-LACY: Well, what did they finally offer?

MR BRENNAN: They offered to match the Brisbane offer as was outlined by me at the Richmond meeting.

Greg Basto asked in view of the fact that North Melbourne and Fitzroy were given a deadline of twelve noon Friday to merge why there was so much 'indecent haste'?

MR BRENNAN: My position in this matter was that I believed that the league had the power to control the licence. I submitted to the league two offers and if you care to refer to my report you will see that I said to the league, 'In view of all the circumstances I do not mind which merger offer you accept, as long as you accept a merger offer. You should also be aware that if there was no merger there would be no Fitzroy playing on the

---

11. What I had in mind was an action by Bondborough against the administrator. Bondborough received only 27c in the dollar from a debt of more than $500,000 owing to it by the Football Club. We claimed a North Melbourne-Fitzroy merge would have returned 100c in the dollar.

CHAPTER 10

Saturday. I had not an indemnity from the league and therefore I wasn't going to field the team.

MR BASTO: But there was no doubt that there was a merger going to take place. Is a deadline a deadline or is a deadline not a deadline?

MR BRENNAN: Well, I think you should direct those questions to the commission. It was the commission, who's the governing body of the AFL, that made the decision at that time.

MR BASTO: Is your consideration only financial in this matter or do you take into account the people involved, the number of directors involved, where they have got to conduct their business from, or is your consideration just financial?

MR BRENNAN: It's primarily financial.

MR BASTO: Have you taken any of those other things into consideration?

MR BRENNAN: Yes, but you have also got to know that I knew the directors of Fitzroy were talking to Brisbane.

...

MR BRENNAN: Mr de Rauch.

MR DE RAUCH: Right, I just want to clear up a point here for the creditor's sake. I think there has been a total misunderstanding and I think a bit of creative accounting. The North offer on Thursday night was $3.9 million. It was increased by a million. So $3.9 million was the North offer at that night, plus reading your report with a bit of creative accounting you have added the $1.3 million that was coming from dividends from the league onto the Brisbane offer. That was never in our offer because that was automatically to be paid to the players as the season continued. So therefore the North offer, using the same creative accounting and not using your $300,000 fee – our offer then was $5.2 million to the creditors.

MR BRENNAN: Right, well, I think I have already responded to those comments, Mr de Rauch.

MR DE RAUCH: Which means I think that a decision was

made without the correct information. So I really think the creditors should know that the North offer was higher, because you're stating the North offer was $4.5 million because you said it was equal with the Bears, plus the $300,000 for your fee. But the North offer was $5.2 million and then plus your $300,000 so that the North offer was a lot higher and I think that's what the creditors should have accepted.

MR BRENNAN: Excuse me a minute. Right, well, I think we have dealt with that matter considerably. Are there any other questions?

Earlier on, Brennan said he knew the Fitzroy directors were having discussions with Fitzroy. I asked him how he knew the Fitzroy board was holding discussions with Brisbane, and he admitted his knowledge of the Fitzroy merger arrangements had come totally from information supplied by the Bears.

MR HORE-LACY: ... You said that you knew directors of Fitzroy were talking to Brisbane. How did you know that?

MR BRENNAN: I don't think it's my place to tell you the people that were involved.

MR HORE-LACY: Yes, I think it is, because you have been filled up with a lot of misleading facts by Brisbane, I know, and possibly by other parties. I think you should disclose who told you that we were talking to Brisbane.

MR BRENNAN: Well, Brisbane told me that they were talking to Fitzroy.

MR HORE-LACY: All right, and what did they tell you the contents of that conversation was?

MR BRENNAN: That they had reasonable discussions with you, and they have also told me certain facts that could only have come from the then directors of Fitzroy.

MR HORE-LACY: What did they tell you? That's what I'm asking you.

MR BRENNAN: They told me than on the information provided by the directors of Fitzroy, their offer was formulated so

CHAPTER 10

as to pay out all of the unsecured creditors 100 cents in the dollars because Bondborough wasn't going to prove and that the unsecured creditors were only $1.5 million and therefore the $1,000,000 would pay out all the unsecured creditors. That's why their offer features the $1,000,000 and also the proposal that Bondborough wouldn't prove. [12]

MR HORE-LACY: So that's the sum total of the discussions you believe Brisbane had with Fitzroy, is it?

MR BRENNAN: No, Dyson.

MR HORE-LACY: Well, that was the question. What was the content of the discussions you believe Brisbane had had with Fitzroy?

MR BRENNAN: They had had merger discussions.

MR HORE-LACY: What was the context of it?

MR BRENNAN: Simply that. They had discussed merging with Fitzroy, with the Fitzroy directors.

MR HORE-LACY: That's all you have been told, was it?

MR BRENNAN: Yes

MR HORE-LACY: They discussed merging?

MR BRENNAN: Yes

MR HORE-LACY: Well, what do you draw from that?

MR BRENNAN: That the Fitzroy directors were discussing with Brisbane the possibility of a merger.

MR HORE-LACY: But not qualified by any circumstances, such as if the North Melbourne merger fell over in the last moment?

MR BRENNAN: It wasn't of concern to me, Dyson.

MR HORE-LACY: All right, Did you discuss with any Fitzroy director what the attitude of the Fitzroy directors was towards a

---

12. It was never contemplated by the Fitzroy directors that Bondborough would not prove (i.e. put in a claim to the administrator for the money Bondborough was owed by Fitzroy Football Club). First, only Elaine Findlay and I as directors of Bondborough, could come to such a decision, and secondly such a decision would be contrary to our duty as directors of Bondborough Pty Ltd., to act in its best interests.

merger with Brisbane or North Melbourne.

MR BRENNAN: No, Dyson, I didn't. because I knew it implicitly.

MR HORE-LACY: Well, in one breath you say that you knew Fitzroy was having discussions with Brisbane about mergers. Now you say you didn't discuss that with Fitzroy directors because you knew it implicitly. Now, what are you saying you knew implicitly, what the directors' attitude was to a merger with Brisbane?

MR BRENNAN: I didn't say that, Dyson. I knew what the attitude of the Fitzroy directors was to a merger with North Melbourne. I didn't know of their attitude to a merger with Brisbane.

MR HORE-LACY: Well, in that case I wonder why you mentioned the fact that we were having discussions with Brisbane at all about mergers? I mean, that seems to be suggesting that you believe that some Fitzroy directors at least were keen to merge with Brisbane, which was not the case. I will move on to the next question if I may. Did you discuss at any time – bearing in mind I was at the presidents' meeting and at AFL House when this business was going on – did you discuss at any time, with any Fitzroy directors, as to whether or not we had completed an agreement with North Melbourne at that stage?

MR BRENNAN: No, because I knew you had not.

MR HORE-LACY: In fact we had, How did you know we had not?

MR BRENNAN: Mr Casey told me.

MR HORE-LACY: When did he tell you that?

MR BRENNAN: 5(pm) o'clock.

MR HORE-LACY: Well, I can tell you we came to an agreement at about 12 o'clock, as Mr de Rauch will verify, with North Melbourne on every issue. I don't believe you when you're saying Mr Casey told you that they hadn't ageed with us. If he told you that, he was misinformed.

MR BRENNAN: Well, I think we have just got to note that

CHAPTER 10

fact, that Mr Casey and Mr Miller were in my office at 2.30pm and they didn't tell me then they had a done deal. They said, "We still haven't done the deal."

MR HORE-LACY: At 2.30pm. How about at 4 or 5 o'clock?

MR BRENNAN: Well, Mr Miller was still at the meeting. He didn't confirm to me that you had done a deal.

MR HORE-LACY: All right. Is this being recorded, incidentally, what you're saying?

MR BRENNAN: Yes.

MR HORE-LACY: Thank you. Did you speak to anybody about the effect on fundraising and revenue raising of orchestrating a merge with the AFL against the wishes of the Fitzroy directors?

MR BRENNAN: I think I take exception to the word "orchestrating", Dyson.

MR HORE-LACY: Well, that seems to be a pretty fair description of it but if you prefer something else then take it as said.

MR BRENNAN: Yes, we did.

MR HORE-LACY: What advice did you get?

MR BRENNAN: Indeed, with our projections with North Melbourne we had allowed $100,000 as the net revenue from fundraising.

MR HORE-LACY: How about your projections with Brisbane?

MR BRENNAN: Zero[13]

MR HORE-LACY: When you say zero, you mean you hadn't anything or you projected no money at all?

MR BRENNAN: We knew there was certain money that we would get but we didn't take into account any net benefit.

MR HORE-LACY: Did you seek advice from anybody at Fitzroy concerning the possible effect of – I'm trying to think of another word – negotiating a merger with the AFL against the unanimous wishes of the Fitzroy directors?

---

13. If North Melbourne had offered to match the Brisbane offer it is hard to see, from what Brennan, said why the creditors would not have been at least $100,000 better off had Brennan gone with North Melbourne.

MR BRENNAN: Yes, we were generally aware of the impact.

MR HORE-LACY: No, I asked you did you discuss it with anybody.

MR BRENNAN: With anybody at Fitzroy?

MR HORE-LACY: With anybody at all. No doubt you did with Brisbane but with anybody at Fitzroy.

MR BRENNAN: We would have had some discussions with the chief executive, Dyson.

MR HORE-LACY: What did he tell you?

MR BRENNAN: He told me that – or he told my staff, I didn't discuss it with him – that a merger with another club may not be as popular as a merger with North.

MR HORE-LACY: So you appreciated then, did you, that the merger with Brisbane would not be as popular with a merger with North Melbourne?

MR BRENNAN: May not be as popular.

MR HORE-LACY: May not be, all right.

MR BRENNAN: Dyson, I think we really have to let some other people ask questions.

MR HORE-LACY: Certainly.

MR DE RAUCH: Is there any comment to my question? I didn't get a comment back for my question.

MR BRENNAN: Sorry?

MR DE RAUCH: There was no comment back on my question whether the North offer was correct or not?

MR BRENNAN: I don't believe your version of events, I'm sorry.

MR DE RAUCH: Happens to be true, sir.

MR BRENNAN: I don't want to be a smart arse….

MR HORE-LACY: Well, you're doing a pretty good job.

MR BRENNAN: – but they didn't have any letterhead there. So things that were written on letterheads –

MR DE RAUCH: Do you think you might have kept it in your files seeing it was so important?

CHAPTER 10

MR BRENNAN: It was a document submitted to the league. Questions from other creditors please? Yes, sir.

MR TROTTER: Graham Trotter. From your comment previously, an acceptance of the merger you said wasn't your decision but was a decision of the AFL directors.

MR BRENNAN: The AFL Commission.

MR TROTTER: Commission, and therefore they shut the gate before the final deadline which had been set, as we understand from what we have read in papers, of the midday on the Friday.

MR BRENNAN: Yes.

MR TROTTER: Therefore they weren't concerned whether creditors had a better chance of getting a better return than the deal with Brisbane and yet that would be your position as administrator, to work for the creditors to get the best return.

MR BRENNAN: Yes.

MR TROTTER: So the problem lies with the AFL Commission and their actions.

MR BRENNAN: Are there any further question? Mrs Graham, isn't it?

MRS GRAHAM: My name is Janet Graham, yes. My question is, speaking also as a member of the Fitzroy Football Club as well as a creditor, did it ever occur to you that it might be a good idea to find out the members' opinions on the merger situation or is your consideration simply financial and without any regard to what the members feel? I think you might agree, having I believe attended the meeting last night which I saw news reports of, there is a great welter of opinion against the Brisbane merger. Furthermore, is it in your power – and I suggest it should be – to overturn the Brisbane-Fitzroy merger and reconsider the North-Fitzroy merger?

MR BRENNAN: I don't think that I would be reconsidering the arrangements made, in view of the interests of creditors at large. In relation to your earlier question about the attitude of the Fitzroy supporters, I think I was generally aware that there may have been a majority in favour of merging with North.

The administrator seemed to be openly acknowledging the role played by the AFL.

'MR BRENNAN: There is a question down the back. Yes, Colin Hobbs.

MR HOBBS: In view of the question from Mr Trotter previously about your obligation as administrator, pursuing the best deal for the creditors, why did you not continue to pursue the deal until Friday midday?

MR BRENNAN: Because the holder of the licence told me that they wished to make a decision on that evening and therefore would I procure final and best bids from both bidders.

MR HOBBS: And you did that?

MR BRENNAN: I did that. You know, you have got to understand that the AFL had me on notice that the licence was terminable at will and therefore, whereas I may have wanted to dispute that, I had neither the power, the money – or I perhaps had the power – but I didn't have the time or money to do it.

MR HOBBS: What you must understand, that we have also been dealing with the AFL much longer and we sympathise with you in view of the fact that the AFL had you on notice. We sympathise with you in that regard.

MR BRENNAN: Thank you.

MR HORE-LACY: Did they virtually threaten that they were going to pull the licence straightaway unless you made a decision that night?

MR BRENNAN: Yes.

MR HORE-LACY: Thank you.

MR HOBBS: It's a disgrace.

MR BRENNAN: Well, I'm sorry, that was implicit.

Brennan confirmed that the AFL decision was shutting the gate before the final deadline was set. The AFL later publicly denied this threat. Brennan's answer also confirmed that it was the AFL who made the decision to merge with Brisbane – for 'strategic reasons,' readers will recall.

CHAPTER 10

He also admitted, in response to a question from Mr Aris Zafiriou of the Australian Tax Office, that he had not researched any potential Fitzroy claim on AFL (or old VFL) assets. He was under attack from all sides – except Brisbane and the AFL.

As the meeting was winding up, I raised the question of Brennan's administrative expenses.

MR HORE-LACY: The $350,000 I am told by North Melbourne that you didn't disclose to them, that Brisbane had offered you $350,000 for your administration expenses or something like that. Could you make a comment on that?[14]

MR BRENNAN: I certainly didn't disclose it to North Melbourne, no.

MR HORE-LACY: Don't you think it would have been prudent to do that to give them an opportunity to match it?

MR BRENNAN: Not when you ask people to, 'Put in your final and best bid.'

MR HORE-LACY: I thought you said North Melbourne said they would match Brisbane's offer.

MR BRENNAN: In relation to the unsecured creditors.

MR HORE-LACY: Well, how can they match Brisbane's offer if they don't know about this apparently secret – well, let's call it an offer to pay you – we will call it expenses for the purpose of the question – but if they don't even know of the existence of it. I mean, they might have offered a million dollars to you.

MR BRENNAN: In which case they may very well have been directed to merge with Fitzroy.

The meeting soon ended. Greg Basto left in tears.

After about 12 months, and after all the Fitzroy unsecured creditors had been paid their 27 cents in the dollar (with Nauru getting paid in full), the administrator moved out and the club returned to the control of the directors.

I'm not suggesting that Brennan was not trying to do what he

---

14. The actual amount was $300,000.

thought was best for the Fitzroy creditors. To be fair to him, whatever the position regarding the offers, he could be excused for thinking that to some extent the AFL had him over a barrel. Without the AFL's $6 million merger inducement (of which Brisbane eventually received somewhere between $3 million and $4 million) Fitzroy's creditors' including Nauru would have received nothing. The only weapon Brennan had, and that was not insignificant, was the possible legal action against the AFL which he had mentioned at the AFL president's meeting held at Richmond on July 4. It is apparent from what he said at the creditors' meeting that he was under pressure from the AFL to come to an arrangement that night.

On any view, it would seem that ultimate responsibility to merge Fitzroy with Brisbane lay at the feet of the AFL. Brennan was aware that the merger with Brisbane would be less popular with Fitzroy supporters than a merger with North Melbourne. Why then did the AFL do it?

The AFL and Nauru assigned the Nauru debt to Brisbane who immediately put a charge over Fitzroy Football Club for that debt, even though Nauru had been paid out of the merger money. The charge means that there is a registered debt against Fitzroy Football Club Ltd and although this charge hangs like the 'Sword of Damocles' over its neck, Fitzroy Football Club has not been killed off and it still operates essentially through the same directors who were in place on July 4, 1996: Elaine Findlay, John Stewart, John Petinella, Colin Hobbs, Robert Eales, David McMahon, Kevin Ryan and Dyson Hore-Lacy.

The Fitzroy directors have stayed on and have remained friends. They have been joined by Bill Atherton, a well known and extremely competent accountant who has worked tirelessly in keeping the club going, both in the preparation of necessary corporate returns and documentation in organising almost everything that involves the club.

Not one of the directors has had anything to do with the

CHAPTER 10

Brisbane Lions. This is significant in view of the claim by Noel Gordon on July 4 to the other AFL club directors that there were a number of Fitzroy directors who supported a union with Brisbane.

As administrator Michael Brennan attempted to acquire the hotel from Elaine and me. As a consequence of the administrator's action, we organised a meeting with all the hotel investors at the Fitzroy Club Hotel. There the issues relating to the hotel were canvassed in full and the investors were unanimous in the view that we should not hand it over or sell it to Brisbane. In any event we could not, as Elaine and I knew that what Brisbane was offering was well below what the asset was worth and, as directors of Bondborough Pty Ltd, we could only act in the best interests of Bondborough.

The result was that Brennan, funded by money that Brisbane received from the merger, sued Elaine and myself in the Supreme Court. Brisbane must have spent hundreds of thousands of dollars on the case. During the trial of the action, Elaine and I were publicly accused of fraud in the setting up of the hotel, a scurrilous allegation and one which was totally rejected by the trial judge, who in her judgment, I am pleased to say, formally found me to be a 'witness of truth'. Elaine was not required to give evidence. The administrator, of course, had access to all Fitzroy's records. I was cross-examined for a day in a futile attempt to discredit me.

The administrator's case had no chance from the outset, according to the advice we had received from Peter Buchanan, QC. Neither Elaine nor I had or ever did have any beneficial interest in the hotel whatsoever but we stood to lose hundreds of thousands of dollars in costs, and possibly our reputations, if we had lost.

On the day judgment was delivered in the Supreme Court all the Brisbane hierarchy had assembled eagerly anticipating a great victory. Noel Gordon, Andrew Ireland and the administrator were there, and a number of partners from the law firm of our opponents. They lost.

Immediately after judgement was delivered, Colin Hobbs turned around to offer heartfelt condolences to Brennan and Co, only to see them disappearing very quickly through the doors of the Supreme Court.

Brennan then appealed to the Victoria Court of Appeal. After Brennan's counsel presented their argument, our counsel (Bernard Bongiorno QC and Richard Attiwell) were not even called upon to reply – such was the strength of our case. Judgment was given on the spot upholding Justice Balmford's decision in the Supreme Court. As I was leaving the court I heard Brennan's junior counsel suggest to his senior counsel that they appeal to the High Court. 'I don't think that would be a realistic option,' was the understated reply.

This exercise in futility was particularly stressful for Elaine, who is a person of great integrity and for whom the court action must have seemed like a nightmare. For me it was not so bad as I understood the process and was always extremely confident of the outcome.

As a tactical ploy, it is difficult to understand Brisbane's motives. It is hard to imagine an action more calculated to alienate me, Elaine and all the Fitzroy directors permanently from the 'Brisbane Lions.' After Noel Gordon's appearance on the *Footy Show*, one would have thought that Brisbane would want all the help it could get to win over Fitzroy members and supporters. Suing the two leaders of the club would not have seemed, to an impartial observer, to be one of the best ways of going about this – especially when the chairman and vice-chairman had the support of all other directors.

Brisbane may have believed, along with the AFL, that we, the Fitzroy directors, were irrelevant and that our members and supporters would be won over to Brisbane by the sweet smiles of Ross Oakley, Michael Brennan and Noel Gordon. This strange attitude seemed to overlook the obvious fact that we had been elected by those very same supporters and members to lead their club.

CHAPTER 10

There was, however, another serious downside to the administrator's action over the hotel. Readers will recall that we had an agreement in place with the Mathieson Group that projected a $500,000 minimum profit per annum to Bondborough which Fitzroy would have had access to.

When Brennan commenced his action, Bruce Mathieson could not progress the agreement because of the question mark over the ownership of the hotel. Well before the court action had been finalised we felt compelled to sell our lease to the Mathieson company. Part of this agreement was that we would take a sixteen-year lease of the West Brunswick Hotel on the corner of Grantham Street and Brunswick Road, Brunswick as a replacement. Later this agreement was varied and Bondborough now has an agreement with the Mathieson Group to take the Rising Sun Hotel in Nicholson Street, North Carlton. At the time of writing our various licence applications are being processed.

After Bondborough sold its lease of the Fitzroy Club Hotel to Mathieson, it was left with a surplus of about $70,000. We have used this to give support where we can to the new alliance – the Coburg-Fitzroy Lions – now playing in the VFL. At the moment, our arrangement is one of financial and membership support but later it may develop more. We have also supported in a modest way the Fitzroy Redz in the Amateur competition and the Fitzroy juniors in the Yarra Junior Football League. We hope to continue to support worthwhile non-profit community football clubs from the proceeds of our new social club to be formed at the Rising Sun Hotel.[15]

One last mystery from the final year needs to be mentioned. The ASC inquiry into Fitzroy's trading was taken no further. One day, hopefully, we will find out who instigated the action against us.

---

15. All creditors' of Bondborough (totalling about $1,000, 000) were paid in full. The only people connected with Fitzroy who lost any money were the unsecured creditors (the largest, and constituting about 70% of the total) being Bondborough and the Taxation Office. They received 27 cents in the dollar.

FITZROY

Very few of the Fitzroy members have gone over to Brisbane. Many, if not most, Fitzroy people have drifted away from AFL football completely. Between us, the directors, we would not have seen more than a dozen games of AFL football since the events of 1996. I have seen three.

Shortly following our attempt to merge with North Melbourne, the Hawthorn Football Club and Melbourne Football Club attempted the same thing with AFL backing. This was a debacle with vitriol flying publicly and constantly for the six weeks or so leading up to the official vote. In the end, Melbourne Football Club voted for and Hawthorn Football Club voted against, so defeating the proposal. Both clubs have recovered, but I think that particular fiasco put an end to the AFL's enthusiasm to merge Melbourne clubs.

Back in 1996, however, merger speculation and interest was widespread. When it became known publicly that Fitzroy and North Melbourne Football clubs were in serious discussions about merging, a number of AFL clubs publicly expressed a view attempting to put a dampener on the deal. Collingwood was one in particular who suggested that Fitzroy would not be a good merger partner.

The hypocrisy demonstrated by some of these clubs was mind boggling. Particularly Collingwood.

Shortly before 'the agreement' with North Melbourne was signed, the Collingwood hierarchy approached us with a view to a merge. They actually put their offer in writing. First it was Collingwood-Fitzroy Magpies. We said that if Collingwood was going to keep its emblem (Magpies) our name had to appear first, that is Fitzroy-Collingwood Magpies. They said they believed that would be okay. There would be a home strip (Collingwood colours) and an away strip (Fitzroy colours).

As mentioned before one of our directors was initially keen to explore this possibility, but the rest of us thought that one way or another Collingwood would devour us. Furthermore, we didn't

CHAPTER 10

think the proposal had a hope of getting past the Collingwood members in any event, let alone the unpopularity such a move would have engendered with our members. Collingwood believed there would not be a problem with their members. We asked Collingwood to give us a million dollars worth of insurance to compensate us for the damage done if we came to some sort of agreement but at the eleventh hour had the deal knocked back by their members (as subsequently happened to the Hawthorn-Melbourne merger). Later on Collingwood said they could probably provide $500,000 worth of insurance. We were not interested.

I had an approach from St Kilda which went no further than the enquiry stage. I also received a detailed offer from Geelong to create the 'Geelong Lions' that was both Melbourne-based and Geelong-based. An even more detailed approach was made by Hawthorn for the 'Hawthorn Lions.'

One of the most generous offers came from Footscray. Fitzroy and Footscray would merge and become known as the Western Bulldogs! Richmond also submitted a very attractive deal where by our two clubs would merge, and play in the AFL as Richmond and in the VFL as Fitzroy. I said to Leon Daphne, Richmond's president at the time, who made the offer, that we may accept his offer but it would be on the condition that he bought me a flat in Moscow. 'Why is that?' asked Leon. I replied, 'Because that is where I and my family would have to live if I entered into a deal like that!'

We even had a nibble from Adelaide, keen to cement a Melbourne supporter base. We received a detailed proposal from the South Australia Cricket Association (SACA) which controlled the Adelaide Oval. They were desperate to get a second team in Adelaide playing at the Adelaide Oval to maximise the use of that venue. At that time they were keen for us to merge with Norwood. Of course the AFL would have no part of that arrangement. In any event, it had already decided, I suspect, to admit Port Adelaide

FITZROY

Football Club as the next team regardless. Writing of Port Adelaide, I am reminded of one of the more interesting proposals from Graeme Samuel. That was to merge Fitzroy with Port Adelaide. I received it on September 10, 1995. This document was headed 'Re Port Power Football Club (P.P.F.C.) and Fitzroy Football Club (FFC) – Joint Venture.' Extracts from this document follow:

Memorandum

RE: PORT POWER FOOTBALL CLUB ('PPFC') AND FITZROY FOOTBALL CLUB ('FFC')– Joint Venture

The following notes outline a proposal for a joint venture between PPFC and FFC to form a new club. The Port Power Lions, to participate in the AFL competition in substitution for PPFC and FFC.

It is proposed that the joint venture be implemented in the following manner.

   A) A company limited by guarantee called the Port Power Lions, be formed.

   B) Members of this company limited by guarantee would be:

      – 'A' class members with no voting rights other than detailed below in relation to the appointment and removal of their own nominees to the Board of Directors – PPFC and FFC.

   ...

   D) PPFC and FFC would enter into a joint venture agreement under which:

     1. FFC would surrender their licence to play in the AFL competition subject to The Port Power Lions being granted a new licence by the AFL.

     2. PPFC and FFC would continue as independent entitles with their own members and their own board of directors. However, all members of PPFC and FFC would automatically become members of The Port Power Lions. PPFC and FFC would retain their social clubs but they would carry the banners of The Port Power Lions. The net profit of each social club would be contributed to the Port Power Lions.

     ...and so on...'

CHAPTER 10

There was no mention of what would happen to Fitzroy Football Club's creditors. We were not greatly interested in becoming the 'power lines'.

One of the greatest ironies occurred later. During 1996 there was a bloodless coup in Nauru which ended up with Kinza Clodumar becoming President of the Republic of Nauru. If this had occurred a few months earlier, the course of history may have been different as far as Fitzroy Football Club was concerned.

Newspaper headlines that appear throughout this book tell their own story. For many years the AFL has operated with a largely unquestioning press. Various headlines in 1999 – three years after the merger – indicate that some elements of the press may now be re-examining the role of the AFL and the wisdom of some of the decisions made.

Many are beginning to realise the AFL has evolved from a suburban football competition into a corporate giant, where grass root supporters are treated as being largely irrelevant except for their capacity to provide an income stream to the AFL. Whether this income is from television rights or money through the turnstiles seems to be irrelevant as far as football's governing body is concerned.

Loyal fans deserve their Lions' share

Mike Sheahan
Herald Sun
15/4/99

Lions fans lose: AFL

Michael Manley
The Sunday Age
9/5/99

For Victorians, the Lions' share is next to nothing
Patrick Smith
The Age
10/5/99

Fears for death of Lions union
Rod Nicholson
Sunday Herald Sun
12/3/00

As I write this in June 2000 there have been many changes in football, but in many ways things have remained the same – the AFL stumbles along from controversy to crisis. Carlton is locked in Supreme Court proceedings over TV rights to Optus Oval. Colonial Stadium, which only the AFL seemed to want, has now commenced operations at the expense of Waverley Park. We read reports that the clubs playing home games at the venue need a crowd of 34,0000 to break even. Where is the money going?

The AFL is also embroiled in controversy over perceived conflicts of interest. Channel 7 is part of a consortium of companies which operate Colonial stadium and the ground manager Nation Wide Venue Management is a wholly-owned subsidiary of Spotless Catering whose managing director is, coincidentally, Ron Evans, the chairman of the AFL Commission. Graeme Samuel is on the Docklands Trust which granted the successful tender to the Channel 7 consortium to operate the stadium. Kerry Stokes, Channel 7 supremo, is reported as being a major shareholder in Ticketmaster, which manages ticketing.

Some issues never change. On March 10, 1995, I received a letter signed by John Kennedy, chairman of the AFL which reads:

> Dear Dyson,
> I have an extract of a comment that you made on radio 3AK recently, which reads:
>
> > "It just makes one wonder who is exactly running football.
> > I think there is a very strong argument that TV rights

CHAPTER 10

should go out to tender and it shouldn't be just a renewing of an agreement, especially with the reported relationship between the hierarchy of the AFL and Channel 7."

Our advice is that members of the Commission, and in particular our Chief Executive Officer, could take defamation action against you for this comment.

More importantly however, I am disappointed at your apparent distrust of Commissioners and the Chief Executive Officer. Your public questioning our integrity may suit some purpose but it certainly does not further the interests of football.

I can only appeal to you to keep the public discussion of your differences with the Commission (and we appreciate that there will be disagreements) on an impersonal level.

Yours sincerely,
John Kennedy (Chairman)

For whatever reasons, AFL football is at the crossroads. Country football appears to be slowly dying, with famous and historical clubs disappearing. At the school my son Andrew attends, for the first time in its ninety-year history, there are more students playing soccer in Year 9 than are playing Aussie Rules Football. At the school there are 19 soccer teams in total and only eight Aussie Rules teams.

I was once asked by a journalist if I ever regretted becoming involved with Fitzroy. My first inclination was to laugh. Do I regret six years of almost constant stress? Then I reflected on the question.

For most Fitzroy supporters, during the time I was a director, winning was of secondary importance. Survival was the dominant consideration coupled with a steely determination not to let outside forces defeat us. It was Fitzroy's very survival that prompted the AFL to consider introducing a minimum salary cap. The only way we were surviving, so it thought, was by saving money on player payments.

But there were other factors which helped make the stress bearable for all of us. The family lives of many of Fitzroy's supporters revolved around the club, crisis or not. The match on

Saturday afternoon was the focus, but the very existence of the club, with all its trimmings, constituted a large part of their lives.

I met a range of wonderful people at Fitzroy – from university lecturers to people who held the most menial of jobs or who were unemployed. I recall Frank Hardy, one of Australia's greatest authors, at the Fitzroy Club Hotel after we beat Carlton one day decked out like a Christmas tree in Fitzroy beanie and scarf. Frank's son and daughter, Alan Hardy and Shirley Hardy, were two of our closest supporters. Former Minister Tom Roper was a good supporter of the club. Tom, a keen Carlton man, was no doubt, under some sort of compulsion from his wife Anita, an avid Fitzroy supporter. Former Premier John Cain helped the club at a number of functions, including the 'Ins and Outs' every Thursday night, and his wife Nancye was an icon around the place, attending many functions and always offering support. Parliamentarians from both side of politics were regulars– Tom Reynolds and Frank Wilkes to name two.

And I can never forget the hundreds of ordinary supporters who offered donations both big and small, or those who ran minor raffles or rattled tins. Some were known to me, but many were not. Their loyalty, generosity and good spirit was inspiring. One rarely heard Fitzroy supporters publicly bagging their teams or coach which seems to happen so regularly with some other clubs. I recall one Sunday when we were playing Collingwood at Victoria Park, the Collingwood banner went up first, which exhorted its team to extinguish the life of Fitzroy in some brutal way. The Fitzroy banner went up. It had 'Happy Mother's Day' written on it.

The luckiest Fitzroy supporters are the ones who regard the 'union' between Fitzroy Football Club Limited and Brisbane Bears Football Club Limited as a merger. To those people the directors genuinely say 'good luck' as we in no way discourage our members from supporting the new entity. Whilst the directors have initiated other opportunities for its members and supporters (such as the Coburg-Fitzroy Lions) we also take the view that it is possible for

CHAPTER 10

Fitzroy people to support different teams at different levels.

We believe the vast majority of Fitzroy members, however, regard the club as having been betrayed by the AFL when it forced the shotgun marriage between Brisbane and Fitzroy for 'strategic reasons' and against the unanimous view of the directors and the wishes of the vast majority of Fitzroy supporters.

Of course I regret what happened in the end but as for the journey, I was proud to be part of the struggle. I remember receiving a letter from a supporter which commenced, 'Once more to the barricades.'

That is what it was like – but there were many fine people behind those barricades. Many of whom have been lost to football forever.